DAILY LIGHT

ON THE

DAILY PATH

A DEVOTIONAL TEXT BOOK

FOR

EVERY DAY IN THE YEAR

IN THE VERY WORDS OF SCRIPTURE

The Morning Hour

Multæ terricolis linguæ, cœlestibus una

LONDON : S. BAGSTER & SONS LIMITED
NEW YORK. JAMES POTT & CO.

JANUARY 1.

This one thing I do, forgetting those things which are behind, . . . I press toward the mark for the prize of the high calling of God in Christ Jesus.

FATHER, I will that they . . . whom thou hast given me, be with me where I am ; that they may behold my glory, which thou hast given me. — I know whom I have believed, and am persuaded that he is able to keep that which I have committed unto him against that day. — He which hath begun a good work in you will perform it until the day of Jesus Christ.

Know ye not that they which run in a race run all, but one receiveth the prize? So run, that ye may obtain. And every man that striveth for the mastery is temperate in all things. Now they do it to obtain a corruptible crown ; but we an incorruptible. — Let us lay aside every weight, and the sin which doth so easily beset us, and let us run with patience the race that is set before us, looking unto Jesus.

PHIL. 3. 13, 14   John 17. 24. — 2 Tim. 1. 12 —
    Phil. 1. 6.   1 Cor. 9. 24, 25 — Heb. 12. 1, 2.
    M   •

JANUARY 2.

Sing unto the Lord a new song

SING aloud unto God our strength; make a joyful noise unto the God of Jacob. Take a psalm, and bring hither the timbrel, the pleasant harp with the psaltery.—He hath put a new song in my mouth, even praise unto our God: many shall see it, and fear, and shall trust in the LORD.

Be strong and of a good courage; be not afraid, neither be thou dismayed: for the LORD thy God is with thee whithersoever thou goest.—The joy of the Lord is your strength.—Paul . . . thanked God, and took courage.

Knowing the time, that now it is high time to awake out of sleep: for now is our salvation nearer than when we believed. The night is far spent, the day is at hand: let us therefore cast off the works of darkness, and let us put on the armour of light. Let us walk honestly, as in the day; not in rioting and drunkenness, not in chambering and wantonness, not in strife and envying. But put ye on the Lord Jesus Christ, and make not provision for the flesh, to fulfil the lusts thereof.

Is. 42. 10. Ps. 81. 1, 2.—Ps. 40 3. Jos. 1. 9.
—Neh. 8. 10.—Acts 28. 15 Rom. 13. 11-14.
N

JANUARY 3.

He led them forth by the right way

HE found [Jacob] in a desert land, and in the waste howling wilderness; he led him about, he instructed him, he kept him as the apple of his eye. As an eagle stirreth up her nest, fluttereth over her young, spreadeth abroad her wings, taketh them, beareth them on her wings: so the LORD alone did lead him.—Even to your old age I am he; and even to hoar hairs will I carry you I have made, and I will bear; even I will carry, and will deliver you.

He restoreth my soul: he leadeth me in the paths of righteousness for his name's sake. Yea, though I walk through the valley of the shadow of death, I will fear no evil · for thou art with me; thy rod and thy staff they comfort me.

The LORD shall guide thee continually, and satisfy thy soul in drought, and make fat thy bones : and thou shalt be like a watered garden, and like a spring of water, whose waters fail not. —For this God is our God for ever and ever : he will be our guide even unto death.—Who teacheth like him?

Ps 107 7 Deut. 32 10-12 —Is 46 4 Ps 23. 3, 4. Is 58 11.—Ps 48. 14 —Job 36 22
M

JANUARY 4.

Ye are not as yet come to the rest and to
the inheritance, which the Lord your God
giveth you.

THIS is not your rest —There remaineth therefore a rest to the people of
God.—Within the veil; whither the
forerunner is for us entered, even Jesus.

In my Father's house are many man-
sions if it were not so, I would have told
you. I go to prepare a place for you.
And if I go and prepare a place for you,
I will come again, and receive you unto
myself; that where I am, there ye may be
also.—With Christ; which is far better.

God shall wipe away all tears from
their eyes; and there shall be no more
death, neither sorrow, nor crying, neither
shall there be any more pain: for the
former things are passed away —There
the wicked cease from troubling: and
there the weary be at rest

Lay up for yourselves treasures in
heaven. For where your treasure is,
there will your heart be also.—Set your
affection on things above, not on things
on the earth.

DEUT. 12 9 Mic. 2. 10 —Heb 4 9 —Heb. 6.
19, 20. John 14. 2 3.—Phil 1 23 Rev 21. 4
—Job 3 17. Mat. 6. 20, 21.—Col. 3. 2.
M

JANUARY 5.

We which have believed do enter into rest.

THEY weary themselves to commit iniquity.—I see another law in my members warring against the law of my mind, and bringing me into captivity to the law of sin which is in my members. O wretched man that I am ! who shall deliver me from the body of this death ?

Come unto me, all ye that labour and are heavy laden, and I will give you rest.—Being justified by faith, we have peace with God through our Lord Jesus Christ : by whom also we have access by faith into this grace wherein we stand, and rejoice in hope of the glory of God.

He that is entered into his rest, he also hath ceased from his own works.— Not having mine own righteousness, which is of the law, but that which is through the faith of Christ, the righteousness which is of God by faith — This is the rest wherewith ye may cause the weary to rest ; and this is the refreshing.

HEB. 4. 3.   Jer. 9. 5 —Rom. 7. 23, 24.   Mat. 11.
28.—Rom. 5. 1, 2.   Heb. 4. 10.—Phil. 3 9 —
Is. 28. 12

M   I *

JANUARY 6.

Let the beauty of the Lord our God
be upon us and establish thou
the work of our hands.

THY renown went forth among the heathen for thy beauty : for it was perfect through my comeliness, which I had put upon thee, saith the Lord GOD. —We all, with open face beholding as in a glass the glory of the Lord, are changed into the same image from glory to glory, even as by the Spirit of the Lord.

Blessed is every one that feareth the LORD : that walketh in his ways. For thou shalt eat the labour of thine hands : happy shalt thou be, and it shall be well with thee —Commit thy works unto the LORD, and thy thoughts shall be established.

Work out your own salvation with fear and trembling. For it is God which worketh in you both to will and to do of his good pleasure —Our Lord Jesus Christ himself, and God, even our Father, which hath loved us, and hath given us everlasting consolation and good hope through grace, comfort your hearts, and stablish you in every good word and work.

Ps 90 17   Ezek 16. 14 —2 Cor. 3. 18. Ps
123. 1, 2 —Pro 16 3   Phil 2. 12, 13.—
2 Thes 2 16. 17

M

JANUARY 7.

Think upon me, my God, for good.

THUS saith the LORD; I remember thee, the kindness of thy youth, the love of thine espousals, when thou wentest after me in the wilderness.—I will remember my covenant with thee in the days of thy youth, and I will establish unto thee an everlasting covenant.—I will visit you, and perform my good word toward you.—For I know the thoughts that I think toward you, saith the LORD, thoughts of peace, and not of evil, to give you an expected end.

As the heavens are higher than the earth, so are my ways higher than your ways, and my thoughts than your thoughts.— I would seek unto God, and unto God would I commit my cause : which doeth great things and unsearchable ; marvellous things without number.—Many, O LORD my God, are thy wonderful works which thou hast done, and thy thoughts which are to us-ward : they cannot be reckoned up in order unto thee : if I would declare and speak of them, they are more than can be numbered.

NEH. 5 19 Jer. 2 2 —Ezek. 16. 60.—Jer. 29. 10, 11. Is. 55 9 —Job 5. 8, 9 —Ps. 40. 5.
M

JANUARY 8.

They that know thy name will put their trust in thee; for thou, Lord, hast not forsaken them that seek thee.

THE name of the LORD is a strong tower : the righteous runneth into it, and is safe. — I will trust, and not be afraid : for the LORD JEHOVAH is my strength and my song ; he also is become my salvation.

I have been young, and now am old ; yet have I not seen the righteous forsaken, nor his seed begging bread. — For the LORD loveth judgment, and forsaketh not his saints ; they are preserved for ever : but the seed of the wicked shall be cut off —The LORD will not forsake his people for his great name's sake : because it hath pleased the LORD to make you his people —Who delivered us from so great a death, and doth deliver : in whom we trust that he will yet deliver us.

Be content with such things as ye have : for he hath said, I will never leave thee, nor forsake thee. So that we may boldly say, The Lord is my helper, and I will not fear what man shall do unto me.

Ps. 9. 10. Pro. 13. 10.—Is 12. 2. Ps. 37. 25.—
Ps. 37. 28.—1 Sam. 12 22 —2 Cor. 1 10.
Heb 12. 5. 6.

M

JANUARY 9.

Thou hast given a banner to them that
fear thee, that it may be displayed
because of the truth.

JEHOVAH Nissi (The LORD my banner).—When the enemy shall come
in like a flood, the Spirit of the LORD
shall lift up a standard against him
We will rejoice in thy salvation, and
in the name of our God we will set up
our banners.—The LORD hath brought
forth our righteousness : come, and let
us declare in Zion the work of the LORD
our God.—We are more than conquerors
through him that loved us.—Thanks be
to God, which giveth us the victory through
our Lord Jesus Christ.—The captain of
their salvation.

My brethren, be strong in the Lord,
and in the power of his might.—Valiant
for the truth.—Fight the LORD's battles.
—Be strong, all ye people of the land,
saith the LORD, and work : . . . fear ye
not.—Lift up your eyes, and look on the
fields ; for they are white already to har-
vest.—Yet a little while, and he that
shall come will come, and will not tarry.

Ps. 60 4   Ex. 17 15 —Is. 59 19. Ps 20. 5 —
Jer 51. 10.—Rom. 8. 37.—1 Cor. 15. 57.—Heb.
2. 10.   Eph 5 10 —Jer 9. 3 —1 Sam. 18. 17.
—Hag 2 4, 5.—John 4. 35 —Heb. 10. 37.
M

JANUARY 10.

I pray God your whole spirit and soul and body be preserved blameless unto the coming of our Lord Jesus Christ.

CHRIST loved the church, and gave himself for it ; that he might present it to himself a glorious church, not having spot, or wrinkle, or any such thing ; but that it should be holy and without blemish.—Whom we preach, warning every man, and teaching every man in all wisdom ; that we may present every man perfect in Christ Jesus

The peace of God . . , passeth all understanding.—Let the peace of God rule in your hearts, to the which also ye are called in one body.

Our Lord Jesus Christ himself, and God, even our Father, which hath loved us, and hath given us everlasting consolation and good hope through grace, comfort your hearts, and stablish you in every good word and work.—Who shall also confirm you unto the end, that ye may be blameless in the day of our Lord Jesus Christ.

1 Thes. 5. 23. Eph. 5. 25, 27.—Col. 1. 28. Phil. 4. 7.—Col. 3. 15. 2 Thes. 2. 16, 17.—
1 Cor. 1 8.

M

JANUARY 11.

TO as there is but one God, the Father, of whom are all things, and we in him ; and one Lord Jesus Christ.—All men should honour the Son, even as they honour the Father. He that honoureth not the Son honoureth not the Father which hath sent him.—By him therefore let us offer the sacrifice of praise to God continually, that is, the fruit of our lips giving thanks to his name. — Whoso offereth praise glorifieth me : and to him that ordereth his conversation aright will I shew the salvation of God.

I beheld, and, lo, a great multitude, which no man could number, of all nations, and kindreds, and people, and tongues, stood before the throne, and before the Lamb, clothed with white robes, and palms in their hands ; and cried with a loud voice, saying, Salvation to our God which sitteth upon the throne, and unto the Lamb. Amen · Blessing, and glory, and wisdom, and thanksgiving, and honour, and power, and might, be unto our God for ever and ever. Amen.

Ps. 65. 1 1 Cor 8 6 —John 5. 23.—Heb. 13. 15 —Ps. 50 23 Rev. 7. 9, 10, 12

M

JANUARY 12.

CHRIST Jesus, who of God is made unto us wisdom, and righteousness, and sanctification, and redemption —Canst thou by searching find out God? canst thou find out the Almighty unto perfection? It is as high as heaven; what canst thou do? deeper than hell; what canst thou know?

We speak the wisdom of God in a mystery, even the hidden wisdom, which God ordained before the world unto our glory. — The mystery, which from the beginning of the world hath been hid in God, who created all things by Jesus Christ: to the intent that now unto the principalities and powers in heavenly places might be known, by the church, the manifold wisdom of God.

If any of you lack wisdom, let him ask of God, that giveth to all men liberally, and upbraideth not; and it shall be given him —The wisdom that is from above is first pure, then peaceable, gentle, and easy to be entreated, full of mercy and good fruits, without partiality, and without hypocrisy.

JUDE 25.   1 Cor. 1. 30.—Job 11 7, 8.   1 Cor. 2 7.—Eph. 3 9, 10.   Ja 1 5—Ja. 3 17.
M

JANUARY 13.

Thou wilt keep him in perfect peace,
whose mind is stayed on thee.

CAST thy burden upon the LORD, and
he shall sustain thee ; he shall never
suffer the righteous to be moved.—I will
trust, and not be afraid : for the LORD
JEHOVAH is my strength and my song ;
he also is become my salvation.

Why are ye fearful, O ye of little faith?
—Be careful for nothing ; but in every
thing by prayer and supplication with
thanksgiving let your requests be made
known unto God   And the peace of
God, which passeth all understanding,
shall keep your hearts and minds through
Christ Jesus.—In quietness and in confidence shall be your strength.

The effect of righteousness [shall be]
quietness and assurance for ever.—Peace
I leave with you, my peace I give unto
you : not as the world giveth give I unto
you.   Let not your heart be troubled,
neither let it be afraid.—Peace, from him
which is, and which was, and which is to
come.

Is 26 3. Ps. 55. 22.—Is. 12 2. Mat 8 26.—
Phil. 4. 6, 7.—Is. 30. 15. Is 32. 17.—John
14 27.—Rev. 1. 4

M

My Father is greater than I.

WHEN ye pray say, Our Father which art in heaven. —My Father, and your Father ; . . . my God and your God.

As the Father gave me commandment, even so I do.—The words that I speak unto you I speak not of myself: but the Father that dwelleth in me, he doeth the works.

The Father loveth the Son, and hath given all things into his hand.—Thou hast given him power over all flesh, that he should give eternal life to as many as thou hast given him.

Lord, shew us the Father, and it sufficeth us. Jesus saith unto him, Have I been so long time with you, and yet hast thou not known me, Philip? he that hath seen me hath seen the Father ; and how sayest thou then, Shew us the Father? Believest thou not that I am in the Father, and the Father in me?—I and my Father are one —As the Father hath loved me, so have I loved you : continue ye in my love. If ye keep my commandments, ye shall abide in my love ; even as I have kept my Father's commandments, and abide in His love.

JOHN 14. 28.   Luke 11- 2 —John 20- 17-   John 14. 31-—John 14 10-   John 3- 35—John 17- 2-   John 14. 8-10 —John 10. 30 —John 15- 9, 10.

M

JANUARY 15.

My soul cleaveth unto the dust: quicken thou me according to thy word.

IF ye . . . be risen with Christ, seek those things which are above, where Christ sitteth on the right hand of God. Set your affection on things above, not on things on the earth. For . . . your life is hid with Christ in God.—Our conversation is in heaven; from whence also we look for the Saviour, the Lord Jesus Christ: who shall change our vile body, that it may be fashioned like unto his glorious body, according to the working whereby he is able even to subdue all things unto himself.

The flesh lusteth against the Spirit, and the Spirit against the flesh; and these are contrary the one to the other: so that ye cannot do the things that ye would.—Brethren, we are debtors, not to the flesh, to live after the flesh. For if ye live after the flesh, ye shall die: but if ye through the Spirit do mortify the deeds of the body, ye shall live.— Dearly beloved, I beseech you as strangers and pilgrims, abstain from fleshly lusts, which war against the soul.

Ps. 119. 25. Col. 3. 1-3.—Phil. 3 20, 21. Gal. 5. 17.—Rom. 8. 12. 13.—1 Pet. 2. 11.

M

JANUARY 16.

It pleased the Father, that in him should all fulness dwell.

THE Father loveth the Son, and hath given all things into his hand.—God hath highly exalted him, and given him a name which is above every name: that at the name of Jesus every knee should bow, of things in heaven, and things in earth, and things under the earth; and that every tongue should confess that Jesus Christ is Lord, to the glory of God the Father.—Far above all principality, and power, and might, and dominion, and every name that is named, not only in this world, but also in that which is to come.—By him were all things created, that are in heaven, and that are in earth, visible and invisible, whether they be thrones, or dominions, or principalities, or powers: all things were created by him, and for him

Christ both died, and rose, and re-vived, that he might be Lord both of the dead and living.—And ye are complete in him, which is the head of all principality and power.—Of his fulness have all we received.

CoL. 1. 19. John 3. 35.—Phil. 2. 9-11.—Eph. 1. 21.—Col. 1. 16. Rom. 14. 9.—Col. 2. 10.— John 1. 16.

M

JANUARY 17.

Thou hast in love to my soul delivered
it from the pit of corruption.

GOD sent his only begotten Son into
the world, that we might live through
him Herein is love, not that we loved
God, but that he loved us, and sent his
Son to be the propitiation for our sins.
Who is a God like unto thee, that
pardoneth iniquity, and passeth by the
transgression of the remnant of his heritage? he retaineth not his anger for
ever, because he delighteth in mercy.
He will turn again, he will have compassion upon us; he will subdue our
iniquities; and thou wilt cast all their
sins into the depths of the sea —O LORD
my God, I cried unto thee, and thou
hast healed me O LORD, thou hast
brought up my soul from the grave:
thou hast kept me alive, that I should
not go down to the pit —When my soul
fainted within me I remembered the
LORD; and my prayer came in unto
thee, into thine holy temple.—I waited
patiently for the LORD He brought me
up . . . out of a horrible pit, out of the
miry clay, and set my feet upon a rock.

Is. 33 17. 1 John 4 9, 10. Mic. 7. 18, 19.—
Ps. 30. 2, 3 —Jon 2 7 —Ps. 40 1, 2.
M

JANUARY 18.

JESUS . . made a little lower than the angels for the suffering of death, . . . that he by the grace of God should taste death for every man.—One died for all.—As by one man's disobedience many were made sinners, so by the obedience of one shall many be made righteous.

The first man Adam was made a living soul; the last Adam was made a quickening spirit. That was not first which is spiritual, but that which is natural; and afterward that which is spiritual.—God said, Let us make man in our image, after our likeness. So God created man in his own image, in the image of God created he him.—God . . . hath in these last days spoken unto us by his Son, . . . the brightness of his glory, and the express image of his person.—Thou hast given him power over all flesh

The first man is of the earth, earthy: the second man is the Lord from heaven. As is the earthy, such are they also that are earthy: and as is the heavenly, such are they also that are heavenly.

Rom. 5. 14   Heb 2. 9.—2 Cor. 5. 14.—Rom. 5. 19.   1 Cor. 15. 45, 46.—Gen. 1. 26. 27.—Heb. 1. 1-3.—John 17. 2.   1 Cor. 15. 47, 48.

M

JANUARY 19.

Serving the Lord with all humility
of mind.

WHOSOEVER will be great among
you, let him be your minister ; and
whosoever will be chief among you, let
him be your servant · even as the Son of
man came not to be ministered unto,
but to minister, and to give his life a
ransom for many.

If a man think himself to be some-
thing, when he is nothing, he deceiveth
himself.—I say, through the grace given
unto me, to every man, . . . not to
think of himself more highly than he
ought to think ; but to think soberly,
according as God hath dealt to every
man the measure of faith.—When ye
shall have done all those things which
are commanded you, say, We are unprofitable servants : we have done that
which was our duty to do.

Our rejoicing is this, . . . that in
simplicity and godly sincerity, not with
fleshly wisdom, but by the grace of God,
we have had our conversation in the
world.—We have this treasure in earthen
vessels, that the excellency of the power
may be of God, and not of us.

ACTS 20. 19. Mat. 20. 26-28. Gal. 6 3.—Rom.
12. 3.—Luke 17. 10. 2 Cor. 1. 12.—2 Cor. 4. 7.
M

JANUARY 20.

His name shall be called Wonderful.

THE Word was made flesh, and dwelt among us, (and we beheld his glory, the glory as of the only begotten of the Father,) full of grace and truth —Thou hast magnified thy word above all thy name.

They shall call his name Emmanuel, which being interpreted is, God with us.—JESUS: for he shall save his people from their sins.

All men should honour the Son, even as they honour the Father —God . . . hath highly exalted him, and given him a name which is above every name.—Far above all principality, and power, and might, and dominion, and every name that is named, not only in this world, but also in that which is to come; and hath put all things under his feet.—He had a name written, that no man knew, but he himself . . . KING OF KINGS, AND LORD OF LORDS.

Touching the Almighty, we cannot find him out.—What is his name, and what is his son's name, if thou canst tell?

Is. 9. 6.   John 1. 14.—Ps 138. 2.   Mat. 1. 23.—
Mat. 1. 21.   John 5. 23 —Phil 2. 9.—Eph. 1.
21, 22 —Rev 19. 16.   Job 37. 23.—Pro. 30. 4.
M

JANUARY 21.

Every branch that beareth fruit, he purgeth it.

HE is like a refiner's fire, and like fullers' sope : and he shall sit as a refiner and purifier of silver : and he shall purify the sons of Levi, and purge them as gold and silver, that they may offer unto the LORD an offering in righteousness.

We glory in tribulations : knowing that tribulation worketh patience ; and patience, experience ; and experience, hope : and hope maketh not ashamed ; because the love of God is shed abroad in our hearts by the Holy Ghost which is given unto us.—If ye endure chasten ing, God dealeth with you as with sons ; for what son is he whom the father chasteneth not ? But if ye be without chastisement, whereof all are partakers, then are ye bastards, and not sons. Now no chastening for the present seemeth to be joyous, but grievous : nevertheless afterward it yieldeth the peaceable fruit of righteousness unto them which are exercised thereby. Wherefore lift up the hands which hang down, and the feeble knees.

JOHN 15. 2. Mal. 3. 2, 3. Rom. 5. 3-5 —
Heb 12. 7. 8. 11. 12.

v

JANUARY 22.

This God is our God for ever and ever:
he will be our guide even unto death.

O LORD, thou art my God; I will
exalt thee, I will praise thy name; for
thou hast done wonderful things; thy
counsels of old are faithfulness and
truth.—The LORD is the portion of mine
inheritance, and of my cup.

He leadeth me in the paths of righteousness, for his name's sake. Yea,
though I walk through the valley of the
shadow of death, I will fear no evil.
for thou art with me; thy rod and thy
staff they comfort me.—Thou hast holden
me by my right hand. Thou shalt guide
me with thy counsel, and afterward
receive me to glory. Whom have I in
heaven but thee? and there is none
upon earth that I desire beside thee.
My flesh and my heart faileth : but God
is the strength of my heart, and my portion for ever.—Our heart shall rejoice
in him because we have trusted in his
holy name.—The LORD will perfect that
which concerneth me. thy mercy, O
LORD, endureth for ever : forsake not
the works of thine own hands.

Ps. 48 14   Is. 25. 1.—Ps 16 5   Ps 23. 3, 4.
—Ps. 73 23-26—Ps. 33 21.—Ps 138 8

JANUARY 23.

Hope maketh not ashamed.

I AM the LORD : . . . they shall not be ashamed that wait for me.—Blessed is the man that trusteth in the LORD, and whose hope the LORD is.—Thou wilt keep him in perfect peace, whose mind is stayed on thee : because he trusteth in thee. Trust ye in the LORD for ever : for in the LORD JEHOVAH is everlasting strength.—My soul, wait thou only upon God ; for my expectation is from him. He only is my rock and my salvation : he is my defence ; I shall not be moved. —I am not ashamed, for I know whom I have believed.

God, willing more abundantly to shew unto the heirs of promise the immutability of his counsel, confirmed it by an oath : that by two immutable things, in which it was impossible for God to lie, we might have a strong consolation, who have fled for refuge to lay hold upon the hope set before us ; which hope we have as an anchor of the soul, both sure and sted- fast, and which entereth into that within the veil ; whither the forerunner is for us entered, even Jesus.

ROM. 5. 5. Is. 49. 23.—Jer. 17. 7.—Is. 26. 3, 4 —Ps. 62. 5, 6.—1 Tim. 1. 12. Heb. 6. 17-20

M

JANUARY 24.

The Lord is at hand.

THE Lord himself shall descend from heaven with a shout, with the voice of the archangel, and with the trump of God . and the dead in Christ shall rise first : then we which are alive and remain, shall be caught up together with them in the clouds, to meet the Lord in the air : and so shall we ever be with the Lord. Wherefore comfort one another with these words.—He which testifieth these things saith, Surely I come quickly; Amen. Even so, come, Lord Jesus.

Wherefore, beloved, seeing that ye look for such things, be diligent that ye may be found of him in peace, without spot, and blameless.—Abstain from all appearance of evil. And the very God of peace sanctify you wholly ; and I pray God your whole spirit and soul and body be preserved blameless unto the coming of our Lord Jesus Christ. Faithful is he that calleth you, who also will do it.

Be ye also patient ; stablish your hearts ; for the coming of the Lord draweth nigh.

PHIL. 4. 5   1 Thes. 4 16-18.—Rev 22. 20
2 Pet. 3. 14.—1 Thes. 5. 22-24. Ja. 5 8.
M

JANUARY 25.

The righteousness of God which is by
faith of Jesus Christ unto all and
upon all them that believe.

HE hath made him to be sin for us,
who knew no sin ; that we might be
made the righteousness of God in him —
Christ hath redeemed us from the curse
of the law, being made a curse for us —
Who of God is made unto us wisdom, and
righteousness, and sanctification, and re
demption —Not by works of righteousness which we have done, but according
to his mercy he saved us, by the washing
of regeneration, and renewing of the Holy
Ghost ; which he shed on us abundantly
through Jesus Christ our Saviour.

I count all things but loss for the excellency of the knowledge of Christ Jesus
my Lord : for whom I have suffered the
loss of all things, and do count them but
dung, that I may win Christ, and be
found in him, not having mine own
righteousness, which is of the law, but
that which is through the faith of Christ,
the righteousness which is of God by
faith.

Rom 3. 22   2 Cor. 5. 21 —Gal 3. 13.—1 Cor.
1 30.—Tit 3 5, 6.   Phil 3 & 9.

M

Let us go forth unto him without the camp, bearing his reproach. For here have we no continuing city, but we seek one to come

BELOVED, think it not strange con-cerning the fiery trial which is to try you, as though some strange thing happened unto you : but rejoice, inasmuch as ye are partakers of Christ's sufferings ; that, when his glory shall be revealed, ye may be glad also with exceeding joy.— As ye are partakers of the sufferings, so shall ye be also of the consolation.

If ye be reproached for the name of Christ, happy are ye ; for the Spirit of glory and of God resteth upon you : on their part he is evil spoken of, but on your part he is glorified.

They departed from the presence of the council, rejoicing that they were counted worthy to suffer shame for his name.— Choosing rather to suffer affliction with the people of God, than to enjoy the pleasures of sin for a season ; esteeming the reproach of Christ greater riches than the treasures in Egypt ; for he had re-spect unto the recompence of the reward.

HEB. 13 13, 14 1 Pet. 4 12, 13.—2 Cor 1. 7.
1 Pet. 4 14. Acts 5 41 —Heb 11. 25, 26.
M

JANUARY 27.

Ye know that he was manifested to take away our sins: and in him is no sin.

GOD, . . . hath in these last days spoken unto us by his Son, . . . who being the brightness of his glory, and the express image of his person, and upholding all things by the word of his power, when he had by himself purged our sins, sat down on the right hand of the Majesty on high.—He hath made him to be sin for us, who knew no sin.

Pass the time of your sojourning here in fear : forasmuch as ye know that ye were not redeemed with corruptible things, as silver and gold ; . . . but with the precious blood of Christ, as of a lamb without blemish and without spot : who verily was foreordained before the foundation of the world, but was manifest in these last times for you.—The love of Christ constraineth us ; because we thus judge, that if one died for all, then were all dead : and that he died for all, that they which live should not henceforth live unto themselves, but unto him which died for them, and rose again.

1 JOHN 3 5. Heb 1 1-3 —2 Cor 5 21.
1 Pet, 1 17-20.—2 Cor 5 14, 15.

M

JANUARY 28.

As thy days, so shall thy strength be

WHEN they shall lead you, and deliver you up, take no thought beforehand what ye shall speak, neither do ye premeditate: but whatsoever shall be given you in that hour, that speak ye: for it is not ye that speak, but the Holy Ghost.—Take no thought for the morrow: for the morrow shall take thought for the things of itself. Sufficient unto the day is the evil thereof.

The God of Israel is he that giveth strength and power unto his people. Blessed be God—He giveth power to the faint; and to them that have no might he increaseth strength.

My grace is sufficient for thee: for my strength is made perfect in weakness. Most gladly therefore will I rather glory in my infirmities, that the power of Christ may rest upon me. Therefore I take pleasure in infirmities, in reproaches, in necessities, in persecutions, in distresses for Christ's sake: for when I am weak, then am I strong.—I can do all things through Christ which strengtheneth me.—O my soul, thou hast trodden down strength.

DEUT. 33. 25. Mark 13. 11.—Mat. 6 34. Ps. 68. 35.—Is. 40. 29. 2 Cor. 12. 9, 10.—Phil. 4. 13.—Jud. 5. 21

M

JANUARY 29.

Thou God seest me.

O LORD, thou hast searched me, and known me. Thou knowest my down-sitting and mine uprising, thou under standest my thought afar off. Thou compassest my path and my lying down, and art acquainted with all my ways. For there is not a word in my tongue, but, lo, O LORD, thou knowest it altogether. . . . Such knowledge is too wonderful for me : it is high, I cannot attain unto it.

The eyes of the LORD are in every place, beholding the evil and the good. —The ways of man are before the eyes of the LORD, and he pondereth all his goings —God knoweth your hearts : for that which is highly esteemed among men is abomination in the sight of God. —The eyes of the LORD run to and fro throughout the whole earth, to shew himself strong in the behalf of them whose heart is perfect toward him

Jesus . . knew all men, and needed not that any should testify of man : for he knew what was in man —Lord, thou knowest all things; thou knowest that I love thee

GEN. 16 13 Ps. 139 1-4, 6. Pro. 15. 3 —Pro. 5. 21.—Luke 16. 15 —2 Chr. 16. 9. John 2. 24, 25,—John 21 17

JANUARY 30.

Let us run with patience the race that is set before us, looking unto Jesus the author and finisher of our faith.

IF any man will come after me, let him deny himself, and take up his cross daily, and follow me —Whosoever he be of you that forsaketh not all that he hath, he cannot be my disciple.—Let us therefore cast off the works of darkness.

Every man that striveth for the mastery s temperate in all things   Now they do it to obtain a corruptible crown ; but we an incorruptible.   I therefore so run, not as uncertainly ; so fight I, not as one that beateth the air · but I keep under my body, and bring it into subjection : lest that by any means, when I have preached to others, I myself should be a castaway. —Brethren, I count not myself to have apprehended : but this one thing I do, forgetting those things which are behind, and reaching forth unto those things which are before, I press toward the mark for the prize of the high calling of God in Christ Jesus.—Then shall we know, if we follow on to know the LORD.

Heb. 12. 1, 2.   Luke 9 23.—Luke 14 33 —Rom 13 12.   1 Cor. 9 25-27.—Phil 3 13, 14.—
Hos 6 3

M

JANUARY 31.

I ye will not drive out the inhabitants of the land from before you, those which ye let remain of them shall be pricks in your eyes, and thorns in your sides, and shall vex you in the land wherein ye dwell.

FIGHT the good fight of faith —The weapons of our warfare are not carnal, but mighty through God to the pulling down of strong holds; casting down imaginations, . . . and bringing into captivity every thought to the obedience of Christ

Brethren, we are debtors, not to the flesh, to live after the flesh. For if ye live after the flesh, ye shall die : but if ye through the Spirit do mortify the deeds of the body, ye shall live —The flesh lusteth against the Spirit, and the Spirit against the flesh : and these are contrary the one to the other · so that ye cannot do the things that ye would —I see another law in my members, warring against the law of my mind, and bringing me into captivity to the law of sin which is in my members —We are more than conquerors through him that loved us.

Num. 33 55   1 Tim 6 12 —2 Cor 10 4, 5
Rom. 8. 12, 13 —Gal 5 17 —R jm, 7 23 —
Rom. 8 37
M

FEBRUARY 1.

Whom having not seen, ye love.

WE walk by faith, not by sight.—We love him, because he first loved us. —And we have known and believed the love that God hath to us. God is love; and he that dwelleth in love dwelleth in God, and God in him.—In whom ye trusted, after that ye heard the word of truth, the gospel of your salvation: in whom also after that ye believed, ye were sealed with that holy Spirit of promise. —God would make known what is the riches of the glory of this mystery among the Gentiles; which is Christ in you, the hope of glory.

If a man say, I love God, and hateth his brother, he is a liar: for he that loveth not his brother whom he hath seen, how can he love God whom he hath not seen?

Jesus saith unto him, Thomas, because thou hast seen me, thou hast believed: blessed are they that have not seen, and yet have believed.—Blessed are all they that put their trust in him.

1 Pet. 1. 8.   2 Cor. 5. 7.—1 John 4. 19.—1 John 4. 16.—Eph. 1. 13.—Col. 1. 27.   1 John 4 20. John 20. 29.—Ps. 2. 12.

M

FEBRUARY 2.

Oh that thou wouldest keep me from evil.

WHY sleep ye? rise and pray, lest ye enter into temptation.—The spirit indeed is willing, but the flesh is weak.

Two things have I required of thee; deny me them not before I die: remove far from me vanity and lies; give me neither poverty nor riches; feed me with food convenient for me: lest I be full, and deny thee, and say, Who is the LORD? or lest I be poor, and steal, and take the name of my God in vain.

The LORD shall preserve thee from all evil: he shall preserve thy soul.—I will deliver thee out of the hand of the wicked, and I will redeem thee out of the hand of the terrible.—He that is begotten of God keepeth himself, and that wicked one toucheth him not.

Because thou hast kept the word of my patience, I also will keep thee from the hour of temptation, which shall come upon all the world, to try them that dwell upon the earth.—The LORD knoweth how to deliver the godly out of temptations.

1 CHR. 4 10. Luke 22 46.—Mat. 26. 41:
Pro. 30. 7-9. Ps. 121. 7.—Jer. 15. 21.—1 John
5. 18. Rev. 3 10.—2 Pet. 2 9.
M

FEBRUARY 3.

Be strong, and work: for I am with
you, saith the Lord of hosts

I AM the vine, ye are the branches:
he that abideth in me, and I in him,
the same bringeth forth much fruit: for
without me ye can do nothing.—I can
do all things through Christ which
strengtheneth me.—Strong in the Lord,
and in the power of his might.—The
joy of the Lord is your strength.

Thus saith the LORD of hosts; Let
your hands be strong, ye that hear in
these days these words by the mouth of
the prophets.—Strengthen ye the weak
hands, and confirm the feeble knees
Say to them that are of a fearful heart,
Be strong, fear not.—The LORD looked
upon him, and said, Go in this thy might.

If God be for us, who can be against
us?—Therefore seeing we have this
ministry, as we have received mercy, we
faint not.

Let us not be weary in well doing:
for in due season we shall reap, if we
faint not.—Thanks be to God, which
giveth us the victory through our Lord
Jesus Christ.

HAG 2 4 John 15 5 —Phil 4 13 —Eph.
6 10 —Neh 8 10 Zec 8 9 —Is 35. 3, 4 —
Jud. 6 14. Rom 8 31.—2 Cor 4 1 Gal.
6 9 —1 Cor 15 57

M

FEBRUARY 4.

The Lord hath said unto you, Ye shall
henceforth return no more that way.

TRULY if they had been mindful of
that country from whence they came
out, they might have had opportunity
to have returned But now they desire
a better country, that is a heavenly.
Choosing rather to suffer affliction with
the people of God, than to enjoy the
pleasures of sin for a season ; esteeming
the reproach of Christ greater riches
than the treasures in Egypt —The just
shall live by faith : but if any man draw
back, my soul shall have no pleasure
in him. But we are not of them who
draw back unto perdition ; but of them
that believe to the saving of the soul.—
No man, having put his hand to the
plough, and looking back, is fit for the
kingdom of God.

God forbid that I should glory, save
in the cross of our Lord Jesus Christ,
by whom the world is crucified unto me
and I unto the world.—Come out from
among them, and be ye separate, saith
the Lord, .   and I will receive you.

He which hath begun a good work in you
will perform it until the day of Jesus Christ.

DEUT. 17. 16. Heb. 11. 15, 16, 25, 26.—Heb.
10 38, 39.—Luke 9 62 Gal 6 14 —2 Cor.
6. 17   Phil. 1. 6.

M

FEBRUARY 5.

I am come that they might have life, and that they might have it more abundantly

IN the day that thou eatest thereof thou shalt surely die.—She took of the fruit thereof, and gave also unto her husband with her ; and he did eat.

The wages of sin is death; but the gift of God is eternal life through Jesus Christ our Lord.—If by one man's offence death reigned by one , much more they which receive abundance of grace and of the gift of righteousness shall reign in life by one, Jesus Christ.—Since by man came death, by man came also the resurrection of the dead. For as in Adam all die, even so in Christ shall all be made alive.—Our Saviour Jesus Christ, . . . hath abolished death, and hath brought life and immortality to light through the gospel.

God hath given to us eternal life, and this life is in his Son. He that hath the Son hath life ; and he that hath not the Son of God hath not life.—For God sent not his Son into the world to condemn the world ; but that the world through him might be saved.

JOHN 10. 10   Gen. 2 17.—Gen. 3 6.   Rom.'
6. 23 —Rom. 5. 17.—1 Cor. 15. 21, 22.—2 Tim.
1 10   1 John 5 11, 12 — Iohn 3 17

M

FEBRUARY 6.

The grace of our Lord was exceeding
abundant with faith and love
which is in Christ Jesus.

YE know the grace of our Lord Jesus
Christ, that, though he was rich, yet
for your sakes he became poor, that ye
through his poverty might be rich.—
Where sin abounded, grace did much
more abound.

That in the ages to come he might
shew the exceeding riches of his grace in
his kindness toward us through Christ
Jesus. For by grace are ye saved through
faith ; and that not of yourselves . it is
the gift of God : not of works, lest any
man should boast.—Knowing that a man
is not justified by the works of the law,
but by the faith of Jesus Christ, even we
have believed in Jesus Christ, that we
might be justified by the faith of Christ,
and not by the works of the law : for
by the works of the law shall no flesh
be justified.—According to his mercy he
saved us, by the washing of regeneration,
and renewing of the Holy Ghost ; which
he shed on us abundantly through Jesus
Christ our Saviour.

1 TIM. 1. 14. 2 Cor. 8 9.—Rom. 5. 20. Eph.
2. 7-9.—Gal. 2. 16.—Tit. 3 5, 6.
M   2 *

When thou hast eaten and art full, . . .
thou shalt bless the Lord thy God for
the good land which he hath given thee.

BEWARE that thou forget not the
LORD thy God.—One of them, when
he saw that he was healed, turned back,
and with a loud voice glorified God, and
fell down on his face at his feet, giving
him thanks: and he was a Samaritan.
And Jesus answering said, Were there
not ten cleansed? but where are the
nine? There are not found that returned
to give glory to God, save this stranger.

Every creature of God is good, and
nothing to be refused, if it be received
with thanksgiving: for it is sanctified
by the word of God and prayer —He
that eateth, eateth to the Lord, for he
giveth God thanks.—The blessing of the
LORD, it maketh rich, and he addeth no
sorrow with it.

Bless the LORD, O my soul: and all
that is within me, bless his holy name.
Bless the LORD, O my soul, . . . who
forgiveth all thine iniquities; . . . who
crowneth thee with lovingkindness and
tender mercies.

DEUT. 8. 10. Deut. 8. 11.—Luke 17. 15-18.
1 Tim. 4. 4, 5.—Rom. 14. 6.—Pro. 10. 22.
Ps. 103. 1-4.

M

FEBRUARY 8.

Henceforth I call you not servants; for
the servant knoweth not what his lord
doeth: but I have called you friends

THE LORD said, Shall I hide from
Abraham that thing which I do?—It
is given unto you to know the mysteries
of the kingdom of heaven.—God hath
revealed them unto us by his Spirit: for
the Spirit searcheth all things, yea, the
deep things of God—Even the hidden
wisdom, which God ordained before the
world unto our glory.

Blessed is the man whom thou choosest,
and causest to approach unto thee, that
he may dwell in thy courts: we shall
be satisfied with the goodness of thy
house, even of thy holy temple.—The
secret of the LORD is with them that
fear him; and he will shew them his
covenant.—I have given unto them the
words which thou gavest me; and they
have received them, and have known
surely that I came out from thee, and
they have believed that thou didst send
me.

Ye are my friends, if ye do whatsoever
I command you.

JOHN 15 15. Gen. 18. 17 —Mat. 13 11—
1 Cor 2 10 —1 Cor 2 7   Ps. 65. 4—Ps. 25.
14 —John 17 8. John 15 14

K

FEBRUARY 9.

Now he is comforted.

THY sun shall no more go down; neither shall thy moon withdraw itself: for the LORD shall be thine everlasting light, and the days of thy mourning shall be ended.—He will swallow up death in victory; and the LORD God will wipe away tears from off all faces; and the rebuke of his people shall he take away from off all the earth.—These are they which came out of great tribulation, and have washed their robes, and made them white in the blood of the Lamb. Therefore are they before the throne of God, and serve him day and night in his temple: and he that sitteth on the throne shall dwell among them. They shall hunger no more, neither thirst any more; neither shall the sun light on them, nor any heat. For the Lamb which is in the midst of the throne shall feed them, and shall lead them unto living fountains of waters.—God shall wipe away all tears from their eyes; and there shall be no more death, neither sorrow, nor crying, neither shall there be any more pain: for the former things are passed away.

LUKE 16. 25. Is. 60. 20.—Is. 25. 8.—Rev. 7. 14-17.—Rev 21. 4.

M

FEBRUARY 10.

The light of the body is the eye: there-
fore when thine eye is single, thy
whole body also is full of light.

THE natural man receiveth not the
things of the Spirit of God : for they
are foolishness unto him : neither can he
know them, because they are spiritually
discerned.—Open thou mine eyes, that I
may behold wondrous things out of thy
law.

I am the light of the world : he that
followeth me shall not walk in darkness,
but shall have the light of life.—We all,
with open face beholding as in a glass the
glory of the Lord, are changed into the
same image . . . even as by the Spirit
of the Lord.—God, who commanded the
light to shine out of darkness, hath shined
in our hearts, to give the light of the
knowledge of the glory of God in the face
of Jesus Christ.

The God of our Lord Jesus Christ, the
Father of glory, . . . give unto you the
spirit of wisdom and revelation in the
knowledge of him . . . that ye may
know what is the hope of his calling,
and what the riches of the glory of his
inheritance in the saints.

LUKE 11. 34. 1 Cor. 2. 14.—Ps. 119. 18. John
8. 12.—2 Cor. 3, 18.—2 Cor. 4. 6. Eph. 1. 17, 18.

M

FEBRUARY 11.

They that feared the Lord spake often one
to another : and the Lord hearkened, and
heard it, and a book of remembrance was
written before him for them that feared
the Lord, and that thought upon his name.

I T came to pass, that, while they com-
muned together and reasoned, Jesus
himself drew near, and went with them.
—Where two or three are gathered together in my name, there am I in the
midst of them —My fellow-labourers,
whose names are in the book of life

Let the word of Christ dwell in you
richly in all wisdom ; teaching and admonishing one another in psalms and
hymns and spiritual songs, singing with
grace in your hearts to the Lord —Ex-
hort one another daily, while it is called
to day; lest any of you be hardened
through the deceitfulness of sin

Every idle word that men shall speak,
they shall give account thereof in the day
of judgment : for by thy words thou
shalt be justified, and by thy words thou
shalt be condemned.—Behold, it is written before me.

MAL. 3. 16 Luke 24 15 —Mat. 18. 20 —Phil 4.
3. Col 3 16—Heb 3 13 Mat 12 36, 37.
—Is 65. 6.

M

FEBRUARY 12.

They shall be mine, saith the Lord of
hosts, in that day when I make up
my jewels

I HAVE manifested thy name unto the
men which thou gavest me out of the
world : thine they were, and thou gavest
them me , and they have kept thy word.
I pray for them : I pray not for the world,
but for them which thou hast given me ;
for they are thine. And all mine are
thine, and thine are mine ; and I am
glorified in them. Father, I will that
they also, whom thou hast given me, be
with me where I am : that they may
behold my glory, which thou hast given
me : for thou lovedst me before the
foundation of the world.

I will come again, and receive you
unto myself.—He shall come to be glorified in his saints, and to be admired in
all them that believe . . . in that day.
—We which are alive and remain shall
be caught up together with them in the
clouds, to meet the Lord in the air : and
so shall we ever be with the Lord —Thou
shalt also be a crown of glory in the
hand of the LORD, and a royal diadem
in the hand of thy God

MAL. 3 17 John 17 6, 9, 10, 24. John 14 3.
  2 Thes 1 10 —1 Thes 4 17 —Is 62 3
  M

FEBRUARY 13.

Upon the likeness of the throne was the
likeness as the appearance of a man
above upon it

THE man Christ Jesus.—Made in the
likeness of men . . . found in fashion
as a man.—Forasmuch . . as the children are partakers of flesh and blood, he
also himself likewise took part of the
same ; that through death he might destroy him that had the power of death.

I am he that liveth, and was dead ;
and, behold, I am alive for evermore.—
Christ being raised from the dead dieth
no more ; death hath no more dominion
over him. For in that he died, he died
unto sin once : but in that he liveth, he
liveth unto God —What and if ye shall
see the Son of Man ascend up where he
was before ?—He raised him from the
dead, and set him at his own right hand
in the heavenly places.—In him dwelleth
all the fulness of the Godhead bodily

Though he was crucified through weakness, yet he liveth by the power of God.
For we also are weak in him, but we
shall live with him by the power of God.

EZEK 1. 26. 1 Tim 2 5 —Phil. 2 7, 8 —Heb.
2 14 Rev 1. 18.—Rom 6 9, 10 —John 6 62.
—Eph 1 20 —Col. 2. 9. 2 Cor. 13 4
M

FEBRUARY 14.

Suffer it to be so now: for thus it
becometh us to fulfil all righteousness.

I DELIGHT to do thy will, O my God:
yea, thy law is within my heart.

Think not that I am come to destroy
the law, or the prophets : I am not come
to destroy, but to fulfil. For verily I say
unto you, Till heaven and earth pass, one
jot or one tittle shall in no wise pass from
the law, till all be fulfilled —The LORD
is well pleased for his righteousness' sake ;
ue will magnify the law, and make it
honourable —Except your righteousness
shall exceed the righteousness of the
scribes and Pharisees, ye shall in no case
enter into the kingdom of heaven.

What the law could not do, in that it
was weak through the flesh, God sending
his own Son in the likeness of sinful flesh,
and for sin. condemned sin in the flesh :
that the righteousness of the law might
be fulfilled in us, who walk not after the
flesh, but after the Spirit.—Christ is the
end of the law for righteousness to every
one that believeth.

MAT. 3. 15. Ps. 40. 8. Mat. 5. 17, 18.—Is. 42.
21 —Mat. 5. 20. Rom. 8. 3. 4 —Rom. 10. 4.
M

Who can say, I have made my heart clean?

THE LORD looked down from heaven upon the children of men, to see if there were any that did understand, and seek God. They are all gone aside, they are all together become filthy. there is none that doeth good, no, not one —They that are in the flesh cannot please God

To will is present with me; but how to perform that which is good I find not. For the good that I would I do not. but the evil which I would not, that I do.— We are all as an unclean thing, and all our righteousnesses are as filthy rags ; and we all do fade as a leaf; and our iniquities, like the wind, have taken us away.

The scripture hath concluded all under sin, that the promise by faith of Jesus Christ might be given to them that believe.—God was in Christ, reconciling the world unto himself, not imputing their trespasses unto them —If we say that we have no sin, we deceive ourselves, and the truth is not in us. If we confess our sins, he is faithful and just to forgive us our sins, and to cleanse us from all unrighteousness.

PRO. 20. 9 Ps 14 2, 3 —Rom 8. 8. Rom 7. 18, 19 —Is. 64 6 Gal. 3. 22 —2 Cor. 5 19. —1 John 1 8, 9.

M

FEBRUARY 16.

Thy name is as ointment poured forth.

CHRIST . . . hath loved us, and hath given himself for us, an offering and a sacrifice to God for a sweetsmelling savour —Unto you therefore which believe he is precious — God also hath highly exalted him, and given him a name which is above every name : that at the name of Jesus every knee should bow.—In him dwelleth all the fulness of the Godhead bodily.

If ye love me, keep my commandments. —The love of God is shed abroad in our hearts by the Holy Ghost which is given unto us.—The house was filled with the odour of the ointment.—They took knowledge of them, that they had been with Jesus.

O LORD our Lord, how excellent is thy name in all the earth ! who hast set thy glory above the heavens —Emmanuel . . . God with us.—His name shall be called Wonderful, Counsellor, The mighty God, The everlasting Father, The Prince of Peace.—The name of the LORD is a strong tower : the righteous runneth into it, and is safe.

CANT 1. 3.   Eph 5 2.—1 Pet. 2 7 —Phil. 2 9, 10.—Col. 2 9   John 14 15.—Rom. 5. 5.—John 12 3.—Acts 4 13   Ps 8 1 — Mat. 1 23 —Is. 9. 6 —Pro 18 10.

M

FEBRUARY 17.

The whole bullock shall he carry forth without the camp unto a clean place, where
the ashes are poured out, and burn him on
the wood with fire.

THEY took Jesus, and led him away.
And he bearing his cross went forth
into a place called the place of a skull,
which is called in the Hebrew Golgotha :
where they crucified him.—The bodies of
those beasts, whose blood is brought into
the sanctuary by the high priest for sin,
are burned without the camp. Wherefore Jesus also, that he might sanctify the
people with his own blood, suffered without the gate. Let us go forth therefore
unto him without the camp, bearing his
reproach.—The fellowship of his sufferings.

Rejoice, inasmuch as ye are partakers
of Christ's sufferings : that, when his
glory shall be revealed, ye may be glad
also with exceeding joy.—Our light affliction, which is but for a moment, worketh for us a far more exceeding and
eternal weight of glory.

Lev. 4. 12. John 19. 16-18.—Heb. 13. 11-13.—
    Phil. 3. 10. 1 Pet. 4. 13.—2 Cor. 4. 17.
M

FEBRUARY 18.

Thou art my hope in the day of evil.

THERE be many that say, Who will shew us any good? LORD, lift thou up the light of thy countenance upon us. —I will sing of thy power; yea, I will sing aloud of thy mercy in the morning: for thou hast been my defence and refuge in the day of my trouble.

In my prosperity I said, I shall never be moved. Thou didst hide thy face, and I was troubled. I cried to thee, O LORD: and unto the LORD I made supplication What profit is there in my blood, when I go down to the pit? Shall the dust praise thee? shall it declare thy truth? Hear, O LORD, and have mercy upon me: LORD, be thou my helper

For a small moment have I forsaken thee; but with great mercies will I gather thee. In a little wrath I hid my face from thee for a moment; but with everlasting kindness will I have mercy on thee, saith the LORD thy Redeemer —Sorrow shall be turned into joy.—Weeping may endure for a night, but joy cometh in the morning.

JER. 17 17. Ps. 4 6 —Ps. 59 16. Ps. 30 6, 8-10. Is 54. 7, 8 —John 16 20 —Ps 30. 5

M

FEBRUARY 19.

The Lord giveth wisdom: out of his mouth cometh knowledge and understanding.

TRUST in the LORD with all thine heart ; and lean not unto thine own understanding.—If any of you lack wisdom, let him ask of God, that giveth to all men liberally, and upbraideth not ; and it shall be given him.—The foolishness of God is wiser than men ; and the weakness of God is stronger than men.— I will give you a mouth and wisdom, which all your adversaries shall not be able to gainsay nor resist.—God hath chosen the foolish things of the world to confound the wise. . .That no flesh should glory in his presence.

The entrance of thy words giveth light ; it giveth understanding unto the simple. —Thy word have I hid in my heart, that I might not sin against thee.

All bare him witness, and wondered at the gracious words which proceeded out of his mouth.—Never man spake like this man.—Of him are ye in Christ Jesus, who of God is made unto us wisdom, and righteousness, and sanctification, and redemption.

PRO 2. 6.   Pro 3. 5.—Ja. 1. 5.—1 Cor. 1. 25 — Luke 21. 15.—1 Cor. 1. 27, 29. Ps. 119. 130.—Ps. 119. 11.   Luke 4. 22 —Iohn 7. 46.—1 Cor. 1. 30.

M

He shall see of the travail of his soul, and shall be satisfied

JESUS . . . said, It is finished : and he bowed his head, and gave up the ghost. —He hath made him to be sin for us, who knew no sin ; that we might be made the righteousness of God in him. This people have I formed for myself ; they shall shew forth my praise.—To the intent that now unto the principalities and powers in heavenly places might be known by the church the manifold wisdom of God, according to the eternal purpose which he purposed in Christ Jesus our Lord.—That in the ages to come he might shew the exceeding riches of his grace in his kindness toward us through Christ Jesus.

After that ye believed, ye were sealed with that holy Spirit of promise, which is the earnest of our inheritance until the redemption of the purchased possession, unto the praise of his glory.—Ye are a chosen generation, a royal priesthood, a holy nation, a peculiar people ; that ye should shew forth the praises of him who hath called you out of darkness into his marvellous light

Is. 53. 11.   John 19 30 —2 Cor. 5. 21.   Is 43. 21. —Eph. 3. 10. 11.—Eph. 2. 7.   Eph. 1. 13, 14 — 1 Pet 2 9

M

I am the Lord which sanctify you.

I AM the LORD your God, which have separated you from other people Ye shall be holy unto me : for I the LORD am holy, and have severed you from other people, that ye should be mine.

Sanctified by God the Father.—Sanctify them through thy truth : thy word is truth.—The very God of peace sanctify you wholly ; and I pray God your whole spirit and soul and body be preserved blameless unto the coming of our Lord Jesus Christ.

Jesus . . that he might sanctify the people with his own blood, suffered without the gate.—Our Saviour Jesus Christ . . . gave himself for us, that he might redeem us from all iniquity, and purify unto himself a peculiar people, zealous of good works.—Both he that sanctifieth and they who are sanctified are all of one : for which cause he is not ashamed to call them brethren.—For their sakes I sanctify myself, that they also might be sanctified through the truth.—Through sanctification of the Spirit, unto obedience, and sprinkling of the blood of Jesus Christ.

LEV. 20 8   Lev 20 24, 26   Jude 1.—John 17. 17.—1 Thes 5 23.   Heb 13 12.—Tit. 2 13, 14.—Heb 2 11 —John 17 19 —1 Pet 1 2.

M

What man is he that feareth the Lord?
him shall he teach in the way that
he shall choose

THE light of the body is the eye: if
therefore thine eye be single, thy
whole body shall be full of light.

Thy word is a lamp unto my feet, and
a light unto my path.—Thine ears shall
hear a word behind thee, saying, This is
the way, walk ye in it, when ye turn to
the right hand, and when ye turn to the
left.—I will instruct thee and teach thee
in the way which thou shalt go: I will
guide thee with mine eye. Be ye not as
the horse, or as the mule, which have no
understanding · whose mouth must be
held in with bit and bridle, lest they come
near unto thee. Many sorrows shall be
to the wicked · but he that trusteth in the
LORD, mercy shall compass him about.
Be glad in the LORD, and rejoice, ye
righteous : and shout for joy, all ye that
are upright in heart.

O LORD, I know that the way of man
is not in himself: it is not in man that
walketh to direct his steps.

Ps 25 12. Mat. 6 22 Ps 119. 105.—Is. 30. 21.
—Ps. 32 8·11 Jer. 10. 23

M

FEBRUARY 23.

The blood of sprinkling, that speaketh
better things than that of Abel

BEHOLD the Lamb of God, which
taketh away the sin of the world.—
The Lamb slain from the foundation of
the world.—It is not possible that the
blood of bulls and of goats should take
away sins. Wherefore when he cometh
into the world, he saith, Sacrifice and
offering thou wouldest not, but a body
hast thou prepared me. By the which
will we are sanctified through the offering
of the body of Jesus Christ once for all.

Abel . . . brought of the firstlings of his
flock and of the fat thereof. . .The LORD
had respect unto Abel and to his offering.
—Christ . . . hath loved us, and hath
given himself for us, an offering and a
sacrifice to God for a sweetsmelling
savour

Let us draw near with a true heart in
full assurance of faith, having our hearts
sprinkled from an evil conscience, and
our bodies washed with pure water.—
Having . . . boldness to enter into the
holiest by the blood of Jesus.

HEB. 12 24. John 1 29.—Rev. 13. 8.—Heb.
10. 4, 5, 10. Gen. 4 4.—Eph. 5. 2 Heb. 10. 22
—Heb. 10. 19.

M

FEBRUARY 24.

Thus saith the Lord God, I will yet for this be enquired of.

YE have not, because ye ask not. Ask, and it shall be given you ; seek, and ye shall find ; knock, and it shall be opened unto you : for every one that asketh receiveth ; and he that seeketh findeth ; and to him that knocketh it shall be opened —-This is the confidence that we have in him, that, if we ask anything according to his will, he heareth us ; and if we know that he hear us, whatsoever we ask, we know that we have the petitions that we desired of him.—If any of you lack wisdom, let him ask of God, that giveth to all men liberally, and upbraideth not ; and it shall be given him. —Open thy mouth wide, and I will fill it. —Men ought always to pray, and not to faint.

The eyes of the LORD are upon the righteous, and his ears are open unto their cry. The LORD heareth, and delivereth them out of all their troubles.—Ye shall ask in my name ; and I say not unto you, that I will pray the Father for you ; for the Father himself loveth you, because ye have loved me.

EZEK. 36. 37   Ja. 4 2   Mat. 7 7, 8 —1 John
5. 14 15 —Ja 1. 5 —Ps 81 10 —Luke 18. 8.
Ps. 34. 15. ͏ —John 16 26, 27.
M

FEBRUARY 25.

Resist the devil, and he will flee from you.

WHEN the enemy shall come in like a flood, the Spirit of the LORD shall lift up a standard against him.—Get thee hence, Satan : for it is written, Thou shalt worship the Lord thy God, and him only shalt thou serve. Then the devil leaveth him, and, behold, angels came and ministered unto him.

Be strong in the Lord, and in the power of his might. Put on the whole armour of God, that ye may be able to stand against the wiles of the devil.—And have no fellowship with the unfruitful works of darkness, but rather reprove them.—Lest Satan should get an advantage of us : for we are not ignorant of his devices.—Be sober, be vigilant ; because your adversary the devil, as a roaring lion, walketh about, seeking whom he may devour ; whom resist stedfast in the faith, knowing that the same afflictions are accomplished in your brethren that are in the world.

Who shall lay any thing to the charge of God's elect ? It is God that justifieth.

JA. 4 7. Is. 59 19.—Mat. 4 10, 11 Eph. 6. 10, 11.—Eph. 5. 11.—2 Cor. 2. 11.—1 Pet. 5. 8, 9. Rom. 8. 33.

M

FEBRUARY 26.

Let us search and try our ways, and turn again to the Lord

EXAMINE me, O LORD, and prove me; try my reins and my heart.—Behold, thou desirest truth in the inward parts : and in the hidden part thou shalt make me to know wisdom.—I thought on my ways, and turned my feet unto thy testimonies. I made haste, and delayed not to keep thy commandments.—Let a man examine himself, and so let him eat of that bread, and drink of that cup.

If we confess our sins, he is faithful and just to forgive us our sins, and to cleanse us from all unrighteousness.—We have an advocate with the Father, Jesus Christ the righteous : and he is the propitiation for our sins.—Having therefore, brethren, boldness to enter into the holiest by the blood of Jesus, by a new and living way which he hath consecrated for us, through the veil, that is to say, his flesh : and having a high priest over the house of God ; let us draw near with a true heart, in full assurance of faith, having our hearts sprinkled from an evil conscience, and our bodies washed with pure water

LAM. 3. 40. Ps. 26. 2.—Ps. 51. 6.—
Ps. 119. 59, 60.—1 Cor. 11. 28. 1 John 1. 9.—
1 John 2. 1.—Heb. 10. 19-22.

FEBRUARY 27.

Reckon ye yourselves to be dead indeed
unto sin, but alive unto God through
Jesus Christ our Lord

HE that heareth my word, and believeth on him that sent me, hath
everlasting life, and shall not come into
condemnation ; but is passed from death
unto life.—I through the law am dead to
the law, that I might live unto God. I
am crucified with Christ ; nevertheless I
live ; yet not I, but Christ liveth in me :
and the life which I now live in the flesh
I live by the faith of the Son of God, who
loved me, and gave himself for me.

Because I live, ye shall live also.—I
give unto them eternal life : and they
shall never perish, neither shall any man
pluck them out of my hand. My Father,
which gave them me, is greater than all ;
and no man is able to pluck them out of
my Father's hand. I and my Father are
one

If ye then be risen with Christ, seek
those things which are above, where
Christ sitteth on the right hand of God.
. . . For ye are dead, and your life is
hid with Christ in God.

ROM. 6 11 John 5 24 —Gal. 2. 19, 20.
John 14. 19.—John 10. 28-30 Col. 3 1, 3.

61

FEBRUARY 28.

God so loved the world, that he gave his
only begotten Son, that whosoever believeth in him should not perish, but
have everlasting life.

GOD . . . hath reconciled us to himself by Jesus Christ, and hath given
to us the ministry of reconciliation; to
wit, that God was in Christ, reconciling
the world unto himself, not imputing
their trespasses unto them; and hath
committed unto us the word of reconciliation. Now then we are ambassadors
for Christ, as though God did beseech
you by us · we pray you in Christ's stead,
be ye reconciled to God. For he hath
made him to be sin for us, who knew no
sin; that we might be made the righteousness of God in him.

God is love. In this was manifested
the love of God toward us, because that
God sent his only begotten Son into the
world, that we might live through him
Herein is love, not that we loved God,
but that he loved us, and sent his Son to
be the propitiation for our sins Beloved, if God so loved us, we ought also
to love one another.

JOHN 3. 16. 2 Cor 5 18-21 1 John 4. 8-11.
M

FEBRUARY 29.

Boast not thyself of to-morrow, for thou knowest not what a day may bring forth.

BEHOLD, now is the accepted time; behold, now is the day of salvation.— Yet a little while is the light with you. Walk while ye have the light, lest darkness come upon you : for he that walketh in darkness knoweth not whither he goeth. While ye have light, believe in the light, that ye may be the children of light.

Whatsoever thy hand findeth to do, do it with thy might; for there is no work, nor device, nor knowledge, nor wisdom, in the grave, whither thou goest.

Soul, thou hast much goods laid up for many years; take thine ease, eat, drink, and be merry.. Thou fool, this night thy soul shall be required of thee : then whose shall those things be, which thou hast provided ? So is he that layeth up treasure for himself, and is not rich toward God-

The world passeth away, and the lust thereof : but he that doeth the will of God abideth for ever.

Prov. 27. 1. 2 Cor 6. 2.—John 12. 35, 36.
Ecc. 9. 10. Luke 12. 19-21. 1 John 2. 17
N

MARCH 1.

The fruit of the Spirit is love.

GOD is love : and he that dwelleth in
love dwelleth in God, and God in
him.—The love of God is shed abroad
in our hearts by the Holy Ghost which is
given unto us.

Unto you . . . which believe he is
precious.—We love him, because he firs'
loved us

The love of Christ constraineth us ;
because we thus judge, that if one died
for all, then were all dead . and that he
died for all, that they which live should
not henceforth live unto themselves, but
unto him which died for them, and rose
again.

Ye yourselves are taught of God to
love one another —This is my commandment, That ye love one another, as I
have loved you —Above all things have
fervent charity among yourselves : for
charity shall cover the multitude of sins
—Walk in love, as Christ also hath
loved us, and hath given himself for us,
an offering and a sacrifice to God for a
sweetsmelling savour

GAL. 5 22. 1 John 4 16—Rom 5 5. 1 Pet 2 7.
—1 John 4 19 2 Cor 5 14, 15 1 Thes 4 9 ᴸ
John 15 12—1 Pet 4. 8 —Eph 5 2.

3

MARCH 2.

God hath caused me to be fruitful in the
land of my affliction .

BLESSED be God, even the Father of
our Lord Jesus Christ, the Father of
mercies, and the God of all comfort;
who comforteth us in all our tribulation,
that we may be able to comfort them
which are in any trouble, by the comfort
wherewith we ourselves are comforted of
God. For as the sufferings of Christ
abound in us, so our consolation also
aboundeth by Christ.

He shall sit as a refiner and purifier of
silver; and he shall purify the sons of
Levi—Now for a season, if need be, ye
are in heaviness through manifold temptations : that the trial of your faith, being
much more precious than of gold that
perisheth, though it be tried with fire,
might be found unto praise and honour
and glory at the appearing of Jesus
Christ.—The Lord stood with me, and
strengthened me.

Let them that suffer according to the
will of God commit the keeping of their
souls to him in well doing, as unto a
faithful Creator.

* Gen. 41. 52. 2 Cor. 1. 3-5. Mal. 3. 3—
1 Pet. 1. 6, 7.—2 Tim. 4. 17 1 Pet. 4. 19.
M

Trust in the Lord with all thine heart, and lean not unto thine own understanding In all thy ways acknowledge him, and he shall direct thy paths.

TRUST in him at all times ; ye people, pour out your heart before him : God is a refuge for us.

I will instruct thee and teach thee in the way which thou shalt go : I will guide thee with mine eye Be ye not as the horse, or as the mule, which have no understanding : whose mouth must be held in with bit and bridle, lest they come near unto thee. Many sorrows shall be to the wicked · but he that trusteth in the LORD, mercy shall compass him about.—Thine ears shall hear a word behind thee, saying, This is the way, walk ye in it, when ye turn to the right hand, and when ye turn to the left.

If thy presence go not with me, carry us not up hence. For wherein shall it be known here that I and thy people have found grace in thy sight? is it not in that thou goest with us? so shall we be separated, I and thy people, from all the people that are upon the . . . earth.

PROV 3 5, 6 Ps. 62 8 Ps 32 8-10 —
M Is. 30 21 Ex 23 15, 16

MARCH 4.

Set your affection on things above, not on things on the earth.

LOVE not the world, neither the things that are in the world. If any man love the world, the love of the Father is not in him.—Lay not up for yourselves treasures upon earth, where moth and rust doth corrupt, and where thieves break through and steal : but lay up for yourselves treasures in heaven, where neither moth nor rust doth corrupt, and where thieves do not break through nor steal : for where your treasure is, there will your heart be also

We walk by faith, not by sight.—We faint not ; but though our outward man perish, yet the inward man is renewed day by day. For our light affliction, which is but for a moment, worketh for us a far more exceeding and eternal weight of glory : while we look not at the things which are seen, but at the things which are not seen : for the things which are seen are temporal ; but the things which are not seen are eternal.—An inheritance incorruptible, and undefiled, and that fadeth not away, reserved in heaven for you.

Col. 3. 2   1 John 2. 15 —Mat 6. 19-21.
2 Cor. 5. 7.—2 Cor 4 16-18.—1 Pet 1. 4.

MARCH 5.

O Lora, I am oppressed; undertake for me.

UNTO thee I lift up mine eyes, O thou that dwellest in the heavens. Behold, as the eyes of servants look unto the hand of their masters, and as the eyes of a maiden unto the hand of her mistress; so our eyes wait upon the LORD our God — Hear my cry, O God; attend unto my prayer. From the end of the earth will I cry unto thee, when my heart is overwhelmed: lead me to the rock that is higher than I. For thou hast been a shelter for me, and a strong tower from the enemy. I will abide in thy tabernacle for ever : I will trust in the covert of thy wings.—Thou hast been a strength to the poor, a strength to the needy in his distress, a refuge from the storm.

Christ . . . suffered for us, leaving us an example, that ye should follow his steps : who did no sin, neither was guile found in his mouth · who, when he was reviled, reviled not again; when he suffered, he threatened not; but committed himself to him that judgeth righteously.

Is. 38. 14.   Ps. 123. 1, 2 —Ps. 61 1-4 —Is 25. 4.
1 Pet 2. 21-23
M

MARCH 6.

He preserveth the way of his saints.

THE LORD your God . . went in the way before you, to search you out a place to pitch your tents in, in fire by night, to shew you by what way ye should go, and in a cloud by day.—As an eagle stirreth up her nest, fluttereth over her young, spreadeth abroad her wings, taketh them, beareth them on her wings : so the LORD alone did lead him.—The steps of a good man are ordered by the LORD : and he delighteth in his way. Though he fall, he shall not be utterly cast down ; for the LORD upholdeth him with his hand.—Many are the afflictions of the righteous · but the LORD delivereth him out of them all —For the LORD knoweth the way of the righteous ; but the way of the ungodly shall perish.—We know that all things work together for good to them that love God, to them who are the called according to his purpose.—With us is the LORD our God to help us, and to fight our battles

The LORD thy God in the midst of thee is mighty ; he will save, he will rejoice over thee with joy

PRO. 2. 8. Deut. 1. 32, 33.—Deut. 32. 11, 12 —
Ps. 37. 23, 24.—Ps. 34. 19.—Ps. 1. 6.—Rom. 8. 28.
        —2 Chr. 32. 8. Zep. 3. 17.

M

Thy Maker is thine husband, the Lord of hosts is his name.

THIS is a great mystery : but I speak concerning Christ and the church. Thou shalt no more be termed Forsaken . . . but thou shalt be called Hephzi-bah, . for the LORD delighteth in thee And as the bridegroom rejoiceth over the bride, so shall thy God rejoice over thee — He hath sent me . . . to comfort all that mourn ; to appoint unto them that mourn in Zion, to give unto them beauty for ashes, the oil of joy for mourning, the garment of praise for the spirit of heaviness

I will greatly rejoice in the LORD, my soul shall be joyful in my God ; for he hath clothed me with the garments of salvation, . as a bridegroom decketh himself with ornaments, and as a bride adorneth herself with her jewels.

I will betroth thee unto me for ever ; yea, I will betroth thee unto me in righteousness, and in judgment, and in lovingkindness, and in mercies.

Who shall separate us from the love of Christ ?

Is. 54. 5   Eph 5 32.   Is 62. 4, 5.—Is. 61. 1-3.
    Is. 61. 10   Hos 2 19.   Rom 8 35.

M

MARCH 8.

Thou hast cast all my sins behind thy back.

WHO is a God like unto thee, that pardoneth iniquity, and passeth by the transgression of the remnant of his heritage? he retaineth not his anger for ever, because he delighteth in mercy. He will turn again, he will have compassion upon us; he will subdue our iniquities; and thou wilt cast all their sins into the depths of the sea

I will forgive their iniquity, and I will remember their sin no more.

For a small moment have I forsaken thee; but with great mercies will I gather thee. In a little wrath I hid my face from thee for a moment; but with everlasting kindness will I have mercy on thee, saith the LORD thy Redeemer

Blessed is he whose transgression is forgiven, whose sin is covered. Blessed is the man unto whom the LORD imputeth not iniquity, and in whose spirit there is no guile —The blood of Jesus Christ his Son cleanseth us from all sin

Is 38. 17. Mic 7 18, 19 Jer 31 34 Is 54. 7, 8. Ps 32 1, 2 —1 John 1. 7,

M

MARCH 9.

The living God giveth us richly all things to enjoy

BEWARE that thou forget not the LORD thy God, in not keeping his commandments, and his judgments, and his statutes, which I command thee this day : lest when thou hast eaten and art full, and hast built goodly houses, and dwelt therein , . . . then thine heart be lifted up, and thou forget the LORD thy God : . . . for it is he that giveth thee power to get wealth.

Except the LORD build the house, they labour in vain that build it : except the LORD keep the city, the watchman waketh but in vain. It is vain for you to rise up early, to sit up late, to eat the bread of sorrows : for so he giveth his beloved sleep.—They got not the land in possession by their own sword, neither did their own arm save them : but thy right hand, and thine arm, and the light of thy countenance, because thou hadst a favour unto them — There be many that say, Who will shew us any good ? LORD, lift thou up the light of thy countenance upon us.

1 TIM 6. 17   Deut 8. 11, 12, 14, 18.   Ps. 127
1 2 — Ps 44 3.—Ps 4. 6

M   3 *

The Lord will provide

GOD will provide himself a lamb for a burnt offering

Behold, the LORD's hand is not shortened, that it cannot save; neither his ear heavy, that it cannot hear.—There shall come out of Sion the Deliverer, and shall turn away ungodliness from Jacob.

Happy is he that hath the God of Jacob for his help, whose hope is in the LORD his God.—Behold, the eye of the LORD is upon them that fear him, upon them that hope in his mercy; to deliver their soul from death.

My God shall supply all your need, according to his riches in glory by Christ Jesus.—He hath said, I will never leave thee, nor forsake thee. So that we may boldly say, The Lord is my helper, and I will not fear what man shall do unto me. —The LORD is my strength and my shield; my heart trusted in him, and I am helped: therefore my heart greatly rejoiceth: and with my song will I praise him.

GEN 22 14 (*marg*) Gen 22 8 Is 59 1.—
Rom 11. 26. Ps 146. 5—Ps 33. 18, 19.
Phil 4 19—Heb 13 5, 6.—Ps. 28 7
M

The Lord bless thee, and keep thee

THE blessing of the LORD, it maketh rich, and he addeth no sorrow with it. —Thou, LORD, wilt bless the righteous ; with favour wilt thou compass him as with a shield.

He will not suffer thy foot to be moved : he that keepeth thee will not slumber. Behold, he that keepeth Israel shall neither slumber nor sleep. The LORD is thy keeper : the LORD is thy shade upon thy right hand. The LORD shall preserve thee from all evil : he shall preserve thy soul. The LORD shall preserve thy going out and thy coming in from this time forth, and even for evermore.—I the LORD do keep it ; I will water it every moment : lest any hurt it, I will keep it night and day.

Holy Father, keep through thine own name those whom thou hast given me. While I was with them in the world, I kept them in thy name · those that thou gavest me I have kept.

The Lord shall deliver me from every evil work, and will preserve me unto his heavenly kingdom : to whom be glory for ever and ever. Amen.

NUM 6 24 Pro 10. 22 —Ps 5. 12 Ps 121. 3-5, 7, 8 —Is 27. 2. John 17 11, 12 2 Tim. 4 18.
M

The Lord make his face shine upon thee,
and be gracious unto thee. The Lord lift
up his countenance upon thee, and give
thee peace.

NO man hath seen God at any time;
the only begotten Son, which is in
the bosom of the Father, he hath declared
him.—The brightness of his glory, and
the express image of his person.—The
god of this world hath blinded the minds
of them which believe not, lest the light
of the glorious gospel of Christ, who is
the image of God, should shine unto them.

Make thy face to shine upon thy servant : save me for thy mercies' sake. Let
me not be ashamed, O LORD ; for I have
called upon thee.—LORD, by thy favour
thou hast made my mountain to stand
strong : thou didst hide thy face, and I
was troubled.—Blessed is the people that
know the joyful sound : they shall walk,
O LORD, in the light of thy countenance.

The LORD will give strength unto his
people; the LORD will bless his people
with peace.—Be of good cheer ; it is I ;
be not afraid.

NUM. 6. 25, 26   John 1 18.—Heb. 1 3 —
2 Cor 4 4   Ps. 31. 16, 17.—Ps. 30. 7 —
Ps. 89 15   Ps. 29 11 —Mat. 14 27.

M

There is one God, and one mediator
between God and men, the man
Christ Jesus.

FORASMUCH . as the children are
partakers of flesh and blood, he also
himself likewise took part of the same.

Look unto me, and be ye saved, all
the ends of the earth : for I am God,
and there is none else.

We have an advocate with the Father,
Jesus Christ the righteous —In Christ
Jesus, ye who sometime were far off, are
made nigh by the blood of Christ

He is our peace.—By his own blood
he entered in once into the holy place,
having obtained eternal redemption for
us. And for this cause he is the mediator
of the new testament, that by means of
death, for the redemption of the transgressions that were under the first testament, they which are called might receive
the promise of eternal inheritance.—He
is able also to save them to the uttermost
that come unto God by him, seeing he
ever liveth to make intercession for them.

1 Tim 2 5   Heb 2 14   Is 45 22   1 John 2.
1 —Eph 2 13, 14 —Heb 9 12, 15 —Heb 7 25
M

MARCH 14.

Adorn the doctrine of God our Saviour in all things.

LET your conversation be as it becom·
eth the gospel of Christ.—If ye be
reproached for the name of Christ, happy
are ye. But let none of you suffer as a
murderer, or as a thief, or as an evildoer,
or as a busybody in other men's matters
—Be blameless and harmless, the sons of
God, without rebuke, in the midst of a
crooked and perverse nation, among
whom ye shine as lights in the world —
Let your light so shine before men, that
they may see your good works, and
glorify your Father which is in heaven.

Let not mercy and truth forsake thee :
bind them about thy neck ; write them
upon the table of thine heart ; so shalt
thou find favour and good understanding
in the sight of God and man.—Brethren,
whatsoever things are true, whatsoever
things are honest, whatsoever things are
just, whatsoever things are pure, whatso·
ever things are lovely, whatsoever things
are of good report ; if there be any virtue,
and if there be any praise, think on these
things.

Tit. 2 10 Phil. 1. 27.—1 Pet. 4 14, 15.—Phil.
2. 15.—Mat. 5 16 Pro 3 3, 4.—Phil. 4. 8.

M

MARCH 15.

Perfect through sufferings.

MY soul is exceeding sorrowful, even unto death: tarry ye here, and watch with me. And he went a little farther, and fell on his face, and prayed, saying, O my Father, if it be possible, let this cup pass from me: nevertheless not as I will, but as thou wilt.—And being in an agony he prayed more earnestly, and his sweat was as it were great drops of blood falling down to the ground.

The sorrows of death compassed me, and the pains of hell gat hold upon me: I found trouble and sorrow.—Reproach hath broken my heart; and I am full of heaviness: and I looked for some to take pity, but there was none; and for comforters, but I found none.—I looked on my right hand, and beheld, but there was no man that would know me: refuge failed me, no man cared for my soul.

He is despised and rejected of men; a man of sorrows, and acouainted with grief: and we hid as it were our faces from him; he was despised, and we esteemed him not.

HEB 2 10 Mat 26 38, 39.—Luke 22 44. Ps. 116. 3 —Ps 69. 20.—Ps 142. 4. Is. 53 3.

M

MARCH 16.

What is your life? It is even a vapour,
that appeareth for a little time, and then
vanisheth away

M Y days are swifter than a post : they
flee away, they see no good. They
are passed away as the swift ships : as the
eagle that hasteth to the prey —Thou
carriest them away as with a flood ; they
are as a sleep : in the morning they are
like grass which groweth up. In the
morning it flourisheth, and groweth up ;
in the evening it is cut down, and withereth.—Man that is born of a woman is of
few days, and full of trouble He cometh
forth like a flower, and is cut down.

The world passeth away, and the lust
thereof but he that doeth the will of
God abideth for ever

They shall perish, but thou shalt endure : yea, all of them shall wax old like
a garment ; as a vesture shalt thou change
them, and they shall be changed : but
thou art the same, and thy years shall
have no end.—Jesus Christ, the same
yesterday, and to day, and for ever.

Jᴀ 4 14 Job 9 25, 26 —Ps 90 5, 6 —Job 14
3 1 John 2. 17 Ps 102 26, 27.—Heb 13 8
M

MARCH 17.

He shall put his hand upon the head of
the burnt offering, and it shall be
accepted for him to make atonement
for him

YE know that ye were not redeemed
with corruptible things, as silver and
gold, from your vain conversation received by tradition from your fathers;
but with the precious blood of Christ
as of a lamb without blemish and without spot.—Who his own self bare our sins
in his own body on the tree

He hath made us accepted in the
Beloved

As lively stones, . , . built up a
spiritual house, a holy priesthood, to
offer up spiritual sacrifices. acceptable to
God by Jesus Christ.—I beseech you
therefore, brethren, by the mercies of
God, that ye present your bodies a living
sacrifice, holy, acceptable unto God,
which is your reasonable service

Now unto him that is able to keep
you from falling, and to present you
faultless before the presence of his glory
with exceeding joy, to the only wise God
our Saviour, be glory and majesty, dominion and power, both now and ever.

Lev. 1. 4. 1 Pet. 1 18, 19.—1 Pet. 2. 24 Eph.
1. 6 1 Pet. 2 5.—Rom 12 1 Jude 24, 25
M

Mine eyes fail with looking upward

HAVE mercy upon me, O LORD ; for I am weak : O LORD, heal me ; for my bones are vexed My soul is also sore vexed . but thou, O LORD, how long? Return, O LORD, deliver my soul : oh save me for thy mercies' sake.—My heart is sore pained within me : and the terrors of death are fallen upon me. Fearfulness and trembling are come upon me, and horror hath overwhelmed me. And I said, Oh that I had wings like a dove ! for then would I fly away, and be at rest.

Ye have need of patience.

While they looked stedfastly toward heaven as he went up, behold, two men stood by them in white apparel ; which also said, Ye men of Galilee, why stand ye gazing up into heaven? this same Jesus, which is taken up from you into heaven, shall so come in like manner as ye have seen him go into heaven.—Our conversation is in heaven , from whence also we look for the Saviour, the Lord Jesus Christ.—That blessed hope, . . . the glorious appearing of the great God and our Saviour Jesus Christ.

Is 38 14 Ps 6 2-4—Ps 55 4-6 Heb 10 36. Acts 1 10, 11 —Phil 3 20.—Tit 2 13

M

God, having raised up his Son Jesus, sent him to bless you, in turning away every one of you from his iniquities.

BLESSED be the God and Father of our Lord Jesus Christ, which according to his abundant mercy hath begotten us again unto a lively hope by the resurrection of Jesus Christ from the dead

Our Saviour Jesus Christ, who gave himself for us that he might redeem us from all iniquity, and purify unto himself a peculiar people, zealous of good works.—As he which hath called you is holy, so be ye holy in all manner of conversation; because it is written, Be ye holy; for I am holy.

The God and Father of our Lord Jesus Christ, . . . hath blessed us with all spiritual blessings in heavenly places in Christ.—In him dwelleth all the fulness of the Godhead bodily. And ye are complete in him.—Of his fulness have all we received, and grace for grace.

He that spared not his own Son, but delivered him up for us all, how shall he not with him also freely give us all things?

Acts 3 26. 1 Pet 1 3. Tit. 2. 13, 14 —1 Pet. 1 15, 16 Eph. 1 3 —Col 2. 9, 10 —John 1 16. Rom 8 32

M

The entrance of thy words giveth light.

THIS . . . is the message which we have heard of him, and declare unto you, that God is light, and in him is no darkness at all —God, who commanded the light to shine out of darkness, hath shined in our hearts, to give the light of the knowledge of the glory of God in the face of Jesus Christ.—The Word was God In him was life ; and the life was the light of men —If we walk in the light, as he is in the light, we have fellowship one with another, and the blood of Jesus Christ his Son cleanseth us from all sin

Thy word have I hid in mine heart, that I might not sin against thee.—Ye are clean through the word which I have spoken unto you

Ye were sometime darkness, but now are ye light in the Lord. walk as children of light.—Ye are a chosen generation, a royal priesthood, a holy nation, a peculiar people ; that ye should shew forth the praises of him who hath called you out of darkness into his marvellous light.

Ps. 119 130.   1 John 1 5 —2 Cor. 4 6 —John 1. 1, 4 —1 John 1 7 Ps 119 11 —John 15. 3.   Eph. 5 8.—1 Pet 2 9.

M

MARCH 21.

Be watchful, and strengthen the things
which remain, that are ready to die.

THE end of all things is at hand : be
ye therefore sober, and watch unto
prayer.—Be sober, be vigilant ; because
your adversary the devil, as a roaring
lion, walketh about, seeking whom he
may devour.

Take heed to thyself, and keep thy
soul diligently, lest thou forget the things
which thine eyes have seen, and lest
they depart from thy heart all the days
of thy life.—The just shall live by faith :
but if any man draw back, my soul shall
have no pleasure in him. But we are
not of them who draw back unto perdition ; but of them that believe to the
saving of the soul

What I say unto you I say unto all,
Watch.

Fear thou not ; for I am with thee :
be not dismayed ; for I am thy God ; I
will strengthen thee ; yea, I will help
thee ; yea, I will uphold thee with the
right hand of my righteousness. I the
LORD thy God will hold thy right hand.

REV 3 2. 1 Pet. 4 7 —1 Pet 5 8   Deut. 4. 9.—
Heb 10. 38, 39.   Mark 13. 37.   Is. 41 10, 13.
M

MARCH 22.

Lot lifted up his eyes, and beheld all the plain of Jordan, that it was well watered everywhere, before the Lord destroyed Sodom and Gomorrah, even as the garden of the Lord. Then Lot chose him all the plain of Jordan.

JUST Lot . . . that righteous man.

Be not deceived ; God is not mocked : for whatsoever a man soweth, that shall he also reap.—Remember Lot's wife.

Be ye not unequally yoked together with unbelievers . for what fellowship hath righteousness with unrighteousness? and what communion hath light with darkness? Wherefore come out from among them, and be ye separate, saith the Lord, and touch not the unclean thing.

Be not ye . partakers with them. For ye were sometime darkness, but now are ye light in the Lord: walk as children of light . proving what is acceptable unto the Lord And have no fellowship with the unfruitful works of darkness, but rather reprove them.

GEN. 13 10, 11 2 Pet. 2 7, 8 Gal. 6 7.—
Luke 17 32 2 Cor. 6 14, 17 Eph
5 7, 8, 10, 11

M

MARCH 23.

Holy, holy, holy, Lord God Almighty.

THOU art holy, O thou that inhabitest the praises of Israel.—Draw not nigh hither : put off thy shoes from off thy feet, for the place whereon thou standest is holy ground . . . I am the God of thy father, the God of Abraham, the God of Isaac, and the God of Jacob. And Moses hid his face; for he was afraid to look upon God —To whom then will ye liken me, or shall I be equal? saith the Holy One.—I am the LORD thy God, the Holy One of Israel, thy Saviour —I, even I, am the LORD, and beside me there is no saviour.

As he which hath called you is holy, so be ye holy in all manner of conversation; because it is written, Be ye holy ; for I am holy.—Know ye not that your body is the temple of the Holy Ghost which is in you, which ye have of God, and ye are not your own?—Ye are the temple of the living God; as God hath said, I will dwell in them, and walk in them ; and I will be their God, and they shall be my people —Can two walk together, except they be agreed?

REV 4 8   Ps. 22 3 —Ex. 3 5, 6 —Is 40 25
—Is 43 3, 11   1 Pet 1 15. 16.—1 Cor 6 19
—2 Cor. 6. 16 —Amos 3 3

M

MARCH 24.

Abraham believed in the Lord, and he
counted it to him for righteousness

HE staggered not at the promise of
God through unbelief; but was strong
in faith, giving glory to God ; and being
fully persuaded that, what he had promised, he was able also to perform-
And therefore it was imputed to him for
righteousness. Now it was not written
for his sake alone, that it was imputed
to him   but for us also, to whom it shall
be imputed, if we believe on him that
raised up Jesus our Lord from the dead.

The promise, that he should be the
heir of the world, was not to Abraham,
or to his seed, through the law, but
through the righteousness of faith.

The just shall live by faith.—Let us
hold fast the profession of our faith
without wavering ; (for he is faithful that
promised)—Our God is in the heavens ;
he hath done whatsoever he hath pleased.
—With God nothing shall be impossible
And blessed is she that believed : for
there shall be a performance of those
things which were told her from the
Lord.

Gen 15 6 Rom 4 20-24 Rom 4 13 Rom.
1. 17 —Heb 10 23.—Ps 115 3 —Luke 1 37, 45.

M

MARCH 25.

I will never leave thee, nor forsake thee.

SO that we may boldly say, The Lord is my helper, and I will not fear what man shall do unto me.

Behold, I am with thee, and will keep thee in all places whither thou goest, and will bring thee again into this land; for I will not leave thee, until I have done that which I have spoken to thee of —Be strong and of a good courage, fear not, nor be afraid of them · for the LORD thy God, he it is that doth go with thee; he will not fail thee, nor forsake thee.

Demas hath forsaken me, having loved this present world At my first answer no man stood with me, but all men for-sook me Notwithstanding the Lord stood with me, and strengthened me —When my father and my mother forsake me, then the Lord will take me up

Lo, I am with you alway, even unto the end of the world —I am he that liv-eth, and was dead; and, behold, I am alive for evermore. —I will not leave you comfortless : I will come to you.

HEB. 13. 5. Heb. 13 6 Gen. 28 15.—Deut.
31. 6 2 Tim. 4 10, 16, 17.—Ps. 27 10 Mat.
28 20.—Rev 1 13 —John 14 18.

M

The kingdom of heaven is as a man travelling into a far country, who called his
own servants, and delivered unto them
his goods . to every man according to
his several ability.

KNOW ye not, that to whom ye yield
yourselves servants to obey, his servants ye are to whom ye obey?

All these worketh that one and the
selfsame Spirit, dividing to every man
severally as he will. The manifestation
of the Spirit is given to every man to
profit withal.—As every man hath received the gift, even so minister the same
one to another, as good stewards of the
manifold grace of God.—It is required in
stewards, that a man be found faithful.

Unto whomsoever much is given, of
him shall be much required · and to
whom men have committed much, of
him they will ask the more.

Who is sufficient for these things?—I
can do all things through Christ which
strengtheneth me

MAT. 25 14, 15. Rom 6 16. 1 Cor 12 11, 7.
—1 Pet. 4. 10.—1 Cor. 4. 2 Luke 12. 48
2 Cor 2 16.—Phil. 4 13

M

MARCH 27.

To him that soweth righteousness shall be
a sure reward.

AFTER a long time the lord of those
servants cometh, and reckoneth with
them. And so he that had received five
talents came and brought other five
talents, saying, Lord, thou deliveredst
unto me five talents : behold, I have
gained beside them five talents more.
His lord said unto him, Well done, thou
good and faithful servant : thou hast
been faithful over a few things, I will
make thee ruler over many things : enter
thou into the joy of thy lord.
We must all appear before the judgment seat of Christ ; that every one may
receive the things done in his body, according to that he hath done, whether it
be good or bad.
I have fought a good fight, I have
finished my course, I have kept the faith :
henceforth there is laid up for me a crown
of righteousness, which the Lord, the
righteous judge, shall give me at that day.
Behold, I come quickly : hold that fast
which thou hast, that no man take thy
crown.

PRO. 11 18. Mat. 25. 19-21. 2 Cor. 5 10.
2 Tim. 4 7, 8. Rev. 3 11.

M

Be strong and of a good courage

THE LORD is my light and my salvation · whom shall I fear? the LORD is the strength of my life : of whom shall I be afraid?—He giveth power to the faint ; and to them that have no might he increaseth strength. Even the youths shall faint and be weary, and the young men shall utterly fall : but they that wait upon the LORD shall renew their strength ; they shall mount up with wings as eagles ; they shall run, and not be weary ; and they shall walk, and not faint —My flesh and my heart faileth · but God is the strength of my heart, and my portion for ever

If God be for us, who can be against us ?—The LORD is on my side ; I will not fear : what can man do unto me ?

Through thee will we push down our enemies : through thy name will we tread them under that rise up against us.—We are more than conquerors through him that loved us.

Arise therefore, and be doing, and the LORD be with thee

Jos 1. 18. Ps 27. 1.—Is 40 29 31 —Ps 73 26. Rom. 8 31.—Ps 118 6 Ps 44 5 —Rom 8 37. 1 Chr 22 15

M

MARCH 29.

Come, ye blessed of my Father, inherit the kingdom prepared for you from the foundation of the world.

FEAR not, little flock; for it is your Father's good pleasure to give you the kingdom.—Hath not God chosen the poor of this world rich in faith, and heirs of the kingdom which he hath promised to them that love him?—Heirs of God, and joint-heirs with Christ; if so be that we suffer with him, that we may be also glorified together.

The Father himself loveth you, because ye have loved me.—God is not ashamed to be called their God: for he hath prepared for them a city.

He that overcometh shall inherit all things; and I will be his God, and he shall be my son.—There is laid up for me a crown of righteousness, which the Lord, the righteous judge, shall give me at that day: and not to me only, but unto all them also that love his appearing.

He which hath begun a good work in you will perform it until the day of Jesus Christ.

MAT 25. 34. Luke 12. 32.—Ja. 2. 5.—Rom. 8. 17 John 16 27.—Heb 11. 16. Rev 21 7.— 2 Tim 4. 8. Phil 1 6

M

MARCH 30.

Isaac went out to meditate in the field at
the eventide.

LET the words of my mouth, and the
meditation of my heart, be acceptable
in thy sight, O LORD, my strength, and
my redeemer.

When I consider thy heavens, the work
of thy fingers, the moon and the stars,
which thou hast ordained ; what is man,
that thou art mindful of him ? and the son
of man, that thou visitest him ?—The
works of the LORD are great, sought out
of all them that have pleasure therein.

Blessed is the man that walketh not
in the counsel of the ungodly, nor standeth in the way of sinners, nor sitteth in
the seat of the scornful. But his delight
is in the law of the LORD ; and in his
law doth he meditate day and night.—
This book of the law shall not depart out
of thy mouth ; but thou shalt meditate
therein day and night.—My soul shall be
satisfied as with marrow and fatness ;
and my mouth shall praise thee with
oyful lips : when I remember thee upon
my bed, and meditate on thee in the
night watches.

GEN. 24. 63.   Ps. 19. 14   Ps. 8. 3, 4.—Ps. 111.
    2   Ps 1 1, 2 —Jos. 1. 8 —Ps. 63 5, 6.
M

MARCH 31.

My God shall supply all your need
ing to his riches in glory by Christ

SEEK ye first the kingdom of God,
and his righteousness, and all . . .
things shall be added unto you.—He that
spared not his own Son, but delivered
him up for us all, how shall he not with
him also freely give us all things?

All things are your's: whether Paul,
or Apollos, or Cephas, or the world, or
life, or death, or things present, or things
to come; all are your's; and ye are
Christ's; and Christ is God's.—As having
nothing, and yet possessing all things.

The LORD is my shepherd; I shall
not want.—The LORD God is a sun and
shield the LORD will give grace and
glory: no good thing will he withhold
from them that walk uprightly.—The
living God, . . . giveth us richly all things
to enjoy.—God is able to make all grace
abound toward you; that ye, always
having all sufficiency in all things, may
abound to every good work

PHIL. 4. 19. Mat. 6. 33.—Rom. 8. 32. 1 Cor.
3. 21-23.—2 Cor. 6. 10. Ps. 23. 1.—Ps. 84. 11.—
1 Tim. 6. 17.—2 Cor. 9. 8.
M

APRIL 1.

The fruit of the Spirit is joy.

JOY in the Holy Ghost.—Unspeakable and full of glory.

As sorrowful, yet alway rejoicing ; . . exceeding joyful in all our tribulation.— We glory in tribulations.

Jesus the author and finisher of our faith , . . for the joy that was set before him, endured the cross, despising the shame.—These things have I spoken unto you, that my joy might remain in you, and that your joy might be full.— As the sufferings of Christ abound in us, so our consolation also aboundeth by Christ.

Rejoice in the Lord alway : and again I say, Rejoice.—The joy of the LORD is your strength

In thy presence is fulness of joy : at thy right hand there are pleasures for evermore.—For the Lamb which is in the midst of the throne shall feed them, and shall lead them unto living fountains of waters : and God shall wipe away all tears from their eyes

GAL 5. 22. Rom 14. 17.—1 Pet 1 8. 2 Cor. 6. 10 ; 7. 4.—Rom. 5 3. Heb. 12. 2.—John 15. 11. —2 Cor 1. 5. Phil 4. 4.—Neh. 8. 10 Ps. 16. 11.—Rev 7. 17.

M

If ye do return unto the Lord with all your hearts, then put away the strange gods and Ashtaroth from among you, and prepare your hearts unto the Lord, and serve him only

LITTLE children, keep yourselves from idols.—Come out from among them, and be ye separate, saith the Lord, and touch not the unclean thing ; and I will receive you, and will be a Father unto you, and ye shall be my sons and daughters, saith the Lord Almighty.

Ye cannot serve God and Mammon.

Thou shalt worship no other God : for the LORD, whose name is Jealous, is a jealous God.—Serve him with a perfect heart and with a willing mind : for the LORD searcheth all hearts, and understandeth all the imaginations of the thoughts.

Behold, thou desirest truth in the inward parts ; and in the hidden part thou shalt make me to know wisdom.—Man looketh on the outward appearance, but the LORD looketh on the heart.—Beloved, if our heart condemn us not, then have we confidence toward God.

1 SAM. 7. 3   1 John 5. 21 —2 Cor. 6. 17, 18.
Mat. 6. 24.   Ex 34. 14.—1 Chr. 28. 9.   Ps 51. 6.
      —1 Sam. 16. 7 —1 John 3. 21.

M

4

APRIL 3.

Beloved, be not ignorant of this one thing,
that one day is with the Lord as a thousand
years, and a thousand years as one day.
The Lord is not slack concerning his
promise, as some men count slackness.

MY thoughts are not your thoughts,
neither are your ways my ways, saith
the LORD. For as the heavens are higher than the earth, so are my ways higher
than your ways, and my thoughts than
your thoughts. For as the rain cometh
down, and the snow from heaven, and
returneth not thither, but watereth the
earth, . . . so shall my word be that goeth
forth out of my mouth ; it shall not return unto me void, but it shall accomplish
that which I please, and it shall prosper
in the thing whereto I sent it.

God hath concluded them all in un
belief, that he might have mercy upon all.
O the depth of the riches both of the wisdom and knowledge of God I how unsearchable are his judgments, and his ways past
finding out !

2 PET. 3. 8, 9. Is. 55. 8-11. Rom 11. 32, 33.
M

APRIL 4.

Fear not, I am the first and the last

YE are not come unto the mount that might be touched, and that burned with fire, nor unto blackness, and darkness, and tempest, . . but ye are come unto mount Sion, . . . to God the Judge of all, and to the spirits of just men made perfect, and to Jesus the mediator of the new covenant —Jesus the author and finisher of our faith. —We have not a high priest which cannot be touched with the feeling of our infirmities ; but was in all points tempted like as we are, yet without sin. Let us therefore come boldly unto the throne of grace, that we may obtain mercy, and find grace to help in time of need.

Thus saith the LORD the King of Israel, and his redeemer the LORD of hosts ; I am the first, and I am the last; and beside me there is no God —The mighty God, The everlasting Father, The Prince of Peace.

Art thou not from everlasting, O LORD my God, mine Holy One ?—Who is God, save the LORD ? and who is a rock, save our God ?

REV. 1 17   Heb 12 18, 22-24 —Heb. 12 2 —
Heb. 4 15, 16   Is 44 6 —Is. 9 6   HAB 1 12.
                    —2 Sam 22 32
M

APRIL 5.

I will not let thee go, except thou bless me.

LET him take hold of my strength, that he may make peace with me ; and he shall make peace with me

O woman, great is thy faith . be it unto thee even as thou wilt —According to your faith be it unto you —Let him ask in faith, nothing wavering   For he that wavereth is like a wave of the sea driven with the wind and tossed.   For let not that man think that he shall receive any thing of the Lord.

They drew nigh unto the village, whither they went : and [Jesus] made as though he would have gone further.   But they constrained him, saying, Abide with us : . . . he vanished out of their sight And they said one to another, Did not our heart burn within us, while he talked with us by the way, and while he opened to us the scriptures ?—I pray thee, if I have found grace in thy sight, shew me now thy way, that I may know thee, that I may find grace in thy sight —My presence shall go with thee, and I will give thee rest

GEN. 32. 26 Is 27 5   Mat. 15 28 —Mat 9 29.
—Ja. 1. 6, 7   Luke 24 28, 29, 31, 32 —
M   Ex. 33 13 14

APRIL 6.

He ever liveth to make intercession

WHO is he that condemneth? It is
Christ that died ... who also maketh
intercession for us —Christ is not entered
into the holy places made with hands,
which are the figures of the true ; but into heaven itself, now to appear in the
presence of God for us

If any man sin we have an advocate
with the Father, Jesus Christ the righteous.—There is one God, and one mediator between God and men, the man
Christ Jesus.

Seeing .. that we have a great high
priest, that is passed into the heavens,
Jesus the Son of God, let us hold fast our
profession For we have not an high priest
which cannot be touched with the feeling
of our infirmities ; but was in all points
tempted like as we are, yet without sin.
Let us therefore come boldly unto the
throne of grace, that we may obtain mercy,
and find grace to help in time of need.

Through him we .. have access by
one Spirit unto the Father.

HEB. 7 25 Rom 8 34.—Heb 9 24 1 John
2 1 —1 Tim. 2. 5 Heb. 4 14-16. Eph. 2. 18
M

APRIL 7.

As sorrowful, yet alway rejoicing, as poor, yet making many rich ; as having nothing, and yet possessing all things

WE . . . rejoice in hope of the glory of God. And not only so, but we glory in tribulations also.—I am filled with comfort, I am exceeding joyful in all our tribulation.—Believing, ye rejoice with joy unspeakable and full of glory.

In a great trial of affliction the abundance of their joy and their deep poverty abounded unto the riches of their liberality.—Unto me, who am less than the least of all saints, is this grace given, that I should preach among the Gentiles the unsearchable riches of Christ ; and to make all men see what is the fellowship of the mystery, which from the beginning of the world hath been hid in God.

Hath not God chosen the poor of this world rich in faith, and heirs of the kingdom which he hath promised to them that love him ?—God is able to make all grace abound toward you ; that ye, always having all sufficiency in all things, may abound to every good work.

2 COR. 6 10. Rom. 5. 2, 3.—2 Cor. 7 4.—
1 Pet. 1. 8. 2 Cor. 8. 2.—Eph. 3. 8, 9. Ja. 2. 5.
—2 Cor. 9. 8

M

APRIL 8.

In everything ye are enriched by Him.

WHEN we were yet without strength, in due time Christ died for the ungodly.—He that spared not his own Son, but delivered him up for us all, how shall he not with him also freely give us all things?

In him dwelleth all the fulness of the Godhead bodily. And ye are complete in him, which is the head of all principality and power

Abide in me, and I in you. As the branch cannot bear fruit of itself, except it abide in the vine; no more can ye, except ye abide in me I am the vine, ye are the branches: he that abideth in me, and I in him, the same bringeth forth much fruit : for without me ye can do nothing.—To will is present with me; but how to perform that which is good I find not.—Unto every one of us is given grace according to the measure of the gift of Christ.

If ye abide in me, and my words abide in you, ye shall ask what ye will, and it shall be done unto you —Let the word of Christ dwell in you richly in all wisdom.

1 Cor 1. 5 Rom. 5. 6.—Rom. 8. 32. Col.
2. 9, 10. John 15 4, 5 —Rom 7 18 —Eph 4. 7.
John 15 7.—Col 3. 16

M

APRIL 9.

Fear not, for I have redeemed thee

FEAR not; for thou shalt not be ashamed neither be thou confounded : for thou shalt not be put to shame : for thou shalt forget the shame of thy youth, and shalt not remember the reproach of thy widowhood any more. For thy Maker is thine husband; the LORD of hosts is his name ; and thy Redeemer the Holy One of Israel —I have blotted out, as a thick cloud, thy transgressions, and as a cloud, thy sins : return unto me ; for I have redeemed thee —With the precious blood of Christ, as of a lamb without blemish and without spot.

Their Redeemer is strong ; the LORD of hosts is his name : he shall throughly plead their cause —My Father, which gave them me, is greater than all ; and no man is able to pluck them out of my Father's hand

Grace be to you and peace from God the Father, and from our Lord Jesus Christ, who gave himself for our sins, that he might deliver us from this present evil world, according to the will of God and our Father : to whom be glory for ever and ever   Amen.

Is 43 1.   Is 54 4, 5.—Is 44. 22 —1 Pet 1 19
   Jer. 50 34 —John 10. 20   Gal 1. 3-5
M

APRIL 10

I am black, but comely

BEHOLD, I was shapen in iniquity;
and in sin did my mother conceive
me.—Thy renown went forth among the
heathen for thy beauty : for it was perfect
through my comeliness, which I had put
upon thee, saith the Lord GOD

I am a sinful man, O Lord.—Behold,
thou art fair, my love ; behold, thou art
fair.

I abhor myself, and repent in dust and
ashes.—Thou art all fair, my love ; there
is no spot in thee.

When I would do good, evil is present
with me.—Be of good cheer ; thy sins be
forgiven thee.

I know that in me (that is, in my flesh,)
dwelleth no good thing —Ye are complete in him —Perfect in Christ Jesus.

Ye are washed, . . . ye are sanctified,
. . ye are justified in the name of the
Lord Jesus, and by the Spirit of our God.
—That ye should shew forth the praises
of him who hath called you out of darkness into his marvellous light

CANT 1 5 Ps 51 5 —Ezek. 16 14 Luke 5. 8.
—Cant. 4 1 Job 42 6.—Cant 4. 7 Rom 7 21.
—Mat 9 2. Rom 7 18 —Col 2 10 :
1 28 1 Cor. 6. 11 —1 Pet. 2. 9

M

4 *

In the multitude of words there wanteth
not sin but he that refraineth his lips
is wise.

MY beloved brethren, let every man be
swift to hear, slow to speak, slow to
wrath.—He that is slow to anger is better than the mighty : and he that ruleth
his spirit than he that taketh a city.—If
any man offend not in word, the same is
a perfect man, and able also to bridle the
whole body.—By thy words thou shalt
be justified, and by thy words thou shalt
be condemned.—Set a watch, O LORD,
before my mouth ; keep the door of my lips

Christ . . suffered for us, leaving us
an example, that ye should follow his
steps : who did no sin, neither was guile
found in his mouth : who when he was
reviled, reviled not again ; when he suffered, he threatened not ; but committed
himself to him that judgeth righteously.
—Consider him that endured such contradiction of sinners against himself, lest
ye be wearied and faint in your minds.

In their mouth was found no guile : for
they are without fault before the throne
of God.

PRO. 10. 19   Ja. 1. 19.—Pro 16. 32.—Ja. 3. 2.
—Mat 12 37 —Ps. 141. 3.   1 Pet. 2 21-23
—Heb. 12 3   Rev. 14 5.
M

What the law could not do, in that it was weak through the flesh, God sending his own Son in the likeness of sinful flesh, and for sin, condemned sin in the flesh.

THE law having a shadow of good things to come, and not the very image of the things, can never with those sacrifices which they offered year by year continually make the comers thereunto perfect. For then would they not have ceased to be offered?—By him all that believe are justified from all things, from which ye could not be justified by the law of Moses.

Forasmuch . . . as the children are partakers of flesh and blood, he also himself likewise took part of the same; that through death he might destroy him that had the power of death, that is the devil; and deliver them who through fear of death were all their lifetime subject to bondage. For verily he took not on him the nature of angels; but he took on him the seed of Abraham. Wherefore in all things it behoved him to be made like unto his brethren.

Rom 8 3   Heb 10. 1, 2.—Acts 13. 39.
Heb. 2 14-17.

M

APRIL 13.

Honour the Lord with thy substance, and with the firstfruits of all thine increase.

HE which soweth sparingly shall reap also sparingly; and he which soweth bountifully shall reap also bountifully.—Upon the first day of the week let every one of you lay by him in store, as God hath prospered him.

God is not unrighteous to forget your work and labour of love, which ye have shewed toward his name, in that ye have ministered to the saints and do minister.

I beseech you, . . . brethren, by the mercies of God, that ye present your bodies a living sacrifice, holy, acceptable unto God, which is your reasonable service.

The love of Christ constraineth us; because we thus judge, that if one died for all, then were all dead: and that he died for all, that they which live should not henceforth live unto themselves, but unto him which died for them, and rose again.—Whether therefore ye eat, or drink, or whatsoever ye do, do all to the glory of God.

Pro. 3 9   2 Cor. 9. 6.—1 Cor. 16. 2   Heb. 6. 10   Rom. 12 1   2 Cor. 5. 14, 15.—1 Cor. 10 31.

M

APRIL 14.

My soul shall be satisfied as with marrow
and fatness; and my mouth shall praise
thee with joyful lips: when I remember
thee upon my bed, and meditate on thee
in the night watches.

HOW precious . . are thy thoughts
unto me, O God ! how great is the
sum of them ! If I should count them,
they are more in number than the sand :
when I awake, I am still with thee.—
How sweet are thy words unto my taste !
yea, sweeter than honey to my mouth !
—Thy love is better than wine.

Whom have I in heaven but thee ? and
there is none upon earth that I desire
beside thee.

As the apple tree among the trees of
the wood, so is my beloved among the
sons   I sat down under his shadow
with great delight, and his fruit was
sweet to my taste   He brought me to
the banqueting house, and his banner
over me was love.—His countenance is
as Lebanon, excellent as the cedars.
His mouth is most sweet : yea, he is
altogether lovely. This is my beloved,
and this is my friend.

Ps. 63 5, 6   Ps. 139 17, 18 —Ps 119 103 —
Cant. 1 2. Ps. 73 25. Cant. 2. 3, 4.—
Cant 5 15, 16.

M

APRIL 15.

I KNOW your manifold transgressions and your mighty sins.—I have laid help upon one that is mighty.—The LORD . . . thy Saviour and thy Redeemer, the mighty one of Jacob.—Mighty to save.—Able to keep you from falling.—Where sin abounded, grace did much more abound.

He that believeth on him is not condemned ; but he that believeth not is condemned already, because he hath not believed in the name of the only begotten Son of God.—He is able . . . to save them to the uttermost that come unto God by him

Is my hand shortened at all, that it cannot redeem ?

Who shall separate us from the love of Christ ? . . . I am persuaded, that neither death, nor life, nor angels, nor principalities, nor powers, nor things present, nor things to come, nor height, nor depth, nor any other creature, shall be able to separate us from the love of God, which is in Christ Jesus our Lord.

JER 50 34. Amos 5. 12.—Ps. 89 19.—Is 49. 26.—Is 63 1.—Jude 24.—Rom. 5 20 John 3. 18.—Heb. 7. 25. Is. 50. 2. Rom. 8 35, 38, 39
M

APRIL 16.

I said in my haste, I am cut off from
before thine eyes · nevertheless thou
heardest the voice of my supplications when I cried unto thee.

I SINK in deep mire, where there is
no standing · I am come into deep
waters, where the floods overflow me.
—Waters flowed over mine head ; ther.
I said, I am cut off. I called upon thy
name, O LORD, out of the low dungeon.
Thou hast heard my voice : hide not
thine ear at my breathing, at my cry
Thou drewest near in the day that I
called upon thee : thou saidst, Fear not.
Will the LORD cast off for ever ? and
will he be favourable no more? Is his
mercy clean gone for ever ? doth his
promise fail for evermore ? Hath God
forgotten to be gracious? hath he in anger
shut up his tender mercies ? And I said,
This is my infirmity . but I will remember
the years of the right hand of the most
High. I will remember the works of
the LORD : surely I will remember thy
wonders of old.—I had fainted, unless I
had believed to see the goodness of the
LORD in the land of the living

Ps. 31. 22   Ps. 69 2.—Lam. 3 54-57. Ps.
77 7-11 = Ps 27 13
M

APRIL 17.

LET the word of Christ dwell in you richly in all wisdom; teaching and admonishing one another in psalms and hymns and spiritual songs, singing with grace in your hearts to the Lord And whatsoever ye do in word or deed, do all in the name of the Lord Jesus, giving thanks to God and the Father by him.

Glorify God in your body, and in your spirit, which are God's

Ye are a royal priesthood, . . . that ye should shew forth the praises of him who hath called you out of darkness into his marvellous light —Ye . . . as lively stones, are built up a spiritual house, a holy priesthood, to offer up spiritual sacrifices, acceptable to God by Jesus Christ.—By him . . . let us offer the sacrifice of praise to God continually, that is, the fruit of our lips, giving thanks to his name.

My soul shall make her boast in the LORD: the humble shall hear thereof, and be glad. O magnify the LORD with me, and let us exalt his name together.

Ps 50 23. Col. 3. 16, 17   1 Cor. 6. 20.   1 Pet.
2 9 —1 Pet 2 5 —Heb 13 15.   Ps. 34 2, 3.
M

APRIL 18.

I will raise them up a Prophet from among their brethren, like unto thee.

I [MOSES] stood between the LORD and you at that time, to shew you the word of the LORD : for ye were afraid.—There is one God, and one mediator between God and men, the man Christ Jesus.

Now the man Moses was very meek, above all the men which were upon the face of the earth.—Take my yoke upon you, and learn of me ; for I am meek and lowly in heart : and ye shall find rest unto your souls —Let this mind be in you, which was also in Christ Jesus : who, being in the form of God, thought it not robbery to be equal with God ; but made himself of no reputation, and took upon him the form of a servant, and was made in the likeness of men.

Moses verily was faithful in all his house, as a servant, for a testimony of those things which were to be spoken after ; but Christ as a son over his own house ; whose house are we, if we hold fast the confidence and the rejoicing of the hope firm unto the end.

DEUT. 18. 18. Deut 5. 5 —1 Tim. 2. 5. Num. 12 3.—Mat. 11. 29.—Phil. 2. 5-7. Heb. 3. 5, 6.

M

APRIL 19

Verily, verily, I say unto you, I am
the door of the sheep

THE veil of the temple was rent in
twain from the top to the bottom.—
Christ . . . hath once suffered for sins, the
just for the unjust, that he might bring
us to God —The way into the holiest of
all was not yet made manifest, while as
the first tabernacle was yet standing

I am the door : by me if any man
enter in, he shall be saved, and shall go
in and out, and find pasture.

No man cometh unto the Father, but
by me.—Through him we . . . have
access by one Spirit unto the Father.
Now therefore ye are no more strangers
and foreigners, but fellowcitizens with the
saints, and of the household of God —
Having . . . boldness to enter into the
holiest by the blood of Jesus, by a new
and living way, which he hath conse
crated for us, through the veil, that is
to say, his flesh.—We have peace with
God through our Lord Jesus Christ : by
whom also we have access by faith into
this grace wherein we stand, and rejoice
in hope of the glory of God.

JOHN 10 7. Mat. 27 51 —1 Pet. 3. 18—Heb.
9 8 John 10. 8 John 14 6.—Eph. 2 18, 19.
—Heb 10 19, 20 —Rom 5 1.

M

APRIL 20.

There shall cleave nought of the cursed thing to thine hand.

COME out from among them, and be ye separate, saith the Lord, and touch not the unclean thing —Dearly beloved, I beseech you as strangers and pilgrims, abstain from fleshly lusts, which war against the soul —Hating even the garment spotted by the flesh.

Beloved, now are we the sons of God, and it doth not yet appear what we shall be : but we know that, when he shall appear, we shall be like him ; for we shall see him as he is And every man that hath this hope in him purifieth himself, even as he is pure —The grace of God that bringeth salvation hath appeared to all men, teaching us that, denying ungodliness and worldly lusts, we should live soberly, righteously, and godly, in this present world ; looking for that blessed hope, and the glorious appearing of the great God and our Saviour Jesus Christ who gave himself for us, that he might redeem us from all iniquity, and purify unto himself a peculiar people, zealous of good works

DEUT. 13. 17 2 Cor. 6. 17.—1 Pet. 2 11.—
Jude 23 1 John 3. 2, 3.—Tit 2 11-14

APRIL 21.

Stand fast in the Lord

MY foot hath held his steps, his way have I kept, and not declined —The LORD loveth judgment, and forsaketh not his saints ; they are preserved for ever. —The LORD shall preserve thee from all evil : he shall preserve thy soul.

The just shall live by faith : but if any man draw back, my soul shall have no pleasure in him.   But we are not of them who draw back unto perdition ; but of them that believe to the saving of the soul —If they had been of us, they would no doubt have continued with us : but they went out, that they might be made manifest that they were not all of us.

If ye continue in my word, then are ye my disciples indeed —He that shall endure unto the end, the same shall be saved.—Watch ye, stand fast in the faith, quit you like men, be strong —Hold that fast which thou hast, that no man take thy crown.—He that overcometh, the same shall be clothed in white raiment ; and I will not blot out his name out of the book of life.

PHIL 4 1.   Job 23 11.—Ps 37. 28 —Ps. 121. 7
Heb. 10. 38, 39 —1 John 2 19   John 8. 31.—
Mat. 24 13.—1 Cor 16 13 —Rev 3. 11 ⌐
Rev 3. 5

M

APRIL 22.

If his offering be a burnt sacrifice of the herd, let him offer a male without blemish: he shall offer it of his own voluntary will. And he shall put his hand upon the head of the burnt offering; and it shall be accepted for him to make atonement for him.

GOD will provide himself a lamb for a burnt offering.—Behold the Lamb of God, which taketh away the sin of the world.—We are sanctified through the offering of the body of Jesus Christ once for all.—A ransom for many.

No man taketh it from me, but I lay it down of myself. I have power to lay it down, and I have power to take it again.

I will love them freely.—The Son of God . . . loved me, and gave himself for me.

He hath made him to be sin for us, who knew no sin ; that we might be made the righteousness of God in him.—He hath made us accepted in the beloved.

Lev. 1 3, 4. Gen. 22. 8.—John 1. 29—Heb. 10. 10.—Mat. 20 28. John 10. 18 Hos. 14 4. —Gal. 2. 20 2 Cor 5 21.—Eph. 1 6.

M

APRIL 23

The Lord was my stay.

TRULY in vain is salvation hoped for from the hills, and from the multitude of mountains : truly in the LORD our God is the salvation of Israel —The LORD is my rock, and my fortress, and my deliverer ; my God, my strength, in whom I will trust ; my buckler, and the horn of my salvation, and my high tower.

Cry out and shout, thou inhabitant of Zion ; for great is the Holy One of Israel in the midst of thee

The angel of the LORD encampeth round about them that fear him, and delivereth them The righteous cry, and the LORD heareth, and delivereth them out of all their troubles.—The eternal God is thy refuge, and underneath are the everlasting arms.—So that we may boldly say, The Lord is my helper, and I will not fear what man shall do unto me.— For who is God save the LORD ? or who is a rock save our God ? It is God that girdeth me with strength, and maketh my way perfect.

By the grace of God I am what I am.

Ps 18 18   Jer. 3 23 —Ps. 13 2   Is 12 6.
Ps 34 7, 17 —Deut 33 27.—Heb. 13 6.
—Ps 18 31, 32.   1 Cor. 15 10

M

APRIL 24.

The Lord visited Sarah as he had said, and
the Lord did unto Sarah as he had
spoken

TRUST in him at all times ; ye people,
pour out your heart before him God
is a refuge for us.—David encouraged himself in the LORD his God.—God will
surely visit you, and bring you out of this
land unto the land which he sware to
Abraham, to Isaac, and to Jacob.—I have
seen, I have seen the affliction of my
people which is in Egypt, and I have
heard their groaning, and am come down
to deliver them. He brought them out,
after that he had shewed wonders and
signs in the land of Egypt, and in the
Red sea, and in the wilderness forty years.
—There failed not ought of any good
thing which the LORD had spoken unto
the house of Israel ; all came to pass.

He is faithful that promised.—Hath he
said, and shall he not do it ? or hath he
spoken, and shall he not make it good ?
—Heaven and earth shall pass away, but
my words shall not pass away —The grass
withereth, the flower fadeth ; but the
word of our God shall stand for ever.

GEN. 21 1. Ps 62 8 —1 Sam. 30. 6.—Gen.
50. 24.—Acts 7 34, 36.—Jos 21. 45. Heb 10. 23.
—Num 23 19 —Mat 24. 35.—Is 40 8

M

APRIL 25.

Thou shalt call his name JESUS: for he
shall save his people from their sins.

YE know that he was manifested to
take away our sins —That we, being
dead to sins, should live unto righteousness.—He is able also to save them to
the uttermost that come unto God by him.

He was wounded for our transgressions,
he was bruised for our iniquities: the
chastisement of our peace was upon him;
and with his stripes we are healed...The
LORD hath laid on him the iniquity of us
all —Thus it behoved Christ to suffer,
.. that repentance and remission of sins
should be preached in his name among
all nations.—He appeared to put away
sin by the sacrifice of himself.

Him hath God exalted with his right
hand to be a Prince and a Saviour, . . .
to give repentance.—Through this man
is preached unto you the forgiveness of
sins: and by him all that believe are
justified from all things, from which ye
could not be justified by the law of Moses.
—Your sins are forgiven you for his
name's sake

MAT. 1 21. 1 John 3 5 —1 Pet. 2 24 —Heb.
7 25. Is 53 5, 6 —Luke 24. 46, 47 —Heb. 9 26.
Acts 5. 31.—Acts 13 38 39 —1 John 2. 12.

APRIL 26.

His left hand is under my head, and his
right hand doth embrace me.

UNDERNEATH are the everlasting
arms.—When [Peter] saw the wind
boisterous, he was afraid ; and beginning
to sink, he cried, saying, Lord, save me.
And immediately Jesus stretched forth
his hand, and caught him, and said unto
him, O thou of little faith, wherefore
didst thou doubt ?

The steps of a good man are ordered
by the LORD : and he delighteth in his
way. Though he fall, he shall not be
utterly cast down : for the LORD upholdeth him with his hand.

The beloved of the LORD shall dwell
in safety by him ; and the LORD shall
cover him all the day long, and he shall
dwell between his shoulders.—Casting all
your care upon Him, for he careth for
you.—He that toucheth you, toucheth
the apple of his eye

They shall never perish, neither shall
any man pluck them out of my hand.
My Father, which gave them me, is
greater than all.

CANT. 2. 6. Deut. 33 27.—Mat. 14 30, 31
Ps 37 23, 24. Deut. 33 12.—1 Pet. 5 7.—
Zec. 2. 8 John 10. 28, 29.

M

APRIL 27.

Brethren, the time is short.

MAN that is born of a woman is of few days, and full of trouble. He cometh forth like a flower, and is cut down : he fleeth also as a shadow, and continueth not. —The world passeth away, and the lust thereof : but he that doeth the will of God abideth for ever.—As in Adam all die, even so in Christ shall all be made alive. Death is swallowed up in victory.—Whether we live, we live unto the Lord ; and whether we die, we die unto the Lord : whether we live therefore, or die, we are the Lord's.

To live is Christ, and to die is gain.

Cast not away . . . your confidence, which hath great recompence of reward. For ye have need of patience, that, after ye have done the will of God, ye might receive the promise. For yet a little while, and he that shall come will come, and will not tarry.—The night is far spent, the day is at hand ; let us therefore cast off the works of darkness, and let us put on the armour of light —The end of all things is at hand : be ye therefore sober, and watch unto prayer.

1 Cor. 7. 29. Job 14. 1, 2 —1 John 2. 17 —
1 Cor 15 22, 54 —Rom. 14 8 Phil. 1. 21
Heb. 10. 35-37.—Rom. 13 12.—1 Pet 4 7
M

APRIL 28.

Behold the Lamb of God.

IT is not possible that the blood of bulls and of goats should take away sins. Wherefore when he cometh into the world, he saith, Sacrifice and offering thou wouldest not, but a body hast thou prepared me: in burnt offerings and sacrifices for sin thou hast had no pleasure. Then said I, Lo, I come (in the volume of the book it is written of me,) to do thy will, O God.—He was oppressed, and he was afflicted, yet he opened not his mouth: he is brought as a lamb to the slaughter, and as a sheep before her shearers is dumb, so he openeth not his mouth.

Ye were not redeemed with corruptible things, as silver and gold, . . . but with the precious blood of Christ, as of a lamb without blemish and without spot . . . manifest in these last times for you who by him do believe in God . . that your faith and hope might be in God.

Worthy is the Lamb that was slain to receive power, and riches, and wisdom, and strength, and honour, and glory, and blessing.

JOHN 1. 29. Heb 10. 4-7.—Is. 53 7. 1 Pet. 1. 18-21. Rev 5 12.

M

APRIL 29.

Consider how great things He hath done
for you

THOU shalt remember all the way
which the LORD thy God led thee
these forty years in the wilderness, to
humble thee, and to prove thee, to know
what was in thine heart, whether thou
wouldest keep his commandments, or no.
Thou shalt also consider in thine heart,
that, as a man chasteneth his son, so the
LORD thy God chasteneth thee.

I know, O LORD, that thy judgments
are right, and that thou in faithfulness
hast afflicted me.—It is good for me that
I have been afflicted ; that I might learn
thy statutes.—Before I was afflicted I
went astray : but now have I kept thy
word.—The LORD hath chastened me
sore : but he hath not given me over
unto death.

He hath not dealt with us after our
sins, nor rewarded us according to our
iniquities For as the heaven is high
above the earth, so great is his mercy
toward them that fear him. He knoweth
our frame ; he remembereth that we are
dust.

2 Sam 12 24   Deut. 8 2, 5. Ps. 119 75, 71, 67.
—Ps 118 18. Ps 103 10, 11, 14

M

APRIL 30.

Whoso keepeth his word, in him verily is
the love of God perfected.

THE God of peace, that brought again
from the dead our Lord Jesus, that
great shepherd of the sheep, through the
blood of the everlasting covenant, make
you perfect in every good work to do his
will, working in you that which is well
pleasing in his sight, through Jesus
Christ; to whom be glory for ever and
ever. Amen.

Hereby we do know that we know
him, if we keep his commandments.—
If a man love me, he will keep my
words: and my Father will love him,
and we will come unto him, and make
our abode with him.—Whosoever abideth in him sinneth not · whosoever sinneth hath not seen him, neither known
him. Little children, let no man deceive
you: he that doeth righteousness is
righteous, even as he is righteous.

Herein is our love made perfect, that
we may have boldness in the day of judgment: because as he is, so are we in this
world.

1 JOHN 2. 5   Heb. 13. 20, 21.   1 John 2. 3.—
John 14. 23—1 John 3. 6, 7.   1 John 4. 17.
M

MAY 1.

The fruit of the Spirit is peace

TO be spiritually minded is life and peace.

God hath called us to peace.—Peace I leave with you, my peace I give unto you : not as the world giveth, give I unto you   Let not your heart be troubled, neither let it be afraid.—The God of hope fill you with all joy and peace in believing, that ye may abound in hope, through the power of the Holy Ghost.

I know whom I have believed, and am persuaded that he is able to keep that which I have committed unto him against that day.—Thou wilt keep him in perfect peace, whose mind is stayed on thee : because he trusteth in thee.

The work of righteousness shall be peace ; and the effect of righteousness quietness and assurance for ever.   And my people shall dwell in a peaceable habitation, and in sure dwellings, and in quiet resting places.—Whoso hearkeneth unto me shall dwell safely, and shall be quiet from fear of evil.

Great peace have they which love thy law.   .

GAL. 5. 22. Rom. 8 6. 1 Cor 7 15 —John 14. 27 —Rom. 15. 13. 2 Tim. 1 12.—Is 26. 3. Is. 32. 17, 18.—Pro. 1. 33 Ps 119 165.

M

MAY 2.

Surely the Lord is in this place; and I
knew it not

WHERE two or three are gathered together in my name, there am I in
the midst of them —Lo, I am with you
alway, even unto the end of the world.—
My presence shall go with thee, and I
will give thee rest.

Whither shall I go from thy spirit? or
whither shall I flee from thy presence?
If I ascend up into heaven, thou art there:
If I make my bed in hell, behold, thou
art there.—Am I a God at hand, saith
the LORD, and not a God afar off? Can
any hide himself in secret places that I
shall not see him? saith the LORD. Do
not I fill heaven and earth? saith the
LORD.

Behold, the heaven and heaven of
heavens cannot contain thee; how much
less this house that I have builded?—
Thus saith the high and lofty One that
inhabiteth eternity, whose name is Holy;
I dwell in the high and holy place, with
him also that is of a contrite and humble
spirit, to revive the spirit of the humble,
and to revive the heart of the contrite
ones.

GEN. 28. 16 Mat. 18 20 —Mat. 28 20.—Ex.
33 14 Ps. 139 7, 8 —Jer 23 23, 24 1 Kings
8 27 —Is 57. 15.

M

MAY 3.

Be ye ... perfect, even as your Father which is in heaven is perfect.

I AM the Almighty God; walk before me, and be thou perfect.—Ye shall be holy unto me : for I the LORD am holy, and have severed you from other people, that ye should be mine.

Ye are bought with a price : therefore glorify God in your body, and in your spirit, which are God's

Ye are complete in him, which is the head of all principality and power.—Who gave himself for us, that he might redeem us from all iniquity.—Be diligent that ye may be found of him in peace, without spot, and blameless

Blessed are the undefiled in the way, who walk in the law of the LORD.— Whoso looketh into the perfect law of liberty, and continueth therein, he being not a forgetful hearer, but a doer of the work, this man shall be blessed in his deed.—Search me, O God, and know my heart : try me, and know my thoughts : and see if there be any wicked way in me, and lead me in the way everlasting.

MAT. 5. 48. Gen 17. 1 —Lev. 20. 26. 1 Cor. 6. 20. Col. 2. 10.—Tit. 2 14.—2 Pet. 3. 14. Ps. 119. 1 —Ja. 1 25 —Ps. 139. 23, 24.

M

MAY 4.

Behold, the Lord's hand is not shortened, that it cannot save; neither his ear heavy, that it cannot hear.

IN the day when I cried thou answeredst me, and strengthenedst me with strength in my soul —While I was speaking in prayer, even the man Gabriel, whom I had seen in .he vision at the beginning, being caused to fly swiftly, touched me about the time of the evening oblation

Hide not thy face far from me ; put not thy servant away in anger ; thou hast been my help, leave me not, neither forsake me, O God of my salvation —Be not thou far from me, O LORD : O my strength, haste thee to help me.

Ah Lord GOD ! behold, thou hast made the heaven and the earth by thy great power and stretched out arm, and there is nothing too hard for thee —Who delivered us from so great a death, and doth deliver : in whom we trust that he will yet deliver us —Shall not God avenge his own elect, which cry day and night unto him, though he bear long with them ? I tell you that he will avenge them speedily.

Is 59 1 Ps 138 3 —Dan 9 21. Ps 27. 9.—
Ps 22 19 Jer 32 17 —2 Cor 1 10 —
Luke 18 7, 8

M

5

MAY 5.

Take no thought, saying, What shall we eat? or, What shall we drink? or, Wherewithal shall we be clothed? for your heavenly Father knoweth that ye have need of all these things

O FEAR the LORD, ye his saints : for there is no want to them that fear him. The young lions do lack, and suffer hunger : but they that seek the LORD shall not want any good thing.—No good thing will he withhold from them that walk uprightly. O LORD of hosts, blessed is the man that trusteth in thee.

I would have you without carefulness. —Be careful for nothing ; but in every thing by prayer and supplication with thanksgiving let your requests be made known unto God

Are not two sparrows sold for a farthing? and one of them shall not fall on the ground without your Father. The very hairs of your head are all numbered Fear ye not therefore, ye are of more value than many sparrows.—Why are ye so fearful? how is it that ye have no faith?—Have faith in God.

MAT 6 31, 32   Ps 34 9, 10 —Ps 84 11, 12
1 Cor 7 32 —Phil 4 6   Mat 10 29-31 —Mark
4 40 —Mark 11 22,

M

MAY 6.

Mercy and truth are met together; righteousness and peace have kissed each other.

A JUST God and a Saviour.
The LORD is well pleased for his righteousness' sake ; he will magnify the law,
and make it honourable.

God was in Christ, reconciling the
world unto himself, not imputing their
trespasses unto them.—Whom God hath
set forth to be a propitiation through
faith in his blood, to declare his righteousness for the remission of sins that are
past, through the forbearance of God ;
to declare I say at this time his righteousness : that he might be just, and the justifier of him which believeth in Jesus —
He was wounded for our transgressions,
he was bruised for our iniquities : the
chastisement of our peace was upon him ;
and with his stripes we are healed.—Who
shall lay any thing to the charge of God's
elect ? It is God that justifieth.—To him
that worketh not, but believeth on him
that justifieth the ungodly ; his faith is
counted for righteousness.

Ps. 85 10. Is. 45, 21. Is 42 21 2 Cor. 5 19.
—Rom. 3. 25, 26.—Is. 53. 5.—Rom. 8. 33 —
Rom 4 5
M

MAY 7.

Ye shall hear of wars and rumours of
wars : see that ye be not troubled.

GOD is our refuge and strength, a very
present help in trouble. Therefore
will not we fear, though the earth be removed, and though the mountains be
carried into the midst of the sea ; though
the waters thereof roar and be troubled,
though the mountains shake with the
swelling thereof.—Come, my people, enter thou into thy chambers, and shut thy
doors about thee : hide thyself as it were
for a little moment, until the indignation
be overpast —For, behold, the LORD
cometh out of his place to punish the
inhabitants of the earth for their iniquity.
—In the shadow of thy wings will I make
my refuge, until these calamities be overpast.—Your life is hid with Christ in
God.

He shall not be afraid of evil tidings :
his heart is fixed, trusting in the LORD.

These things I have spoken unto you,
that in me ye might have peace. In the
world ye shall have tribulation : but be
of good cheer; I have overcome the
world.

MAT. 24. 6. Ps. 46. 1-3 —Is 26 20, 21.—Ps.
57 1 —Col 3 3. Ps 112. 7. John 16. 33.
M

MAY 8.

It pleased the Lord to bruise him; he hath put him to grief.

NOW is my soul troubled; and what shall I say? Father, save me from this hour : but for this cause came I unto this hour Father, glorify thy name. Then came there a voice from heaven, saying, I have both glorified it, and will glorify it again.—Father, if thou be willing, remove this cup from me : nevertheless not my will, but thine, be done. And there appeared an angel unto him from heaven, strengthening him.

Being found in fashion as a man, he humbled himself, and became obedient unto death, even the death of the cross.— Therefore doth my Father love me, because I lay down my life, that I might take it again.—For I came down from heaven, not to do mine own will, but the will of him that sent me.—The cup which my Father hath given me, shall I not drink it?

The Father hath not left me alone ; for I do always those things that please him. —My beloved Son, in whom I am well pleased.—Mine elect, in whom my soul delighteth.

Is. 53 10. John 12. 27, 28.—Luke 22. 42, 43.
Phil 2 8 —John 10 17 —John 6 38 —John 18 11.
John 8 29 —Mat. 3 17 —Is 42 1

M

MAY 9.

Faith is the substance of things hoped for, the evidence of things not seen.

IF in this life only we have hope in Christ, we are of all men most miserable.

Eye hath not seen, nor ear heard, neither have entered into the heart of man, the things which God hath prepared for them that love him. But God hath revealed them unto us by his Spirit —After that ye believed, ye were sealed with that holy Spirit of promise, which is the earnest of our inheritance until the redemption of the purchased possession

Jesus saith unto him, Thomas, because thou hast seen me, thou hast believed : blessed are they that have not seen, and yet have believed —Whom having not seen, ye love ; in whom, though now ye see him not, yet believing, ye rejoice with joy unspeakable and full of glory ; receiving the end of your faith, even the salvation of your souls

We walk by faith. not by sight —Cast not away therefore your confidence, which hath great recompence of reward.

Heb. 11. 1. 1 Cor. 15 19. 1 Cor. 2 9, 10 — Eph 1 13, 14 John 20 29 —1 Pet 1 8, 9

M   2 Cor 5 7 —Heb 10 35.

MAY 10.

For this purpose the Son of God was manifested, that he might destroy the works of the devil.

WE wrestle not against flesh and blood, but against principalities, against powers, against the rulers of the darkness of this world, against spiritual wickedness in high places.—Forasmuch . . . as the children are partakers of flesh and blood, he also himself likewise took part of the same; that through death he might destroy him that had the power of death, that is, the devil.—And having spoiled principalities and powers he made a shew of them openly, triumphing over them.—I heard a loud voice saying in heaven, Now is come salvation, and strength, and the kingdom of our God, and the power of his Christ : for the accuser of our brethren is cast down, which accused them before our God day and night. And they overcame him by the blood of the Lamb, and by the word of their testimony , and they loved not their lives unto the death.

Thanks be to God, which giveth us the victory through our Lord Jesus Christ.

1 John 3 8 Eph. 6. 12 —Heb. 2 14.—Col. 2. 15 —Rev 12 10 11. 1 Cor. 15. 57

M

MAY 11.

YE are all the children of light, and the children of the day. Therefore let us not sleep, as do others ; but let us watch and be sober.

It is high time to awake out of sleep : for now is our salvation nearer than when we believed. The night is far spent, the day is at hand : let us therefore cast off the works of darkness, and let us put on the armour of light. — Wherefore take unto you the whole armour of God, that ye may be able to withstand in the evil day, and having done all, to stand. —Cast away from you all your transgressions, whereby ye have transgressed ; and make you a new heart and a new spirit.—Lay apart all filthiness and superfluity of naughtiness, and receive with meekness the engrafted word, which is able to save your souls.

Little children, abide in him ; that, when he shall appear, we may have confidence, and not be ashamed before him at his coming. If ye know that he is righteous, ye know that every one that doeth righteousness is born of him.

2 Cor. 15 34   1 Thes. 5 5, 6   Rom. 13. 11, 12.
—Eph. 6 13 —Ezek 18 31 —Ja. 1 21.
1 John 2 28, 29

M

Beloved, let us love one another: for love is of God, and every one that loveth is born of God, and knoweth God.

THE love of God is shed abroad in our hearts by the Holy Ghost, which is given unto us.—Ye have not received the spirit of bondage again to fear; but ye have received the Spirit of adoption, whereby we cry, Abba, Father. The Spirit itself beareth witness with our spirit, that we are the children of God.—He that believeth on the Son of God hath the witness in himself.

In this was manifested the love of God toward us, because that God sent his only begotten Son into the world, that we might live through him.—In whom we have redemption through his blood, the forgiveness of sins, according to the riches of his grace.—That in the ages to come he might shew the exceeding riches of his grace in his kindness toward us through Christ Jesus.

Beloved, if God so loved us, we ought also to love one another.

1 JOHN 4. 7. Rom. 5 5.—Rom. 8 15, 16.—1 John 5 10. 1 John 4. 9.—Eph. 1. 7.— Eph. 2. 7. 1 John 4. 11

M   5 *

MAY 13.

Pray every where, lifting up holy hands,
without wrath and doubting.

THE true worshippers shall worship the Father in spirit and in truth : for the Father seeketh such to worship him. God is a Spirit : and they that worship him must worship him in spirit and in truth.— Then shalt thou call, and the LORD shall answer ; thou shalt cry, and he shall say, Here I am.—When ye stand praying, forgive, if ye have ought against any.

Without faith it is impossible to please him : for he that cometh to God must believe that he is, and that he is a re warder of them that diligently seek him. —Let him ask in faith, nothing wavering. For he that wavereth is like a wave of the sea, driven with the wind and tossed. For let not that man think that he shall receive any thing of the Lord.

If I regard iniquity in my heart, the Lord will not hear me—My little children, these things write I unto you, that ye sin not. And if any man sin, we have an advocate with the Father, Jesus Christ the righteous.

1 TIM. 2 8. John 4 23, 24 —Is. 58 9 — Mark 11. 25 Heb. 11 6.—Ja. 1 6, 7. Ps. 66. 18 —1 John 2 1.

M

MAY 14.

The fellowship of his sufferings

IT is enough for the disciple that he be as his master, and the servant as his lord

He is despised and rejected of men ; a man of sorrows, and acquainted with grief: and we hid as it were our faces from him ; he was despised, and we esteemed him not. —Because ye are not of the world, but I have chosen you out of the world, therefore the world hateth you.

I looked for some to take pity, but there was none.—At my first answer no man stood with me, but all men forsook me.

The foxes have holes, and the birds of the air have nests ; but the Son of man hath not where to lay his head —Here have we no continuing city, but we seek one to come

Let us run with patience the race that is set before us, looking unto Jesus the author and finisher of our faith ; who for the joy that was set before him endured the cross, despising the shame and is set down at the right hand of the throne of God.

PHIL. 3. 10. Mat. 10. 25 Is 53 3 —John 15 19.
Ps. 69. 20.—2 Tim. 4 16 Mat. 8. 20 —
Heb 13. 14 Heb. 12. 1, 2

M

MAY 15.

God shall wipe away all tears ; . . . there shall be no more death, neither sorrow, . . for the former things are passed away

H E will swallow up death in victory; and the Lord GOD will wipe away tears from off all faces ; and the rebuke of his people shall he take away from off all the earth : for the LORD hath spoken it.—Thy sun shall no more go down ; neither shall thy moon withdraw itself : for the LORD shall be thine everlasting light, and the days of thy mourning shall be ended.—The inhabitant shall not say, I am sick : the people that dwell therein shall be forgiven their iniquity — The voice of weeping shall be no more heard in her, nor the voice of crying.—Sorrow and sighing shall flee away.

I will ransom. them from the power of the grave ; I will redeem them from death : O death, I will be thy plagues ; O grave, I will be thy destruction.—The last enemy that shall be destroyed is death. —Then shall be brought to pass the saying that is written, Death is swallowed up in victory.

REV. 21. 4   Is. 25 8.—Is 60. 20.—Is 33 24.—
Is. 65. 19 —Is. 35. 10. Hos 13. 14 —
1 Cor. 15 26; 54

M

MAY 16.

A servant of Jesus Christ.

YE call me Master and Lord and ye say well; for so I am.—If any man serve me, let him follow me, and where I am, there shall also my servant be : if any man serve me, him will my Father honour.—Take my yoke upon you, and learn of me; for I am meek and lowly in heart. and ye shall find rest unto your souls. For my yoke is easy, and my burden is light

What things were gain to me, those I counted loss for Christ — Being made free from sin, and become servants to God, ye have your fruit unto holiness, and the end everlasting life

Henceforth I call you not servants; for the servant knoweth not what his lord doeth : but I have called you friends; for all things that I have heard of my Father, I have made known unto you.— Thou art no more a servant, but a son.

Stand fast therefore in the liberty wherewith Christ hath made us free, and be not entangled again with the yoke of bondage. For, brethren, ye have been called unto liberty; only use not liberty for an occasion to the flesh.

Rom 1 1. John 13. 13.—John 12. 26.— Mat. 11 29, 30. Phil 3 7 —Rom 6 22. John 15 15 —Gal 4. 7. Gal. 5. 1, 13.
M

MAY 17.

I am the Lord your God, walk in my
statutes, and keep my judgments,
and do them

AS he which hath called you is holy,
so be ye holy in all manner of conversation —He that saith he abideth in
him ought himself also so to walk, even
as he walked. If ye know that he is
righteous, ye know that every one that
doeth righteousness is born of him —
Circumcision is nothing, and uncircumcision is nothing, but the keeping of the
commandments of God. — Whosoever
shall keep the whole law, and yet offend
in one point, he is guilty of all.

Not that we are sufficient of ourselves
to think any thing, as of ourselves ; but
our sufficiency is of God.—Teach me, O
LORD, the way of thy statutes.

Work out your own salvation with fear
and trembling. For it is God which
worketh in you both to will and to do of
his good pleasure.—The God of peace,
. . make you perfect in every good
work to do his will, working in you that
which is well pleasing in his sight, through
Jesus Christ

EZEK 20. 19   1 Pet 1 15.—1 John 2. 6, 29.—
1 Cor. 7 19 —Ja. 2 10. 2 Cor. 3. 5 —Ps 119 33.
Phil 2. 12, 13.—Heb 13. 20, 21

M

MAY 18.

As the Father hath life in himself; so hath he given to the Son to have life in himself.

OUR Saviour Jesus Christ, . . . hath abolished death, and hath brought life and immortality to light through the gospel.—I am the resurrection, and the life.—Because I live, ye shall live also.— We are made partakers of Christ.—Partakers of the Holy Ghost.—Partakers of the divine nature.—The first man Adam was made a living soul; the last Adam was made a quickening spirit.—Behold, I shew you a mystery; We shall not all sleep, but we shall all be changed, in a moment, in the twinkling of an eye, at the last trump: for the trumpet shall sound, and the dead shall be raised incorruptible, and we shall be changed.

Holy, holy, holy, Lord God Almighty, which was, and is, and is to come.— Who liveth for ever and ever.—The blessed and only Potentate, the King of kings, and Lord of lords; who only hath immortality.—Unto the King eternal, . . . be honour and glory for ever and ever.   Amen.

JOHN 5. 26   2 Tim. 1. 10.—John 11. 25.— John 14. 19.—Heb. 3. 14.—Heb. 6. 4.—2 Pet. 1. 4. —1 Cor. 15. 45; 51, 52.   Rev. 4. 8, 9.— 1 Tim. 6. 15, 16.—1 Tim. 1. 17.

M

MAY 19.

Wash me throughly from mine iniquity.

I WILL cleanse them from all their iniquity, whereby they have sinned against me ; and I will pardon all their iniquities, whereby they have sinned, and whereby they have transgressed against me. — Then will I sprinkle clean water upon you, and ye shall be clean ; from all your filthiness, and from all your idols, will I cleanse you.

Except a man be born of water and of the Spirit, he cannot enter into the kingdom of God.—If the blood of bulls and of goats, and the ashes of a heifer sprinkling the unclean, sanctifieth to the purifying of the flesh : how much more shall the blood of Christ, who through the eternal Spirit offered himself without spot to God, purge your conscience from dead works to serve the living God ?

He saved them for his name's sake, that he might make his mighty power to be known.—Not unto us, O LORD, not unto us, but unto thy name give glory, for thy mercy, and for thy truth's sake.

Ps. 51. 2.   Jer. 33. 8.—Ezek. 36. 25.   John 3. 5. —Heb. 9. 13, 14.   Ps. 106. 8.—Ps. 115. 1.
M

MAY 20.

Take heed unto thyself

EVERY man that striveth for the mastery is temperate in all things. Now they do it to obtain a corruptible crown; but we an incorruptible I therefore so run, not as uncertainly; so fight I, not as one that beateth the air : but I keep under my body, and bring it into subjec tion · lest that by any means, when I have preached to others, I myself should be a castaway.

Put on the whole armour of God, that ye may be able to stand against the wiles of the devil. For we wrestle not against flesh and blood, but against principalities, against powers, against the rulers of the darkness of this world, against spiritual wickedness in high places.

They that are Christ's have crucified the flesh with the affections and lusts. If we live in the Spirit, let us also walk in the Spirit.—For as many as are led by the Spirit of God, they are the sons of God.—Meditate upon these things ; give thyself wholly to them ; that thy profiting may appear to all.

1 TIM. 4. 16. 1 Cor 9 25-27. Eph. 6. 11, 12. Gal 5. 24, 25 —Rom. 8. 14 —1 Tim. 4. 15.
M

MAY 21.

My brethren, be strong in the Lord, and
in the power of his might.

MY grace is sufficient for thee : for my
strength is made perfect in weakness. Most gladly therefore will I rather
glory in my infirmities, that the power of
Christ may rest upon me. Therefore I
take pleasure in infirmities, in reproaches,
in necessities, in persecutions, in distresses for Christ's sake : for when I am
weak, then am I strong.—I will go in
the strength of the Lord GOD : I will
make mention of thy righteousness, even
of thine only.—The gospel of Christ . . .
is the power of God unto salvation.

I can do all things through Christ
which strengtheneth me.—I also labour,
striving according to his working, which
worketh in me mightily.—We have this
treasure in earthen vessels, that the excellency of the power may be of God,
and not of us.

The joy of the LORD is your strength.
—Strengthened with all might, according to his glorious power, unto all patience
and longsuffering with joyfulness.

EPH. 6. 10. 2 Cor. 12. 9, 10.—Ps. 71. 16.—
Rom. 1. 16. Phil. 4. 13.—Col. 1. 29.—2 Cor. 4. 7.
Neh. 8. 10.—Col. 1. 11

MAY 22.

Peace I leave with you, my peace I give
unto you. not as the world giveth,
give I unto you.

THE world passeth away, and the lust
thereof—Surely every man walketh in
a vain shew : surely they are disquieted in
vain . he heapeth up riches, and knoweth
not who shall gather them.—What fruit
had ye then in those things whereof ye
are now ashamed? for the end of those
things is death.

Martha, Martha, thou art careful and
troubled about many things : but one
thing is needful : and Mary hath chosen
that good part, which shall not be taken
away from her.

I would have you without carefulness.

These things I have spoken unto you,
that in me ye might have peace. In the
world ye shall have tribulation : but be
of good cheer; I have overcome the
world—The Lord of peace himself give
you peace always by all means.—The
LORD bless thee, and keep thee : the
LORD make his face shine upon thee,
and be gracious unto thee : the LORD
lift up his countenance upon thee, and
give thee peace.

JOHN 14. 27. 1 John 2 17.—Ps 39. 6.—
Rom. 6. 21. Luke 10. 41, 42. 1 Cor. 7. 32.
John 16 33 —2 Thes. 3 16 —Num. 6. 24-26.
M

MAY 23.

Thou shalt put the two stones upon the shoulders of the ephod for stones of memorial unto the children of Israel and Aaron shall bear their names before the Lord.

JESUS . . . because he continueth ever, hath an unchangeable priesthood. Wherefore he is able also to save them to the uttermost that come unto God by him, seeing he ever liveth to make intercession for them.—Him that is able to keep you from falling, and to present you faultless before the presence of his glory.

Seeing . . . that we have a great high priest, that is passed into the heavens, Jesus the Son of God, let us hold fast our profession. For we have not a high priest which cannot be touched with the feeling of our infirmities ; but was in all points tempted like as we are, yet without sin. Let us therefore come boldly unto the throne of grace.

The beloved of the LORD shall dwell in safety by him ; and the LORD shall cover him all the day long, and he shall dwell between his shoulders.

Ex. 28. 12. Heb. 7. 24, 25.—Jude 24
Heb 4. 14-16 Deut. 33. 12

M

MAY 24.

Grieve not the holy Spirit of God,
whereby ye are sealed unto the
day of redemption.

THE love of the Spirit. —The Comforter, which is the Holy Ghost. —In all their affliction he was afflicted, and the angel of his presence saved them : in his love and in his pity he redeemed them ; and he bare them, and carried them all the days of old. But they rebelled, and vexed his holy Spirit : therefore he was turned to be their enemy, and he fought against them.

Hereby know we that we dwell in him, and he in us, because he hath given us of his Spirit. —After that ye believed, ye were sealed with that holy Spirit of promise, which is the earnest of our inheritance until the redemption of the purchased possession —This I say then, Walk in the Spirit, and ye shall not fulfil the lust of the flesh. For the flesh lusteth against the spirit, and the spirit against the flesh · and these are contrary the one to the other · so that ye cannot do the things that ye would.

The Spirit helpeth our infirmities

EPH. 4 30   Rom. 15 30 —John 14. 26 —
Is 63. 9, 10.   1 John 4 13 —Eph 1 13, 14 —
    Gal. 5 16 17   Rom 8. 26

M

MAY 25.

How great is thy goodness, which thou hast laid up for them that fear thee!

SINCE the beginning of the world men have not heard, nor perceived by the ear, neither hath the eye seen, O God, beside thee, what he hath prepared for him that waiteth for him.—Eye hath not seen, nor ear heard, neither have entered into the heart of man, the things which God hath prepared for them that love him. But God hath revealed them unto us by his Spirit.—Thou wilt shew me the path of life : in thy presence is fulness of joy ; at thy right hand there are pleasures for evermore.

How excellent is thy loving kindness, O God ! therefore the children of men put their trust under the shadow of thy wings. They shall be abundantly satis-fied with the fatness of thy house ; and thou shalt make them drink of the river of thy pleasures.

Godliness is profitable unto all things, having promise of the life that now is, and of that which is to come.

Ps. 31. 19 Is. 64. 4.—1 Cor. 2. 9, 10.—
Ps 16 11. Ps 36 7, 8 1 Tim 4. 8.
M

**Our Lord Jesus, that great shepherd
of the sheep**

I AM the good shepherd, and know my sheep, and am known of mine. My sheep hear my voice, and I know them, and they follow me : and I give unto them eternal life ; and they shall never perish, neither shall any man pluck them out of my hand.

The LORD is my shepherd ; I shall not want. He maketh me to lie down in green pastures : he leadeth me beside the still waters. He restoreth my soul : he leadeth me in the paths of righteousness for his name's sake.

All we like sheep have gone astray ; we have turned every one to his own way ; and the LORD hath laid on him the iniquity of us all.—I am the good shepherd : the good shepherd giveth his life for the sheep.—I will seek that which was lost, and bring again that which was driven away, and will bind up that which was broken, and will strengthen that which was sick.—Ye were as sheep going astray ; but are now returned unto the Shepherd and Bishop of your souls.

HEB 13. 20. John 10 14, 27, 28 Ps 23. 1-3,
Is 53 6—John 10 11—Ezek 34 16—
1 Pet. 2. 25

M

MAY 27.

The Lord is good, a strong hold in the
day of trouble, and he knoweth
them that trust in him.

PRAISE the LORD of hosts: for the
LORD is good ; for his mercy endureth
for ever.—God is our refuge and strength,
a very present help in trouble.—I will say
of the LORD, He is my refuge and my
fortress : my God ; in him will I trust.—
Who is like unto thee, O people saved
by the LORD, the shield of thy help, and
who is the sword of thy excellency !—As
for God, his way is perfect ; the word of
the LORD is tried · he is a buckler to all
them that trust in him.   For who is God,
save the LORD ? and who is a rock, save
our God ?

If any man love God, the same is
known of him.—The foundation of God
standeth sure, having this seal, The Lord
knoweth them that are his.   And, Let
every one that nameth the name of Christ
depart from iniquity.—The LORD knoweth the way of the righteous : but the
way of the ungodly shall perish —Thou
hast found grace in my sight, and I know ⁄
thee by name.

NAH. 1. 7.   Jer. 33. 11.—Ps. 46. 1.—Ps 91 2 —
Deut. 33. 29.—2 Sam. 22. 31, 32.   1 Cor. 8 3.—
2 Tim 2. 19.—Ps 1. 6.—Ex. 33 17

M

MAY 28.

We look for the Saviour.

THE grace of God that bringeth salvation hath appeared to all men, teaching us that, denying ungodliness and worldly lusts, we should live soberly, righteously, and godly, in this present world ; looking for that blessed hope, and the glorious appearing of the great God and our Saviour Jesus Christ ; who gave himself for us, that he might redeem us from all iniquity, and purify unto himself a peculiar people zealous of good works. —We, according to his promise, look for new heavens and a new earth, wherein dwelleth righteousness. Wherefore, beloved, seeing that ye look for such things, be diligent that ye may be found of him in peace, without spot, and blameless.

Christ was once offered to bear the sins of many ; and unto them that look for him shall he appear the second time without sin unto salvation.—And it shall be said in that day, Lo, this is our God ; we have waited for him, and he will save us : this is the LORD ; we have waited for him, we will be glad and rejoice in his salvation.

PHIL. 3. 20. TIT. 2 11-14.—2 PeL 3 13, 14.
Heb 9. 28 —Is. 25 9.

ν

MAY 29.

The life of the flesh is in the blood: and I
have given it to you upon the altar to
make an atonement for your souls: for it
is the blood that maketh an atonement
for the soul

BEHOLD the Lamb of God, which
taketh away the sin of the world.—
The blood of the Lamb.—The precious
blood of Christ, as of a lamb without
blemish and without spot.

Without shedding of blood is no re
mission.—The blood of Jesus Christ his
Son cleanseth us from all sin.

By his own blood he entered in once
into the holy place, having obtained eternal redemption for us—Having therefore,
brethren, boldness to enter into the holiest
by the blood of Jesus, by a new and living
way, which he hath consecrated for us,
through the veil, that is to say, his flesh ;
let us draw near with a true heart in full
assurance of faith.

Ye are bought with a price : therefore
glorify God in your body, and in your
spirit, which are God's.

Lev 17. 11. John 1. 29.—Rev. 7 14.—
1 Pet. 1. 19. Heb 9. 22.—1 John 1. 7.
Heb. 9. 12.—Heb. 10. 19, 20, 22. 1 Cor 6 20.
M

MAY 30.

Let us labour to enter into that rest.

ENTER ye in at the strait gate : for wide is the gate, and broad is the way, that leadeth to destruction : . . strait is the gate, and narrow is the way, which leadeth unto life, and few there be that find it.—The kingdom of heaven suffereth violence, and the violent take it by force.—Labour not for the meat which perisheth, but for that meat which endureth unto everlasting life, which the Son of man shall give unto you.

Give diligence to make your calling and election sure . . . for so an entrance shall be ministered unto you abundantly into the everlasting kingdom of our Lord and Saviour Jesus Christ.—So run, that ye may obtain. And every man that striveth for the mastery is temperate in all things. Now they do it to obtain a corruptible crown ; but we an incorruptible.

For he that is entered into his rest, he also hath ceased from his own works, as God did from his.—The LORD shall be unto thee an everlasting light, and thy God thy glory.

HEB 4 11 Mat 7 13, 14 —Mat. II. 12 — John 6. 27. 2 Pet. 1 10, 11.—1 Cor. 9. 24, 25. Heb 4. 10 —Is 60 19.

M

MAY 31,

Thy name shall be called Israel : for as
a prince hast thou power with God
and with men, and hast prevailed.

BY his strength he had power with
God : yea, he had power over the
angel, and prevailed : he wept, and made
supplication unto him.—[Abraham] stag
gered not at the promise of God through
unbelief ; but was strong in faith, giving
glory to God

Have faith in God.   For verily I say
unto you, That whosoever shall say unto
this mountain, Be thou removed, and be
thou cast into the sea ; and shall not
doubt in his heart, but shall believe that
those things which he saith shall come to
pass ; he shall have whatsoever he saith.
Therefore I say unto you, What things
soever ye desire, when ye pray, believe
that ye receive them, and ye shall have
them.—If thou canst believe, all things
are possible to him   that believeth —
Blessed is she that believed · for there
shall be a performance of those things
which were told her from the Lord.

Lord, increase our faith.

GEN. 32. 28.   Hos. 12 3, 4 —Rom. 4 20,
Mark 11 22-24 —Mark 9 23 —Luke 1 45
Luke 17 5.

M

JUNE 1.

The fruit of the Spirit is longsuffering, gentleness.

THE LORD, the LORD God, merciful and gracious, longsuffering, and abundant in goodness and truth. Walk worthy of the vocation wherewith ye are called with all lowliness and meekness, with longsuffering, forbearing one another in love.—Be ye kind one to another, tenderhearted, forgiving one another, even as God for Christ's sake hath forgiven you.—The wisdom that is from above is first pure, then peaceable, gentle, and easy to be intreated, full of mercy and good fruits, without partiality, and without hypocrisy.—Charity suffereth long, and is kind.

In due season we shall reap, if we faint not —Be patient therefore, brethren, unto the coming of the Lord. Behold, the husbandman waiteth for the precious fruit of the earth, and hath long patience for it, until he receive the early and latter rain. Be ye also patient; stablish your hearts: for the coming of the Lord draweth nigh

GAL. 5. 22 Ex 34 6 Eph. 4. 1, 2.—Eph. 4. 32 —Ja. 3 17—1 Cor 13. 4 Gal. 6 9 — Ja 5 7, 8

M

JUNE 2.

Thus shall ye eat it, with your loins
girded, and ye shall eat it in haste
it is the Lord's passover

A RISE ye, and depart; for this is not
your rest.—Here have we no continuing city, but we seek one to come —
There remaineth therefore a rest to the
people of God.

Let your loins be girded about, and
your lights burning; and ye yourselves
like unto men that wait for their lord,
when he will return from the wedding;
that when he cometh and knocketh, they
may open unto him immediately. Blessed
are those servants, whom the lord when
he cometh shall find watching.—Gird up
the loins of your mind, be sober, and
hope to the end for the grace that is to
be brought unto you at the revelation of
Jesus Christ.

This one thing I do, forgetting those
things which are behind, . I press toward the mark for the prize of the high
calling of God in Christ Jesus. Let us
therefore as many as be perfect, be thus
minded

Ex 12 11. Mic. 2 10 —Heb 13 14.—Heb 4 9
Luke 12 35-37 —1 Pet. 1. 13   Phil 3 13-15
M

JUNE 3.

Watch, for ye know neither the day nor the hour wherein the Son of man cometh.

TAKE heed to yourselves, lest at any time your hearts be overcharged with surfeiting, and drunkenness, and cares of this life, and so that day come upon you unawares. For as a snare shall it come on all them that dwell on the face of the earth. Watch ye, therefore, and pray always, that ye may be counted worthy to escape all these things that shall come to pass, and to stand before the Son of man.

The day of the Lord so cometh as a thief in the night. For when they shall say, Peace and safety; then sudden destruction cometh upon them, as travail upon a woman with child; and they shall not escape. But ye, brethren, are not in darkness, that that day should overtake you as a thief. Ye are all the children of light, and the children of the day; we are not of the night, nor of darkness. Therefore let us not sleep, as do others; but let us watch and be sober.

MAT. 25. 13. Luke 21. 34-36. 1 Thes. 5 2-6.
M

JUNE 4.

The glory of this latter house shall be greater than of the former, and in this place will I give peace.

THE house that is to be builded for the LORD must be exceeding magnifical, of fame and of glory throughout all countries.—The glory of the LORD . . . filled the LORD's house.

Destroy this temple, and in three days I will raise it up. He spake of the temple of his body.—That which was made glorious had no glory in this respect, by reason of the glory that excelleth — The Word was made flesh, and dwelt among us, (and we beheld his glory, the glory as of the only begotten of the Father,) full of grace and truth —God . . . hath in these last days spoken unto us by his Son, whom he hath appointed heir of all things, by whom also he made the worlds.

Glory to God in the highest, and on earth peace, good will toward men.—The Prince of Peace —He is our peace. —The peace of God, which passeth all understanding, shall keep your hearts and minds through Christ Jesus

HAG 2 9   1 Chr. 22 5 —2 Chr 7 2   John 2 19, 21 —2 Cor. 3 10 —John 1 14 —Heb 1 1, 2 Luke 2 14 —Is 9 6 —Eph 2 14 —Phil 4 7
M

JUNE 5.

When ye shall have done all those things which are commanded you, say, We are unprofitable servants.

WHERE is boasting then? It is excluded. By what law? of works? Nay : but by the law of faith.—What hast thou that thou didst not receive? now if thou didst receive it, why dost thou glory, as if thou hadst not received it ?—By grace are ye saved through faith ; and that not of yourselves : it is the gift of God : not of works, lest any man should boast. For we are his workmanship, created in Christ Jesus unto good works, which God hath before ordained that we should walk in them.

By the grace of God I am what I am : and his grace which was bestowed upon me was not in vain ; but I laboured more abundantly than they all · yet not I, but the grace of God which was with me.— For of him, and through him, and to him, are all things.—Of thine own have we given thee.

Enter not into judgment with thy servant : for in thy sight shall no man living be justified.

LUKE 17. 10. Rom. 3. 27.—1 Cor. 4. 7.—
Eph. 2. 8-10. 1 Cor. 15. 10.—Rom. 11. 36.—
1 Chr. 29. 14. Ps. 143. 2.

M

6

JUNE 6.

He will rest in his love

THE LORD did not set his love upon you, nor choose you, because ye were more in number than any people; for ye were the fewest of all people : but because the LORD loved you—We love him, because he first loved us—You . . . hath he reconciled in the body of his flesh through death, to present you holy and unblameable and unreproveable in his sight.

Herein is love, not that we loved God, but that he loved us, and sent his Son to be the propitiation for our sins—God commendeth his love toward us, in that while we were yet sinners, Christ died for us.

Lo, a voice from heaven, saying, This is my beloved Son, in whom I am well pleased—Therefore doth my Father love me, because I lay down my life, that I might take it again—His Son . . . who being the brightness of his glory, and the express image of his person, and upholding all things by the word of his power, when he had by himself purged our sins, sat down on the right hand of the Majesty on high.

Zep. 3 17. Deut. 7 7, 8 —1 John 4 19 —
Col. 1. 21, 22 1 John 4 10 —Rom 5 8
Mat. 3 17 —John 10. 17.—Heb 1. 2, 3.

M

JUNE 7.

Men ought always to pray, and not
to faint.

WHICH of you shall have a friend,
and shall go unto him at midnight,
and say unto him, Friend, lend me three
loaves ; for a friend of mine in his journey
is come to me, and I have nothing to set
before him ? And he from within shall
answer and say, Trouble me not : the
door is now shut, and my children are
with me in bed , I cannot rise and give
thee. I say unto you, Though he will
not rise and give him because he is his
friend, yet because of his importunity he
will rise and give him as many as he
needeth.—Praying always with all prayer
and supplication in the Spirit, and watching thereunto with all perseverance and
supplication for all saints.

I will not let thee go, except thou bless
me.—As a prince hast thou power with
God and with men.—Continue in prayer,
and watch in the same with thanksgiving.

[Jesus] went out into a mountain to
pray, and continued all night in prayer
to God

LUKE 18 1 Luke 11 5-8.—Eph 6 18
Gen 32 26 : 28 — Col 4 2. Luke 6. 12.

JUNE 8.

The Lord made all that he did to prosper
in his hand.

BLESSED is every one that feareth
the LORD , that walketh in his ways.
For thou shalt eat the labour of thine
hands : happy shalt thou be, and it shall
be well with thee.—Trust in the LORD,
and do good ; so shalt thou dwell in the
land, and verily thou shalt be fed.   Delight thyself also in the LORD ; and he
shall give thee the desires of thine heart.
—Be not afraid, neither be thou dismayed : for the LORD thy God is with
thee whithersoever thou goest.

Seek ye first the kingdom of God, and
his righteousness ; and all these things
shall be added unto you.

As long as he sought the LORD, God
made him to prosper.—Beware that thou
forget not the LORD thy God, in not
keeping his commandments, and his judgments, and his statutes, which I command
thee this day · and thou say in thine
heart, My power and the might of mine
hand hath gotten me this wealth

Is not the LORD your God with you ?
and hath he not given you rest on every
side ?

GEN. 39. 3   Ps 128. 1, 2 —Ps. 37. 3, 4.—
Jos. 1 9   Mat. 6 33   2 Chr 26 5.—
Deut 8 11, 17.   1 Chr. 22 18
M

JUNE 9.

Never man spake like this man

THOU art fairer than the children of men · grace is poured into thy lips: therefore God hath blessed thee for ever. —The Lord GOD hath given me the tongue of the learned, that I should know how to speak a word in season to him that is weary —His mouth is most sweet. yea, he is altogether lovely. This is my beloved, and this is my friend.

All bare him witness, and wondered at the gracious words which proceeded out of his mouth —He taught them as one having authority, and not as the scribes.

Let the word of Christ dwell in you richly in all wisdom. —The sword of the Spirit . . . is the word of God —The word of God is quick, and powerful, and sharper than any two-edged sword —The weapons of our warfare are not carnal, but mighty through God to the pulling down of strong holds; casting down imaginations, and every high thing that exalteth itself against the knowledge of God, and bringing into captivity every thought to the obedience of Christ.

JOHN 7 46 Ps 45. 2 —Is. 50. 4 —Cant 5. 16.
Luke 4. 22 —Mat. 7. 29 Col. 3. 16.—
Eph. 6. 17.—Heb. 12.—2 Cor. 10. 4, .·
M

JUNE 10.

The younger son took his journey into a
far country, and there wasted his
substance with riotous living.

SUCH were some of you : but ye are
washed, but ye are sanctified, but ye
are justified in the name of the Lord
Jesus, and by the Spirit of our God.

We . . . were by nature the children
of wrath, even as others. But God, who
is rich in mercy, for his great love where
with he loved us, even when we were
dead in sins, hath quickened us together
with Christ, (by grace ye are saved ,) and
hath raised us up together, and made us
sit together in heavenly places in Christ
Jesus.

Herein is love, not that we loved God,
but that he loved us, and sent his Son to
be the propitiation for our sins.

God commendeth his love toward us,
in that, while we were yet sinners, Christ
died for us. If, when we were enemies,
we were reconciled to God by the death
of his Son, much more, being reconciled,
we shall be saved by his life

LUKE 15. 13.   1 Cor. 6. 11.   Eph. 2. 3-6.
1 John 4 10   Rom 5. 8, 10.

M

JUNE 11.

He arose, and came to his father. But
when he was yet a great way off, his
father saw him, and ran, and fell on his
neck, and kissed him.

THE LORD is merciful and gracious,
slow to anger, and plenteous in mercy.
He will not always chide : neither will
he keep his anger for ever. He hath
not dealt with us after our sins ; nor rewarded us according to our iniquities
For as the heaven is high above the
earth, so great is his mercy toward them
that fear him. As far as the east is from
the west, so far hath he removed our
transgressions from us. Like as a father
pitieth his children, so the LORD pitieth
them that fear him.

Ye have received the Spirit of adoption, whereby we cry, Abba, Father.
The Spirit itself beareth witness with our
spirit, that we are the children of God.
—Ye who sometime were far off are made
nigh by the blood of Christ.—Now therefore ye are no more strangers and foreigners, but fellowcitizens with the saints,
and of the household of God.

LUKE 15 20. Ps. 103. 8-13. Rom. 8 15, 16.
—Eph 2 13, 19.
M

JUNE 12.

Every thing that may abide the fire, ye shall make it go through the fire, and it shall be clean.

THE LORD your God proveth you, to know whether ye love the LORD your God with all your heart, and with all your soul.—He shall sit as a refiner and purifier of silver ; and he shall purify the sons of Levi, and purge them as gold and silver, that they may offer unto the LORD an offering in righteousness.—Every man's work shall be made manifest : for the day shall declare it, because it shall be revealed by fire ; and the fire shall try every man's work of what sort it is

I will turn my hand upon thee, and purely purge away thy dross, and take away all thy tin.—I will melt them, and try them.

Thou, O God, hast proved us ; thou hast tried us, as silver is tried. We went through fire and through water : but thou broughtest us out into a wealthy place.

When thou walkest through the fire, thou shalt not be burned ; neither shall the flame kindle upon thee.

NUM 31. 23   Deut. 13. 3.—Mal. 3. 3.—
1 Cor. 3 13   Is. 1. 25.—Jer. 9. 7.
Ps 66. 10. 12.   Is. 43 2.

M

JUNE 13.

Abide in me, and I in you.

I AM crucified with Christ: nevertheless I live ; yet not I, but Christ liveth in me : and the life which I now live in the flesh I live by the faith of the Son of God, who loved me, and gave himself for me.

I know that in me (that is, in my flesh,) dwelleth no good thing : for to will is present with me ; but how to perform that which is good I find not. O wretched man that I am! who shall deliver me from the body of this death? I thank God through Jesus Christ our Lord.

If Christ be in you, the body is dead because of sin; but the Spirit is life because of righteousness.—If ye continue in the faith grounded and settled, and be not moved away from the hope of the gospel, which ye have heard.

Little children, abide in him; that, when he shall appear, we may have con-fidence, and not be ashamed before him at his coming.—He that saith he abideth in him ought himself also so to walk, even as he walked.

JOHN 15. 4. Gal. 2. 20. Rom. 7. 18, 24, 25. Rom. 8. 10.—Col. 1. 23. 1 John 2. 28 —1 John 2. 6.
M
6 *

JUNE 14.

As the sufferings of Christ abound in us, so our consolation also aboundeth by Christ

THE fellowship of his sufferings.—Rejoice, inasmuch as ye are partakers of Christ's sufferings ; that, when his glory shall be revealed, ye may be glad also with exceeding joy.—For if we be dead with him, we shall also live with him.— If children, then heirs , heirs of God, and joint-heirs with Christ ; if so be that we suffer with him, that we may be also glorified together.

God, willing more abundantly to shew unto the heirs of promise the immutability of his counsel, confirmed it by an oath : that by two immutable things, in which it was impossible for God to lie, we might have a strong consolation, who have fled for refuge to lay hold upon the hope set before us.—Our Lord Jesus Christ himself, and God, even our Father, which hath loved us, and hath given us everlasting consolation and good hope through grace, comfort your hearts, and stablish you in every good word and work.

2 Cor. 1. 5. Phil 3. 10.—1 Pet. 4. 13 — 2 Tim. 2. 11.—Rom 8 17. Heb. 6. 17, 18. —2 Thes. 2. 16, 17.

JUNE 15.

The secret things belong unto the Lord our
God : but those which are revealed
belong unto us.

LORD, my heart is not haughty, nor
mine eyes lofty · neither do I exercise
myself in great matters, or in things too
high for me. Surely I have behaved and
quieted myself, as a child that is weaned
of his mother : my soul is even as a
weaned child.

The secret of the LORD is with them
that fear him : and he will shew them his
covenant —There is a God in heaven that
revealeth secrets.

Lo, these are parts of his ways · but
how little a portion is heard of him ?

Henceforth I call you not servants ; for
the servant knoweth not what his lord
doeth . but I have called you friends ; for
all things that I have heard of my Father
I have made known unto you.—If ye love
me, keep my commandments. And I
will pray the Father, and he shall give
you another Comforter, that he may abide
with you for ever ; even the Spirit of truth.

DEUT· 29. 29   Ps· 131· 1, 2·   Ps· 25· 14·—Dan·
2· 28.   Job 26. 14   John 15· 15·—John 14. 15-17.
M

See that ye walk circumspectly, not as
fools, but as wise, redeeming the time,
because the days are evil

TAKE diligent heed to do the commandment and the law, . . . to love the
LORD your God, and to walk in all his
ways, and to keep his commandments,
and to cleave unto him, and to serve him
with all your heart and with all your soul.
—Walk in wisdom toward them that are
without, redeeming the time. Let your
speech be alway with grace, seasoned
with salt, that ye may know how ye
ought to answer every man. — Abstain
from all appearance of evil.

While the bridegroom tarried, they all
slumbered and slept. And at midnight
there was a cry made, Behold, the bridegroom cometh ; go ye out to meet him.—
Watch therefore, for ye know neither the
day nor the hour when the Son of man
cometh.

Brethren, give diligence to make your
calling and election sure ; for if ye do
these things, ye shall never fall.—Blessed
are those servants, whom the lord when
he cometh shall find watching.

EPH. 5. 15, 16. Jos. 22. 5 —Col. 4 5, 6 —
1 Thes 5. 22. Mat. 25. 5, 6, 13. 2 Pet. 1 10.
—Luke 12 37.

M

JUNE 17.

In every thing by prayer and supplication with thanksgiving let your requests be made known unto God.

I LOVE the LORD, because he hath heard my voice and my supplications. Because he hath inclined his ear unto me, therefore will I call upon him as long as I live.

When ye pray, use not vain repetitions, as the heathen do: for they think that they shall be heard for their much speaking.—The Spirit . . . helpeth our infirmities: for we know not what we should pray for as we ought : but the Spirit itself maketh intercession for us with groanings which cannot be uttered.

I will therefore that men pray every where, lifting up holy hands, without wrath and doubting.—Praying always with all prayer and supplication in the Spirit, and watching thereunto with all perseverance and supplication for all saints.

If two of you shall agree on earth as touching any thing that they shall ask, it shall be done for them of my Father which is in heaven.

PHIL. 4. 6 Ps. 116. 1, 2. Mat. 6. 7.—Rom 8. 26.
1 Tim. 2. 8.—Eph. 6. 18. Mat 18- 19

JUNE 18.

Thou shalt put the mercy seat above upon the ark, and there I will meet with thee.

THE way into the holiest of all was not yet made manifest.—Jesus, when he had cried again with a loud voice, yielded up the ghost. And, behold, the veil of the temple was rent in twain from the top to the bottom.

Having . . . brethren, boldness to enter into the holiest by the blood of Jesus, by a new and living way, which he hath consecrated for us, through the veil, that is to say, his flesh ; . . . let us draw near with a true heart in full assurance of faith, having our hearts sprinkled from an evil conscience, and our bodies washed with pure water.—Let us therefore come boldly unto the throne of grace, that we may obtain mercy, and find grace to help in time of need.

Christ Jesus : whom God hath set forth to be a propitiation [mercy seat] through faith in his blood, to declare his righteousness for the remission of sins that are past, through the forbearance of God.—Through him we . . . have access by one Spirit unto the Father.

Ex. 25. 21, 22. Heb. 9. 8.—Mat. 27. 50, 51.
Heb. 10. 19, 20, 22.—Heb. 4. 16.
Rom. 3. 24. 25.—Eph. 2. 18.

M

Holiness, without which no man shall
see the Lord.

EXCEPT a man be born again; he cannot see the kingdom of God.—There
shall in no wise enter into it any thing
that defileth.—There is no spot in thee

Ye shall be holy : for I the LORD your
God am holy.—As obedient children, not
fashioning yourselves according to the
former lusts in your ignorance : but as he
which hath called you is holy, so be ye
holy in all manner of conversation ; because it is written, Be ye holy ; for I am
holy. And if ye call on the Father, who
without respect of persons judgeth according to every man's work, pass the time of
your sojourning here in fear.

Put off concerning the former conversation the old man, which is corrupt according to the deceitful lusts ; and be renewed
in the spirit of your mind ; and . . . put
on the new man, which after God is
created in righteousness and true holiness.
—He hath chosen us in him before the
foundation of the world, that we should
be holy and without blame before him in
love.

HEB 12, 14   John 3 3 —Rev 21 27.—Cant 4 7
  Lev. 19 2.—1 Pet. 1. 14-17 Eph 4 22-24.
              —Eph 1 4
  M

JUNE 20.

Take this child away, and nurse it for me, and I will give thee thy wages

GO ye . . . into the vineyard, and what-soever is right I will give you —Who-soever shall give you a cup of water to drink in my name, because ye belong to Christ, verily I say unto you, he shall not lose his reward

The liberal soul shall be made fat : and he that watereth shall be watered also himself —God is not unrighteous to forget your work and labour of love, . . . in that ye have ministered to the saints, and do minister.

Every man shall receive his own reward according to his own labour.

Lord, when saw we thee an hungered, and fed thee? or thirsty, and gave thee drink? When saw we thee a stranger, and took thee in? or naked, and clothed thee? And the King shall answer and say unto them, . . . Inasmuch as ye have done it unto one of the least of these my brethren, ye have done it unto me. Come, ye blessed of my Father, inherit the king-dom prepared for you from the foundation of the world.

Ex. 2 9 Mat. 20 4 —Mark 9 41. Pro 11. 25, —Heb. 6. 10. 1 Cor. 3. 8 Mat. 25 37, 38, 40, 34
M

JUNE 21.

Christ suffered for us, leaving us an
example that ye should follow his steps.

EVEN the Son of man came not to be
    ministered unto, but to minister.—
Whosoever of you will be the chiefest,
shall be servant of all.

Jesus of Nazareth . . . went about
doing good.—Bear ye one another's burdens, and so fulfil the law of Christ.

The meekness and gentleness of Christ.
—In lowliness of mind let each esteem
other better than themselves.

Father, forgive them : for they know
not what they do.—Be ye kind one to
another, tender-hearted, forgiving one
another, even as God for Christ's sake
hath forgiven you.

He that saith he abideth in him,
ought himself also so to walk, even as
he walked.—Looking unto Jesus the
author and finisher of our faith; who
for the joy that was set before him endured the cross, despising the shame,
and is set down at the right hand of the
throne of God.

1 PET. 2. 21.   Mark 10. 45.—Mark 10 44
Acts 10. 38.—Gal. 6. 2   2 Cor. 10. 1.—Phil. 2. 3
Luke 23. 34.—Eph. 4. 32   1 John 2. 6.—
Heb 12. 2.

M

JUNE 22.

Ye are dead, and your life is hid with
Christ in God.

HOW shall we, that are dead to sin,
live any longer therein?—I am crucified with Christ, nevertheless I live;
yet not I, but Christ liveth in me: and
the life which I now live in the flesh, I
live by the faith of the Son of God, who
loved me, and gave himself for me.—He
died for all, that they which live should
not henceforth live unto themselves, but
unto him which died for them, and rose
again.—If any man be in Christ, he is a
new creature: old things are passed away;
behold, all things are become new.

We are in him that is true, even in his
Son Jesus Christ.—As thou, Father, art
in me, and I in thee, that they also may
be one in us.—Ye are the body of Christ,
and members in particular.—Because I
live, ye shall live also.

To him that overcometh will I give to
eat of the hidden manna, and will give
him a white stone, and in the stone a new
name written, which no man knoweth
saving he that receiveth it.

Col. 3. 3. Rom. 6. 2.—Gal 2. 20.—2 Cor 5. 15.
—2 Cor 5. 17. 1 John 5. 20.—John 17. 21.—
1 Cor. 12. 27.—John 14. 19. Rev 2. 17

M

JUNE 23.

I will pray the Father, and he shall
give you another Comforter, even
the Spirit of truth.

IT is expedient for you that I go away •
for if I go not away, the Comforter
will not come unto you ; but if I depart,
I will send him unto you.

The Spirit itself beareth witness with
our spirit, that we are the children of
God.—Ye have not received the spirit of
bondage again to fear ; but ye have received the Spirit of adoption, whereby
we cry, Abba, Father.—The Spirit . . .
helpeth our infirmities for we know not
what we should pray for as we ought :
but the Spirit itself maketh intercession
for us with groanings which cannot be
uttered.

The God of hope fill you with all joy
and peace in believing, that ye may
abound in hope, through the power of
the Holy Ghost. — Hope maketh not
ashamed ; because the love of God is
shed abroad in our hearts by the Holy
Ghost which is given unto us

Hereby know we that we dwell in him,
and he in us, because he hath given us of
his Spirit.

JOHN 14 16, 17 John 16 7 Rom 8. 16 —
Rom 8 15 —Rom. 8 26 Rom 15 13 —
Rom 5. 5 1 John 4 13

M

JUNE 24.

The ark of the covenant of the Lord
went before them to search out a
resting place for them

MY times are in thy hand.—He shall
choose our inheritance for us.

Lead me, O LORD, in thy righteousness ; . . . make thy way straight before
my face.

Commit thy way unto the LORD ; trust
also in him ; and he shall bring it to pass.
—In all thy ways acknowledge him, and
he shall direct thy paths.—Thine ears
shall hear a word behind thee, saying,
This is the way, walk ye in it, when ye
turn to the right hand, and when ye turn
to the left.

The LORD is my shepherd ; I shall not
want. He maketh me to lie down in
green pastures he leadeth me beside the
still waters —Like as a father pitieth his
children so the LORD pitieth them that
fear him. For he knoweth our frame ;
be remembereth that we are dust.—Your
heavenly Father knoweth that ye have
need of all these things. —Casting all
your care upon him ; for he careth for
you.

NUM. 10. 33. Ps. 31. 15 —Ps. 47 4 Ps. 5. 8.
Ps. 37. 5.—Pro. 3 6 —Is 30. 21. Ps 23 1, 2
—Ps 103. 13, 14 —Mat 6 32.—1 Pet 5. 7.

JUNE 25.

When ne shall appear, we shall be
like him; for we shall see
him as he is

A S many as received him, to them gave
he power to become the sons of God,
even to them that believe on his name —
Whereby are given unto us exceeding
great and precious promises: that by
these ye might be partakers of the divine
nature, having escaped the corruption that
is in the world through lust.

Since the beginning of the world men
have not heard, nor perceived by the ear,
neither hath the eye seen, O God, beside
thee, what he hath prepared for him that
waiteth for him

Now we see through a glass, darkly;
but then face to face: now I know in
part; but then shall I know even as also
I am known.—Christ . . . shall change
our vile body, that it may be fashioned
like unto his glorious body, according to
the working whereby he is able even to
subdue all things unto himself —As for
me, I will behold thy face in righteousness: I shall be satisfied, when I awake,
with thy likeness.

1 John 3. 2. John 1. 12 —2 Pet. 1. 4. Is. 64. 4
1 Cor 13. 12 —Phil. 3. 20. 21 —Ps 17 15.
M

JUNE 26.

Oh that thou wouldest bless me indeed, . . . and that thou wouldest keep me from evil! . . . And God granted him that which he requested

THE blessing of the LORD, it maketh rich, and he addeth no sorrow with it.—When he giveth quietness, who then can make trouble? and when he hideth his face, who then can behold him?

Salvation belongeth unto the LORD: thy blessing is upon thy people.—How great is thy goodness, which thou hast laid up for them that fear thee; which thou hast wrought for them that trust in thee before the sons of men!—I pray not that thou shouldest take them out of the world, but that thou shouldest keep them from the evil.

Ask, and it shall be given you, seek, and ye shall find; knock, and it shall be opened unto you. for every one that asketh receiveth; and he that seeketh findeth; and to him that knocketh it shall be opened.—The LORD redeemeth the soul of his servants and none of them that trust in him shall be desolate

1 Chr 4. 10 Pro 10 22 —Job 34 29 Ps 3 8.
—Ps 31 19 —John 17 15 Mat 7 7, 8 —
Ps 34 22.

M

JUNE 27.

Who shall be able to stand?

WHO may abide the day of his coming? and who shall stand when he appeareth? for he is like a refiner's fire, and like fullers' sope.

I beheld, and, lo, a great multitude, which no man could number, of all nations, and kindreds, and people, and tongues, stood before the throne, and before the Lamb, clothed with white robes, and palms in their hands. These are they which came out of great tribulation, and have washed their robes, and made them white in the blood of the Lamb. They shall hunger no more, neither thirst any more ; neither shall the sun light on them, nor any heat. For the Lamb, which is in the midst of the throne, shall feed them, and shall lead them unto living fountains of waters · and God shall wipe away all tears from their eyes.

There is . . . no condemnation to them which are in Christ Jesus, who walk not after the flesh, but after the Spirit.—Stand fast therefore in the liberty wherewith Christ hath made us free

REV 6. 17. Mal 3 2. Rev 7. 9, 14-17
Rom. 8 1.—Gal 5 1.

M

JUNE 28.

IF, when we were enemies, we were reconciled to God by the death of his Son, much more, being reconciled, we shall be saved by his life.—This man, because he continueth ever, hath an un-changeable priesthood. Wherefore he is able also to save them to the uttermost that come unto God by him, seeing he ever liveth to make intercession for them

Because I live, ye shall live also.—If in this life only we have hope in Christ, we are of all men most miserable. But now is Christ risen from the dead, and become the firstfruits of them that slept.

The Redeemer shall come to Zion, and unto them that turn from trans-gression in Jacob, saith the LORD.—We have redemption through his blood, the forgiveness of sins, according to the riches of his grace.—Ye were not redeemed with corruptible things, as silver and gold, from your vain conversation received by tradition from your fathers, but with the precious blood of Christ, as of a lamb without blemish and without spot.

JOB 19. 25. Rom. 5 10 —Heb 7. 24, 25
John 14 19 —1 Cor 15 19, 20 Is. 59. 20 —
Eph 1. 7 —1 Pet 1 18, 19.

M

His commandments are not grievous

THIS is the will of him that sent me, that every one which seeth the Son, and believeth on him, may have everlasting life.—Whatsoever we ask, we receive of him, because we keep his commandments, and do those things that are pleasing in his sight

My yoke is easy, and my burden is light.—If ye love me, keep my commandments —He that hath my commandments and keepeth them, he it is that loveth me: and he that loveth me shall be loved of my Father, and I will love him, and will manifest myself to him.

Happy is the man that findeth wisdom, and the man that getteth understanding. —Her ways are ways of pleasantness, and all her paths are peace —Great peace have they which love thy law: and nothing shall offend them —I delight in the law of God after the inward man.

This is his commandment, That we should believe on the name of his Son Jesus Christ, and love one another — Love worketh no ill to his neighbour : therefore love is the fulfilling of the law.

1 JOHN 5 3. John 6 40.—1 John 3 22 Mat. 11. 30 —John 14. 15, 21. Pro 3 13, 17 —Ps 119. 165 —Rom 7 22. 1 John 3 23 —Rom. 13 10

M

JUNE 30.

As many as I love, I rebuke and chasten.

MY son, despise not thou the chastening of the Lord, nor faint when thou art rebuked of him for whom the Lord loveth he chasteneth, and scourgeth every son whom he receiveth.—Even as a father the son in whom he delighteth.

He maketh sore, and bindeth up: he woundeth, and his hands make whole. —Humble yourselves therefore under the mighty hand of God, that he may exalt you in due time.—I have chosen thee in the furnace of affliction.

He doth not afflict willingly nor grieve the children of men.—He hath not dealt with us after our sins; nor rewarded us according to our iniquities. For as the heaven is high above the earth, so great is his mercy toward them that fear him. As far as the east is from the west, so far hath he removed our transgressions from us. Like as a father pitieth his children, so the LORD pitieth them that fear him. For he knoweth our frame; he remembereth that we are dust.

REV 3. 19.   Heb 12 5, 6 —Pro 3 12   Job 5. 18 —1 Pet. 5 6.—Is. 48. 10.   Lam 3. 33. —Ps 103. 10-14.

JULY 1.

BE ye . . . followers of God, as dear children.—Love your enemies, bless them that curse you, do good to them that hate you, and pray for them which despitefully use you, and persecute you; that ye may be the children of your Father which is in heaven: for he maketh his sun to rise on the evil and on the good, and sendeth rain on the just and on the unjust.—Be ye therefore merciful, as your Father also is merciful

The fruit of the Spirit is in all goodness and righteousness and truth.

After that the kindness and love of God our Saviour toward man appeared, not by works of righteousness which we have done but according to his mercy he saved us, by the washing of regeneration, and renewing of the Holy Ghost; which he shed on us abundantly through Jesus Christ our Saviour.—The LORD is good to all; and his tender mercies are over all his works.—He that spared not his own Son, but delivered him up for us all, how shall he not with him also freely give us all things?

GAL 5 22. Eph. 5 1.—Mat 5 44 45.—Luke 6. 36. Eph. 5 9 Tit 3 4-6.—Ps 145. 9 —Rom 8. 32.

M

JULY 2.

This is the ordinance of the passover:
There shall no stranger eat thereof.

WE have an altar, whereof they have
no right to eat which serve the tabernacle.—Except a man be born again,
he cannot see the kingdom of God.—At
that time ye were without Christ, being
aliens from the commonwealth of Israel,
and strangers from the covenants of promise. But now, in Christ Jesus, ye who
sometime were far off, are made nigh
by the blood of Christ.

For he is our peace, who hath made
both one, . . . having abolished in his
flesh the enmity, even the law of commandments contained in ordinances; for
to make in himself of twain one new man,
so making peace.

Now therefore ye are no more strangers
and foreigners, but fellowcitizens with
the saints, and of the household of God.

Behold, I stand at the door, and
knock: if any man hear my voice, and
open the door, I will come in to him,
and will sup with him, and he with me.

Ex. 12. 43 Heb. 13. 10.—John 3. 3 —Eph. 2.
12, 13 Eph 2. 14, 15. Eph. 2. 19 Rev. 3. 20.
M

JULY 3.

If children, then heirs ; heirs of God, and joint-heirs with Christ.

IF ye be Christ's, then are ye Abraham's seed, and heirs according to the promise.

Behold, what manner of love the Father hath bestowed upon us, that we should be called the sons of God.—Thou art no more a servant, but a son ; and if a son, then an heir of God through Christ —Having predestinated us unto the adoption of children by Jesus Christ to himself, according to the good pleasure of his will.

Father, I will that they also, whom thou hast given me, be with me where I am ; that they may behold my glory, which thou hast given me.

He that overcometh, and keepeth my works unto the end, to him will I give power over the nations.—To him that overcometh will I grant to sit with me in my throne, even as I also overcame, and am set down with my Father in his throne.

Rom 8. 17. Gal. 3 29. 1 John 3. 1.—Gal. 4. 7 —Eph 1. 5. John 17 24. Rev 2. 26. —Rev. 3. 21.

M

JULY 4.

AS one whom his mother comforteth, so will I comfort you.—They brought young children to him, that he should touch them. And he took them up in his arms, put his hands upon them, and blessed them.

Jesus called his disciples unto him, and said, I have compassion on the multitude, because they continue with me now three days, and have nothing to eat ; and I will not send them away fasting, lest they faint in the way.—A high Priest . . touched with the feeling of our infirmities.—In his love and in his pity he redeemed them.

I will not leave you comfortless (marg orphans) : I will come to you —Can a woman forget her sucking child, that she should not have compassion on the son of her womb? yea, they may forget, yet will I not forget thee

The Lamb which is in the midst of the throne shall feed them, and shall lead them unto living fountains of waters: and God shall wipe away all tears from their eyes

JOHN 13 23 Is 66 13 —Mark 10 13, 16 Mat. 15 32 —Heb 4 15 —Is 63 9 John 14 M 18 —Is 40 15 Rev 7 17.

JULY 5.

We have known and believed the love
that God hath to us

GOD, who is rich in mercy, for his great love wherewith he loved us, even when we were dead in sins, hath quickened us together with Christ, (by grace ye are saved;) and hath raised us up together, and made us sit together in heavenly places in Christ Jesus : that in the ages to come he might shew the exceeding riches of his grace in his kindness toward us through Christ Jesus.

God so loved the world, that he gave his only begotten Son, that whosoever believeth in him should not perish, but have everlasting life — He that spared not his own Son, but delivered him up for us all, how shall he not with him also freely give us all things?—The LORD is good to all . and his tender mercies are over all his works.

We love him, because he first loved us.

Blessed is she that believed : for there shall be a performance of those things which were told her from the Lord.

1 JOHN 4 16. Eph 2 4 7. John 3 16 —Rom. 8 32.—Ps 145 9 1 John 4 19. Luke 1 45

JULY 6.

Let your speech be alway with grace.

A WORD fitly spoken, is like apples of gold in pictures of silver. As an earring of gold, and an ornament of fine gold, so is a wise reprover upon an obedient ear.—Let no corrupt communication proceed out of your mouth, but that which is good to the use of edifying, that it may minister grace unto the hearers.— A good man out of the good treasure of the heart bringeth forth good things: and an evil man out of the evil treasure bringeth forth evil things.—By thy words thou shalt be justified —The tongue of the wise is health

They that feared the LORD spake often one to another and the LORD hearkened, and heard it, and a book of remembrance was written before him for them that feared the LORD, and that thought upon his name.

If thou take forth the precious from the vile, thou shalt be as my mouth — Therefore, as ye abound in every thing, in faith, and utterance, and knowledge, and in all diligence, . . . see that ye abound in this grace also.

COL. 4. 6. Pro 25 11, 12 —Eph 4 29.—Mat. 12 35, 37 —Pro 12 18 Mal 3 16 Jer 15 19.—2 Cor. 8 7

M

JULY 7.

Then was Jesus led up of the spirit into the wilderness to be tempted of the devil.

IN the days of his flesh, when he had offered up prayers and supplications with strong crying and tears unto him that was able to save him from death, and was heard in that he feared ; though he were a Son, yet learned he obedience by the things which he suffered , and being made perfect, he became the author of eternal salvation unto all them that obey him.

We have not an high priest which cannot be touched with the feeling of our infirmities ; but was in all points tempted like as we are, yet without sin.

There hath no temptation taken you but such as is common to man : but God is faithful, who will not suffer you to be tempted above that ye are able ; but will with the temptation also make a way to escape, that ye may be able to bear it.— My grace is sufficient for thee : for my strength is made perfect in weakness.

MAT. 4. 1.   Heb. 5. 7-9   Heb. 4. 15.   1 Cor
10. 13.—2 Cor. 12. 9.

M

JULY 8.

If we confess our sins, he is faithful and just to forgive us our sins, and to cleanse us from all unrighteousness

I ACKNOWLEDGE my transgressions : and my sin is ever before me. Against thee, thee only, have I sinned, and done this evil in thy sight.

And he arose, and came to his father. But when he was yet a great way off, his father saw him, and had compassion, and ran, and fell on his neck, and kissed him.—I have blotted out as a thick cloud, thy transgressions, and, as a cloud, thy sins : return unto me ; for I have re· deemed thee —Your sins are forgiven you for his name's sake —God for Christ's sake hath forgiven you.—That he might be just, and the justifier of him which believeth in Jesus.

Then will I sprinkle clean water upon you, and ye shall be clean.—They shall walk with me in white : for they are worthy

This is he that came by water and blood, even Jesus Christ : not by water only, but by water and blood.

1 JOHN 1. 9 Ps 51. 3, 4. Luke 15 20 —Is 44 22 —1 John 2 12 —Eph 4 32.—Rom. 3 26 Ezek 36 25 —Rev 3 4 1 John 5 6

JULY 9.

I have caused thine iniquity to pass from thee, and I will clothe thee with change of raiment.

BLESSED is he whose transgression is forgiven, whose sin is covered.—We are all as an unclean thing.—I know that in me (that is, in my flesh,) dwelleth no good thing : for to will is present with me ; but how to perform that which is good I find not.

As many of you as have been baptized into Christ have put on Christ.—Ye have put off the old man with his deeds ; and have put on the new man, which is renewed in knowledge after the image of him that created him.—Not having mine own righteousness which is of the law, but . . . the righteousness which is of God by faith.

Bring forth the best robe, and put it on him.—The fine linen is the righteousness of saints.—I will greatly rejoice in the LORD, my soul shall be joyful in my God ; for he hath clothed me with the garments of salvation, he hath covered me with the robe of righteousness.

ZEC. 3 4. Ps. 32. 1 —Is 64. 6 —Rom. 7. 18. Gal 3 27 —Col 3 9, 10.—Phil 3 9. Luke 15 22 —Rev 19 8 —Is 61. 10.

M

JULY 10.

The disciple is not above his master

YE call me Master and Lord ; and ye
say well , for so I am

It is enough for the disciple that he be
as his master, and the servant as his lord.
—If they have persecuted me, they will
also persecute you ; if they have kept my
saying, they will keep your's also.—I
have given them thy word ; and the world
hath hated them, because they are not of
the world, even as I am not of the world.

Consider him that endured such contradiction of sinners against himself, lest
ye be wearied and faint in your minds.
Ye have not yet resisted unto blood,
striving against sin

Let us run with patience the race that
is set before us, looking unto Jesus the
author and finisher of our faith ; who for
the joy that was set before him endured
the cross, despising the shame, and is set
down at the right hand of the throne of
God.—Forasmuch . . . as Christ hath
suffered for us in the flesh, arm yourselves
likewise with the same mind.

MAT. 10. 24   John 13 13   Mat. 10. 25 —John
15. 20.—John 17. 14   Heb. 12 3, 4
Heb. 12. 1, 2.—1 Pet 4. 1

M

I am with thee to save thee

SHALL the prey be taken from the mighty, or the lawful captive delivered? But thus saith the LORD, Even the captives of the mighty shall be taken away, and the prey of the terrible shall be delivered : for I will contend with him that contendeth with thee. And all flesh shall know that I the LORD am thy Saviour and thy Redeemer, the mighty One of Jacob.—Fear thou not ; for I am with thee : be not dismayed ; for I am thy God : I will strengthen thee ; yea, I will help thee ; yea, I will uphold thee with the right hand of my righteousness

We have not a high priest which cannot be touched with the feeling of our infirmities ; but was in all points tempted like as we are, yet without sin.—In that he himself hath suffered being tempted, he is able to succour them that are tempted.

The steps of a good man are ordered by the LORD : and he delighteth in his way. Though he fall, he shall not be utterly cast down : for the LORD upholdeth him with his hand.

JER. 15. 20. Is. 49 24-26.—Is. 41 10. Heb. 4. 15.—Heb. 2 18. Ps 37. 23. 24.

M

JULY 12.

My presence shall go with thee, and I
will give thee rest.

BE strong and of a good courage, fear
not, nor be afraid of them : for the
LORD thy God, he it is that doth go with
thee ; he will not fail thee, nor forsake
thee   The LORD, he it is that doth go
before thee ; he will be with thee, he
will not fail thee, neither forsake thee :
fear not, neither be dismayed.—Have
not I commanded thee ?   Be strong and
of a good courage ; be not afraid, neither
be thou dismayed · for the LORD thy God
is with thee whithersoever thou goest.—
In all thy ways acknowledge him, and he
shall direct thy paths.

He hath said, I will never leave thee,
nor forsake thee   So that we may boldly
say, The Lord is my helper, and I will
not fear what man shall do unto me.—
Our sufficiency is of God

Lead us not into temptation.—O LORD,
I know that the way of man is not in
himself . it is not in man that walketh to
direct his steps.

My times are in thy hand.

Ex. 33· 14.   Deut· 31· 6, 8·—Jos· 1. 9·—Pro 3· 6.
Heb 13· 5, 6 —2 Cor· 3· 5   Mat. 6· 13.—Jer.
10· 23.   Ps. 31 15.

M

JULY 13.

I am my Beloved's, and His desire is
toward me.

I KNOW whom I have believed, and
am persuaded that he is able to keep
that which I have committed unto him
against that day —I am persuaded, that
neither death, nor life, nor angels, nor
principalities, nor powers, nor things
present, nor things to come, nor height,
nor depth, nor any other creature, shall
be able to separate us from the love of
God, which is in Christ Jesus our Lord.
—Those that thou gavest me I have kept,
and none of them is lost.

The LORD taketh pleasure in his people.—My delights were with the sons of
men.—His great love wherewith he loved
us.—Greater love hath no man than this,
that a man lay down his life for his friends.

Ye are bought with a price : therefore
glorify God in your body, and in your
spirit, which are God's.—Whether we
live, we live unto the Lord ; and whether
we die, we die unto the Lord : whether
we live therefore, or die, we are the Lord's

CANT. 7 10. 2 Tim 1 12 —Rom. 8, 38, 39 —
John 17 12 Ps. 149 4 —Pro. 8 31.—Eph. 2 4
—John 15 13. 1 Cor 6, 19.—Rom. 14. 8.
M

JULY 14.

Out of the abundance of the heart the
mouth speaketh.

LET the word of Christ dwell in you
richly in all wisdom.

Keep thy heart with all diligence; for
out of it are the issues of life.—Death and
life are in the power of the tongue.—The
mouth of the righteous speaketh wisdom,
and his tongue talketh of judgment. The
law of his God is in his heart : none of
his steps shall slide.

Let no corrupt communication proceed
out of your mouth, but that which is good
to the use of edifying, that it may minister
grace unto the hearers

We cannot but speak the things which
we have seen and heard.—I believed,
therefore have I spoken.

Whosoever . . . shall confess me before
men, him will I confess also before my
Father which is in heaven.—With the
heart man believeth unto righteousness;
and with the mouth confession is made
unto salvation

MAT 12 34 Col. 3 16 Pro 4 23 —Pro.
18 21—Ps 37 30, 31 Eph. 4. 29. Acts 4 20.
—Ps 116 10. Mat. 10 32 —Rom 10. 10.
M

Thy will be done in earth, as it is in heaven.

BLESS the LORD, ye his angels, that excel in strength, that do his com-mandments, hearkening unto the voice of his word. Bless ye the LORD, all ye his hosts; ye ministers of his that do his pleasure.

I came down from heaven, not to do mine own will, but the will of him that sent me.—I delight to do thy will, O my God : yea, thy law is within my heart.— O my Father, if this cup may not pass away from me, except I drink it, thy will be done.

Not every one that saith unto me, Lord, Lord, shall enter into the kingdom of heaven ; but he that doeth the will of my Father which is in heaven.—Not the hearers of the law are just before God, but the doers of the law shall be justified —If ye know these things, happy are ye if ye do them.—To him that knoweth to do good, and doeth it not, to him it is sin.

Be not conformed to this world : but be ye transformed by the renewing of your mind.

MAT. 6. 10. Ps. 103. 20, 21. John 6. 38.—Ps. 40. 8.—Mat. 26. 42. Mat. 7. 21.—Rom. 2. 13.— John 13. 17.—Ja 4. 17. Rom 12. 2

M

7 *

JULY 16.

Ye shall be unto me a kingdom of priests,
and a holy nation-

THOU wast slain, and hast redeemed us to God by thy blood out of every kindred, and tongue, and people, and nation ; and hast made us unto our God kings and priests.—Ye are a chosen generation, a royal priesthood, a holy nation, a peculiar people ; that ye should shew forth the praises of him who hath called you out of darkness into his marvellous light.

Ye shall be named the Priests of the LORD : men shall call you the Ministers of our God.—Priests of God and of Christ.

Wherefore, holy brethren, partakers of the heavenly calling, consider the Apostle and High Priest of our profession, Christ Jesus.—By him therefore let us offer the sacrifice of praise to God continually, that is, the fruit of our lips giving thanks to his name.

For we are his workmanship, created in Christ Jesus unto good works, which God hath before ordained that we should walk in them.—The temple of God is holy, which temple ye are.

Ex. 19 6 Rev. 5 9, 10.—1 Pet. 2. 9. Is. 61. 6.
—Rev. 20 6. Heb 3. 1.—Heb 13 15 Eph.
2 10.—1 Cor. 3. 17.

M

JULY 17.

Thou art a gracious God, and merciful,
slow to anger, and of great kindness, and
repentest thee of the evil.

I BESEECH thee, let the power of my
Lord be great, according as thou hast
spoken, saying, The LORD is longsuffering, and of great mercy, forgiving iniquity
and transgression, and by no means clear-
ing the guilty; visiting the iniquity of
the fathers upon the children unto the
third and fourth generation

O remember not against us former
iniquities : let thy tender mercies speedily
prevent us. Help us, O God of our salvation, for the glory of thy name : and
deliver us, and purge away our sins, for
thy name's sake.—O LORD, though our
iniquities testify against us, do thou it for
thy name's sake : for our backslidings are
many ; we have sinned aga nst thee.—We
acknowledge, O LORD, our wickedness,
and the iniquity of our fathers : for we
have sinned against thee

If thou, LORD, shouldest mark iniquities,
O LORD, who shall stand? But there is
forgiveness with thee, that thou mayest
be feared.

JON. 4. 2. Num. 14 17, 18. Ps. 79. 8, 9.—Jer.
14. 7, 20. Ps. 130. 3, 4.

He calleth his own sheep by name, and
leadeth them out.

THE foundation of God standeth sure,
having this seal, The Lord knoweth
them that are his; and, Let every one
that nameth the name of Christ, depart
from iniquity.—Many will say to me in
that day, Lord, Lord, have we not pro-
phesied in thy name? and in thy name
have cast out devils? and in thy name
done many wonderful works? And then
will I profess unto them, I never knew
you : depart from me, ye that work ini
quity — The LORD knoweth the way of
the righteous· but the way of the ungodly
shall perish.

Behold, I have graven thee upon the
palms of my hands; thy walls are continually before me.—Set me as a seal
upon thine heart, as a seal upon thine
arm.—The LORD is good, a strong hold
in the day of trouble ; and he knoweth
them that trust in him.

I go to prepare a place for you And
if I go and prepare a place for you, I will
come again, and receive you unto myself;
that where I am, there ye may be also

JOHN 10 3   2 Tim. 2. 19 —Mat. 7 22, 23 —
Ps. 1. 6   Is. 49 16.—Cant. 8 6.—Nah. 1. 7.
John 14 2, 3.

M

JULY 19.

He that is mighty hath done to me great things; and holy is his name.

WHO is like unto thee, O LORD, among the gods? who is like thee, glorious in holiness, fearful in praises, doing wonders?—Among the gods there is none like unto thee, O Lord : neither are there any works like unto thy works. —Who shall not fear thee, O Lord, and glorify thy name? for thou only art holy. —Hallowed be thy name.

Blessed be the Lord God of Israel ; for he hath visited and redeemed his people.

Who is this that cometh from Edom, with dyed garments from Bozrah? this that is glorious in his apparel, travelling in the greatness of his strength? I that speak in righteousness, mighty to save.— I have laid help upon one that is mighty ; I have exalted one chosen out of the people.

Now unto him that is able to do ex· ceeding abundantly above all that we ask or think, according to the power that worketh in us, . . . be glory.

LUKE 1. 49   Ex· 15 11.—Ps. 86 8 —Rev. 15.
4·—Mat 6. 9   Luke 1. 68   Is 63 1.—
Ps. 89 19.   Eph. 3. 20.
M

JULY 20.

They are not of the world, even as I am not of the world

H E is despised and rejected of men ; a man of sorrows, and acquainted with grief.—Ye are partakers of Christ's sufferings ; that when his glory shall be revealed, ye may be glad also with exceeding joy.

Such an high priest became us, who is holy, harmless, undefiled, separate from sinners.—That ye may be blameless and harmless, the sons of God, without rebuke, in the midst of a crooked and perverse nation.

Jesus of Nazareth . . . went about doing good, and healing all that were oppressed of the devil ; for God was with him —As we have therefore opportunity, let us do good unto all men, especially unto them who are of the household of faith.

That was the true Light, which lighteth every man that cometh into the world.—Ye are the light of the world. A city that is set on a hill cannot be hid. Let your light so shine before men, that they may see your good works, and glorify your Father which is in heaven.

JOHN 17. 16. Is. 53 3.—1 Pet. 4. 13. Heb. 7. 26.—Phil. 2. 15. Acts 10 38.—Gal. 6 10. John 1. 9.—Mat. 5. 14. 16.

M

JULY 21.

What profit is there of circumcision?

MUCH every way —Circumcise yourselves to the LORD, and take away
the foreskins of your heart.—If . . . their
uncircumcised hearts be humbled, and
they then accept of the punishment of
their iniquity : then will I remember my
covenant with Jacob, and also my covenant with Isaac, and also my covenant
with Abraham will I remember.

Jesus Christ was a minister of the circumcision for the truth of God, to confirm
the promises made unto the fathers.—In
whom also ye are circumcised with the
circumcision made without hands, in
putting off the body of the sins of the
flesh by the circumcision of Christ.—You,
being dead in your sins and the uncircumcision of your flesh, hath he quickened
together with him, having forgiven you
all trespasses.

Put off concerning the former conversation the old man, which is corrupt
according to the deceitful lusts ; and be
renewed in the spirit of your mind , and
, . . put on the new man, which after
God is created in righteousness and true
holiness.

Rom. 3. 1. Rom. 3 2 —Jer 4. 4.—Lev. 26 41,
42 Rom. 15 8 —Col. 2 11.—Col 2. 13. Eph.
4 22-24.

M

JULY 22.

In that he died, he died unto sin once: but in that he liveth, he liveth unto God.

HE was numbered with the transgressors. — Christ was once offered to bear the sins of many. — Who his own self bare our sins in his own body on the tree, that we, being dead to sins, should live unto righteousness. — By one offering he hath perfected for ever them that are sanctified.

This man, because he continueth ever, hath an unchangeable priesthood. Wherefore he is able also to save them to the uttermost that come unto God by him, seeing he ever liveth to make intercession for them. — While we were yet sinners Christ died for us. Much more then, being now justified by his blood, we shall be saved from wrath through him.

Forasmuch . . . as Christ hath suffered for us in the flesh, arm yourselves likewise with the same mind: for he that hath suffered in the flesh hath ceased from sin; that he no longer should live the rest of his time in the flesh to the lusts of men, but to the will of God.

Rom 6 10. Is. 53 12. — Heb 9. 28. — 1 Pet. 2 24. — Heb 10. 14. Heb 7. 24, 25. — Rom 5 8, 9. 1 Pet 4 1, 2.

JULY 23.

Then cometh the end.

OF that day and that hour knoweth no man, no, not the angels which are in heaven, neither the Son, but the Father. Take ye heed, watch and pray: for ye know not when the time is. And what I say unto you I say unto all, Watch — The Lord is not slack concerning his promise, as some men count slackness; but is longsuffering to us-ward, not willing that any should perish, but that all should come to repentance.—The coming of the Lord draweth nigh. The judge standeth before the door.—Surely I come quickly.

Seeing . . . that all these things shall be dissolved, what manner of persons ought ye to be in all holy conversation and godliness?

The end of all things is at hand : be ye therefore sober, and watch unto prayer.— Let your loins be girded about, and your lights burning; and ye yourselves like unto men that wait for their lord, when he will return from the wedding ; that when he cometh and knocketh, they may open unto him immediately

1 Cor. 15. 24. Mark 13. 32, 33, 37.—2 Pet. 3. 9. —Ja. 5. 8, 9.—Rev. 22. 20. 2 Pet. 3. 11. 1 Pet. 4. 7.—Luke 12. 35, 36.

M

Patient in tribulation.

IT is the LORD : let him do what seemeth him good.—Whom, though I were
righteous, yet would I not answer, but
I would make supplication to my judge.
—The LORD gave, and the LORD hath
taken away ; blessed be the name of the
LORD.—What ? shall we receive good at
the hand of God, and shall we not receive
evil ?

Jesus wept.—A man of sorrows, and
acquainted with grief. Surely he hath
borne our griefs, and carried our sorrows.

Whom the Lord loveth he chasteneth,
and scourgeth every son whom he receiveth. Now no chastening for the pre
sent seemeth to be joyous, but grievous : nevertheless afterward it yieldeth
the peaceable fruit of righteousness unto
them which are exercised thereby.—
Strengthened with all might, according
to his glorious power, unto all patience
and longsuffering with joyfulness.—In the
world ye shall have tribulation : but be
of good cheer ; I have overcome the
world.

ROM 12 12. 1 Sam. 3 18.—Job 9 15.—Job 1,
21.—Job 2. 10 John 11. 35.—Is. 53 3, 4.
Heb. 12. 6, 11.—Col 1. 11.—John 16. 33.
M

We know that we have passed from
death unto life.

HE that heareth my word, and believeth on him that sent me, hath everlasting life, and shall not come into condemnation ; but is passed from death unto
life.—He that hath the Son hath life ;
and he that hath not the Son of God hath
not life.

He which stablisheth us with you in
Christ, and hath anointed us, is God ;
who hath also sealed us, and given the
earnest of the Spirit in our hearts.

Hereby we know that we are of the
truth, and shall assure our hearts before
him   Beloved, if our heart condemn us
not, then have we confidence toward God.
—We know that we are of God, and
the whole world lieth in wickedness.

You hath he quickened, who were
dead in trespasses and sins Quickened
, . together with Christ —Who hath
delivered us from the power of darkness,
and hath translated us into the kingdom
of his dear Son.

1 John 3 14. John 5 24 —1 John 5 12.   2 Cor
 1. 21, 22. 1 John 3. 19, 21.—1 John 5 19.
        Eph. 2. 1, 5 —Col 1 13

M

JULY 26.

By faith Abraham, . . called to go out
into a place which he should after
receive for an inheritance, obeyed.

H E shall choose our inheritance for us.
—He led him about, he instructed
him, he kept him as the apple of his eye.
As an eagle stirreth up her nest, fluttereth
over her young, spreadeth abroad her
wings, taketh them, beareth them on her
wings : so the LORD alone did lead him,
and there was no strange god with him.

I am the LORD thy God which teacheth
thee to profit, which leadeth thee by the
way that thou shouldest go.—Who teach
eth like him?

We walk by faith, not by sight.—Here
have we no continuing city, but we seek
one to come.

Dearly beloved, I beseech you as
strangers and pilgrims, abstain from
fleshly lusts, which war against the soul.
—Arise ye and depart ; for this is not
your rest : because it is polluted, it shall
destroy you, even with a sore destruction.

HEB 11 8. Ps. 47 4.—Deut. 32 10-12 Is.
48 17.—Job 36 22. 2 Cor. 5 7.—Heb. 13.
14. 1 Pet. 2 11.—Mic 2 10.
M

JULY 27.

Christ, who is the image of God.

THE glory of the LORD shall be re-vealed, and all flesh shall see it to-gether.—No man hath seen God at any time ; the only begotten Son, which is in the bosom of the Father, he hath de-clared him. And the Word was made flesh, and dwelt among us, (and we beheld his glory, the glory as of the only begotten of the Father,) full of grace and truth.

He that hath seen me hath seen the Father. —The brightness of his glory, and the express image of his person.— God was manifest in the flesh

In whom we have redemption through his blood, even the forgiveness of sins : who is the image of the invisible God, the firstborn of every creature.—Whom he did foreknow, he also did predestinate to be conformed to the image of his Son, that he might be the firstborn among many brethren

As we have borne the image of the earthy, we shall also bear the image of the heavenly.

2 Cor 4 4. Is 40 5 —John 1 18, 14.
John 14. 9 —Heb. 1 3 —1 Tim. 3. 16
Col 1 14, 15 —Rom. 8. 29. 1 Cor 15 49.

JULY 28.

Walk in love.

A NEW commandment I give unto you,
That ye love one another ; as I have
loved you, that ye also love one another.
—Above all things have fervent charity
among yourselves : for charity shall cover
the multitude of sins.—Love covereth all
sins.

When ye stand praying, forgive, if ye
have ought against any : that your Father
also which is in heaven may forgive you
your trespasses.—Love ye your enemies,
and do good, and lend, hoping for nothing
again. — Rejoice not when thine enemy
falleth, and let not thine heart be glad
when he stumbleth —Not rendering evil
for evil, or railing for railing : but con
trariwise blessing ; knowing that ye are
thereunto called, that ye should inherit
a blessing.—If it be possible, as much as
lieth in you, live peaceably with all men
—Be ye kind one to another, tender-
hearted, forgiving one another, even as
God for Christ's sake hath forgiven you.

My little children, let us not love in
word, neither in tongue ; but in deed and
in truth

Eph 5 2.   John 13. 34.—1 Pet. 4 8 —
Pro. 10 12   Mark 11 25.—Luke 6 35.—
Pro 24 17 —1 Pet 3 9 —Rom 12 18
        —Eph 4. 32   1 John 3. 18.
M

JULY 29.

O that thou wouldest rend the heavens,
that thou wouldest come down.

MAKE haste, my beloved, and be thou
like to a roe or to a young hart upon
the mountains of spices —We ourselves
groan within ourselves, waiting for the
adoption, to wit, the redemption of our
body.—Bow thy heavens, O LORD, and
come down . touch the mountains, and
they shall smoke

This same Jesus, which is taken up
from you into heaven, shall so come in
like manner as ye have seen him go into
heaven —Unto them that look for him
shall he appear the second time without
sin unto salvation.—It shall be said in
that day, Lo, this is our God ; we have
waited for him, and he will save us : this
is the LORD ; we have waited for him,
we will be glad and rejoice in his salvation.

He which testifieth these things saith,
Surely I come quickly. Amen. Even
so, come, Lord Jesus. —That blessed
hope, . . the glorious appearing of the
great God and our Saviour Jesus Christ.
—Our conversation is in heaven.

Is. 64. 1. Cant 8. 14.—Rom 8 23 —Ps. 144. 5.
Acts 1. 11.—Heb 9. 28 —Is 25 9 Rev 22. 20.
—Tit. 2. 13 —Phil 3. 20.

M

JULY 30.

Seek those things which are above, where Christ sitteth on the right hand of God

GET wisdom, get understanding —The wisdom that is from above. — The depth saith, It is not in me : and the sea saith, It is not with me.—We are buried with him by baptism into death : that like as Christ was raised up from the dead by the glory of the Father, even so we also should walk in newness of life. For if we have been planted together in the likeness of his death, we shall be also in the likeness of his resurrection

Let us lay aside every weight, and the sin which doth so easily beset us, and let us run with patience the race that is set before us. — God . . . hath quickened us together with Christ, . . . and hath raised us up together, and made us sit together in heavenly places in Christ Jesus.

They that say such things declare plainly that they seek a country.—Seek ye the LORD, all ye meek of the earth, which have wrought his judgment ; seek right-eousness, seek meekness.

COL. 3. 1. Pro. 4. 5 —Ja 3 17 —Job 28 14 —
Rom. 6 4, 5. Heb 12 1 —Eph 2 4-6
Heb 11 16.—Zep. 2 3
M

JULY 31.

Endure hardness, as a good soldier of Jesus Christ.

I HAVE given him for a witness to the people, a leader and commander to the people.

It became him, for whom are all things, and by whom are all things, in bringing many sons unto glory, to make the captain of their salvation perfect through sufferings.—We must through much tribulation enter into the kingdom of God.

We wrestle not against flesh and blood, but against principalities, against powers, against the rulers of the darkness of this world, against spiritual wickedness in high places. Wherefore take unto you the whole armour of God.—We do not war after the flesh : for the weapons of our warfare are not carnal, but mighty through God to the pulling down of strong holds.

The God of all grace, who hath called us unto his eternal glory by Christ Jesus, after that ye have suffered a while, make you perfect, stablish, strengthen, settle you.

2 TIM. 2. 3.   Is. 55. 4.   Heb. 2. 10.—Acts 14. 22.
Eph. 6. 12, 13 —2 Cor. 10. 3, 4.   1 Pet. 5. 10.
M ·

AUGUST 1.

The fruit of the Spirit is . . . faith.

BY grace are ye saved through faith ; and that not of yourselves : it is the gift of God.—Without faith it is impossible to please him.—He that believeth on him is not condemned : but he that believeth not is condemned already, because he hath not believed in the name of the only begotten Son of God.—Lord, I believe ; help thou mine unbelief.

Whoso keepeth his word, in him verily is the love of God perfected : hereby know we that we are in him. —Faith worketh by love.—Faith without works is dead.

We walk by faith, not by sight.—I am crucified with Christ : nevertheless I live ; yet not I, but Christ liveth in me : and the life which I now live in the flesh I live by the faith of the Son of God, who loved me, and gave himself for me.—Whom having not seen, ye love; in whom, though now ye see him not, yet believing, ye rejoice with joy unspeakable and full of glory; receiving the end of your faith, even the salvation of your souls.

GAL. 5. 22 Eph 2 8 —Heb 11 6.—John 3 18.
—Mar 9 24 1 John 2 5 —Gal. 5. 6.—Ja 2 20.
  2 Cor. 5 7 —Gal. 2. 20.—1 Pet 1 8 9.
M

AUGUST 2.

The Lamb slain from the foundation of the world.

YOUR lamb shall be without blemish, . . . and the whole assembly of the congregation of Israel shall kill it in the evening. And they shall take of the blood, and strike it on the two side posts and on the upper door post of the houses, wherein they shall eat it, . . . and when I see the blood, I will pass over you.—The blood of sprinkling.—Christ our passover is sacrificed for us.—Being delivered by the determinate counsel and foreknowledge of God.—According to his own purpose and grace, which was given us in Christ Jesus before the world began.

We have redemption through his blood, the forgiveness of sins.

Forasmuch then as Christ hath suffered for us in the flesh, arm yourselves likewise with the same mind : for he that hath suffered in the flesh hath ceased from sin ; that he no longer should live the rest of his time in the flesh to the lusts of men, but to the will of God.

Rev. 13. 8. Ex. 12. 5-7, 13.—Heb. 12. 24.—
1 Cor. 5. 7.—Acts 2. 23.—2 Tim. 1. 9. Eph. 1. 7.
1 Pet. 4. 1. 2.

M

AUGUST 3.

His mercy is on them that fear Him.

OH how great is thy goodness, which thou hast laid up for them that fear thee; which thou hast wrought for them that trust in thee before the sons of men! Thou shalt hide them in the secret of thy presence from the pride of man: thou shalt keep them secretly in a pavilion from the strife of tongues.

If ye call on the Father, who without respect of persons judgeth according to every man's work, pass the time of your sojourning here in fear. — The LORD is nigh unto all them that call upon him . . in truth. He will fulfil the desire of them that fear him : he also will hear their cry, and will save them

Because thine heart was tender, and thou hast humbled thyself before the LORD, . . . and hast rent thy clothes, and wept before me ; I also have heard thee, saith the LORD —To this man will I look, even to him that is poor and of a contrite spirit, and trembleth at my word. —The LORD is nigh unto them that are of a broken heart ; and saveth such as be of a contrite spirit.

LUKE 1 50 Ps 31 19, 20. 1 Pet. 1. 17.—
Ps 145 18, 19 2 Kings 22 19 —Is 66. 2 —
Ps 34 18.

M

AUGUST 4.

It is finished : and he bowed his head, and gave up the ghost

JESUS the author and finisher of our faith.—I have glorified thee on the earth : I have finished the work which thou gavest me to do.—We are sanctified through the offering of the body of Jesus Christ once for all And every priest standeth daily ministering and offering oftentimes the same sacrifices, which can never take away sins · but this man, after he had offered one sacrifice for sins for ever, sat down on the right hand of God ; from henceforth expecting till his enemies be made his footstool. For by one offering he hath perfected for ever them that are sanctified.—Blotting out the handwriting of ordinances that was against us, which was contrary to us, and took it out of the way, nailing it to his cross

I lay down my life. that I might take it again. No man taketh it from me, but I lay it down of myself. I have power to lay it down. and I have power to take it again.—Greater love hath no man than this, that a man lay down his life for his friends.

JOHN 19. 30 Heb 12 2 —John 17 4 —
Heb 10. 10-14 —Col 2 14 John 10. 17, 18 —
John 15. 13

M

Walk in newness of life.

AS ye have yielded your members servants to uncleanness and to iniquity unto iniquity; even so now yield your members servants to righteousness unto holiness.—I beseech you, . . . brethren, by the mercies of God, that ye present your bodies a living sacrifice, holy, acceptable unto God, which is your reasonable service. And be not conformed to this world: but be ye transformed by the renewing of your mind.

If any man be in Christ, he is a new creature: old things are passed away; behold, all things are become new.—In Christ Jesus neither circumcision availeth any thing, nor uncircumcision, but a new creature. And as many as walk according to this rule, peace be on them, and mercy.—This I say therefore, and testify in the Lord, that ye henceforth walk not as other Gentiles walk, in the vanity of their mind.—Ye have not so learned Christ; if so be that ye have heard him, and have been taught by him, as the truth is in Jesus.—Put on the new man, which after God is created in righteousness and true holiness.

Rom. 6. 4. Rom. 6. 19—Rom. 12. 1, 2.
2 Cor. 5. 17.—Gal. 6. 15, 16.—Eph. 4 17, 20, 21, 24

M

AUGUST 6.

Whom the Lord loveth he correcteth.

SEE now that I, even I, am he, and there is no god with me · I kill and I make alive ; I wound, and I heal : neither is there any that can deliver out of my hand.

I know the thoughts that I think toward you, saith the LORD, thoughts of peace, and not of evil, to give you an expected end.—My thoughts are not your thoughts, neither are your ways my ways, saith the LORD.

I will allure her, and bring her into the wilderness, and speak comfortably unto her.—As a man chasteneth his son, so the LORD thy God chasteneth thee.—Now no chastening for the present seemeth to be joyous, but grievous : nevertheless afterward it yieldeth the peaceable fruit of righteousness unto them which are exercised thereby. — Humble your-selves therefore under the mighty hand of God, that he may exalt you in due time.

I know, O LORD, that thy judgments are right, and that thou in faithfulness hast afflicted me.

PRO 3 12   Deut 32 39. Jer 29 11 —
Is 55 8   Hos 2. 14.—Deut. 8. 5.—Heb. 12 11
—1 Pet 5. 6. Ps. 119. 75.

M

AUGUST 7.

The Comforter, which is the Holy Ghost, whom the Father will send in my name.

IF thou knewest the gift of God, and who it is that saith to thee, Give me to drink , thou wouldest have asked of him, and he would have given thee living water —If ye . being evil, know how to give good gifts unto your children : how much more shall your heavenly Father give the Holy Spirit to them that ask him ?—Verily, verily, I say unto you, Whatsoever ye shall ask the Father in my name, he will give it you. Hitherto have ye asked nothing in my name ask, and ye shall receive, that your joy may be full

When . . . the Spirit of truth is come, he will guide you into all truth : for he shall not speak of himself; but whatsoever he shall hear, that shall he speak : and he will shew you things to come He shall glorify me for he shall receive of mine, and shall shew it unto you.

They rebelled, and vexed his holy Spirit . therefore he was turned to be their enemy, and he fought against them.

JOHN 14 26. John 4 10.—Luke 11 13 — John 16. 23, 24 John 16 13, 14. Is 63. 10.
M

The path of the just is as the shining
light, that shineth more and more
unto the perfect day

NOT as though I had already attained,
either were already perfect: but I
follow after, if that I may apprehend that
for which also I am apprehended of Christ
Jesus.—Then shall we know, if we follow
on to know the LORD.

Then shall the righteous shine forth as
the sun in the kingdom of their Father.
—We all, with open face beholding as in
a glass the glory of the Lord, are changed
into the same image from glory to glory,
even as by the Spirit of the Lord.—
When that which is perfect is come, then
that which is in part shall be done away.
For now we see through a glass, darkly;
but then face to face. now I know in
part; but then shall I know even as also
I am known

Beloved, now are we the sons of God;
and it doth not yet appear what we shall
be: but we know that, when he shall
appear, we shall be like him; for we
shall see him as he is. And every man
that hath this hope in him purifieth himself, even as he is pure.

PRO. 4. 18.   Phil. 3. 12.—Hos. 6. 3.   Mat. 13. 43.
—2 Cor. 3. 18.—1 Cor. 13. 10, 12.   1 John 3 2, 3.

AUGUST 9.

Thou art all fair, my love; there is
no spot in thee

THE whole head is sick, and the whole
heart faint From the sole of the
foot even unto the head there is no sound-
ness in it ; but wounds, and bruises, and
putrifying sores : they have not been
closed, neither bound up, neither mol-
lified with ointment —We are all as an
unclean thing, and all our righteousnesses
are as filthy rags —I know that in me,
(that is, in my flesh,) dwelleth no good
thing.
Ye are washed, . . . ye are sanctified,
. . . ye are justified in the name of the
Lord Jesus, and by the Spirit of our God.
—The King's daughter is all glorious
within —Perfect through my comeliness,
which I had put upon thee, saith the
Lord GOD
Let the beauty of the LORD our God
be upon us.
These are they which . . have washed
their robes, and made them white in the
blood of the Lamb —A glorious church,
not having spot, or wrinkle, or any such
thing ; but . . holy and without blemish.
—Ye are complete in him.

CANT 4 7   Is. 1 5, 6 —Is 64 6 —Rom 7. 18
  1 Cor. 6 11 —Ps 45 13 —Ezek 16 14
Ps 90 17   Rev. 7 14 —Eph- 5 27.—Col 2 10
  u

AUGUST 10.

I pray not that thou shouldest take them
out of the world, but that thou shouldest
keep them from the evil.

BLAMELESS and harmless, the sons
of God, without rebuke, in the midst
of a crooked and perverse nation, among
whom ye shine as lights in the world.—
Ye are the salt of the earth, . . . the
light of the world.—Let your light so
shine before men, that they may see your
good works, and glorify your Father
which is in heaven.

I also withheld thee from sinning
against me.

The Lord is faithful, who shall stablish you, and keep you from evil.—So
did not I, because of the fear of God.—
Who gave himself for our sins, that he
might deliver us from this present evil
world, according to the will of God and
our Father.—Now unto him that is able
to keep you from falling, and to present
you faultless before the presence of his
glory with exceeding joy, to the only
wise God our Saviour, be glory and
majesty, dominion and power, both now
and ever Amen.

John 17 15. Phil. 2. 15 —Mat. 5. 13, 14. 16.
Gea. 20. 6. 2 Thes. 3. 3.—Neh. 5. 15.—Gal. 1, 4.
м   —Jude 24, 25.

AUGUST 11.

That through death He might destroy
him that had the power of death.

OUR Saviour Jesus Christ . . . hath
abolished death, and hath brought
life and immortality to light through the
gospel.—He will swallow up death in
victory; and the Lord GOD will wipe
away tears from off all faces; and the
rebuke of his people shall he take away
from off all the earth. for the LORD
hath spoken it.—When this corruptible
shall have put on incorruption, and this
mortal shall have put on immortality,
then shall be brought to pass the saying
that is written, Death is swallowed up in
victory O death, where is thy sting?
O grave, where is thy victory? The
sting of death is sin; and the strength of
sin is the law But thanks be to God,
which giveth us the victory through our
Lord Jesus Christ.

God hath not given us the spirit of
fear; but of power, and of love, and of
a sound mind —Yea, though I walk
through the valley of the shadow of
death, I will fear no evil. for thou art
with me; thy rod and thy staff they
comfort me.

HEB. 2. 14 2 Tim 1 10.—Is. 25. 8.—
1 Cor. 15. 54-57 2 Tim 1. 7—Ps 23 4

AUGUST 12.

The Lord will not cast off for ever : but though he cause grief, yet will he have compassion.

FEAR thou not, . . . saith the LORD : for I am with thee ; I will not make a full end of thee, but correct thee in measure —For a small moment have I forsaken thee; but with great mercies will I gather thee. In a little wrath I hid my face from thee for a moment ; but with everlasting kindness will I have mercy on thee, saith the LORD thy Redeemer. For the mountains shall depart, and the hills be removed ; but my kindness shall not depart from thee, neither shall the covenant of my peace be removed, saith the LORD that hath mercy on thee.

O thou afflicted, tossed with tempest, and not comforted, behold, I will lay thy stones with fair colours, and lay thy foundations with sapphires

I will bear the indignation of the LORD, because I have sinned against him, until he plead my cause, and execute judgment for me : he will bring me forth to the light, and I shall behold his righteousness

LAM 3. 31 32 Jer 46 28.—Is 54. 7, 8. 10, 11.
Mic 7 9.
M

AUGUST 13.

Ho hath prepared for them a city.

IF I go and prepare a place for you, I
will come again, and receive you unto
myself; that where I am, there ye may
be also.—An inheritance incorruptible,
and undefiled, and that fadeth not away,
reserved in heaven for you —Here have
we no continuing city, but we seek one
to come.

This same Jesus, which is taken up
from you into heaven, shall so come in
like manner as ye have seen him go into
heaven —Be patient therefore, brethren,
unto the coming of the Lord. Behold,
the husbandman waiteth for the precious
fruit of the earth, and hath long patience
for it, until he receive the early and latter
rain. Be ye also patient ; stablish your
hearts ; for the coming of the Lord draweth
nigh.—Yet a little while, and he that shall
come will come, and will not tarry.

We which are alive and remain shall
be caught up together with them in the
clouds, to meet the Lord in the air :
and so shall we ever be with the Lord.
Wherefore comfort one another with these
words.

HEB 11. 16   John 14 3 —1 Pet. 1 4 —
Heb 13. 14   Acts 1 11 —Ja 5 7, 8.—
Heb 10 37. 1 Thes. 4 17, 10

M

AUGUST 14.

The joy of the Lord is your strength.

SING, O heavens; and be joyful, O earth; and break forth into singing, O mountains: for the LORD hath comforted his people, and will have mercy upon his afflicted.—Behold, God is my salvation; I will trust, and not be afraid: for the LORD JEHOVAH is my strength and my song; he also is become my salvation.

The LORD is my strength and my shield; my heart trusted in him, and I am helped: therefore my heart greatly rejoiceth: and with my song will I praise him.—My soul shall be joyful in my God; for he hath clothed me with the garments of salvation, he hath covered me with the robe of righteousness, as a bridegroom decketh himself with ornaments, and as a bride adorneth herself with her jewels.

I have therefore whereof I may glory through Jesus Christ in those things which pertain to God.—We . . joy in God through our Lord Jesus Christ, by whom we have now received the atonement.—I will joy in the God of my salvation

NEH 8. 10   Is. 49 13 —Is 12 2   Ps 28 7 —
Is. 61 10 Rom 15 17 —Rom 5 11 —Hab. 3. 18
M

AUGUST 15.

The God of peace . . . make you perfect in every good work to do his will.

BE perfect, be of good comfort, be of one mind, live in peace ; and the God of love and peace shall be with you.

By grace are ye saved through faith ; and that not of yourselves : it is the gift of God : not of works, lest any man should boast.—Every good gift and every perfect gift is from above, and cometh down from the Father of lights, with whom is no variableness, neither shadow of turning.

Work out your own salvation with fear and trembling. For it is God which worketh in you both to will and to do of his good pleasure.—Be ye transformed by the renewing of your mind, that ye may prove what is that good, and acceptable, and perfect, will of God.—Being filled with the fruits of righteousness, which are by Jesus Christ, unto the glory and praise of God.

Not that we are sufficient of ourselves to think any thing as of ourselves ; but our sufficiency is of God.

HEB. 13 20, 21. 2 Cor. 13 11 Eph. 2. 8, 9.—
Ja. 1. 17. Phil. 2. 12, 13.—Rom. 12. 2 —
Phil. 1. 11 2 Cor. 3. 5

M

AUGUST 16.

The house that is to be builded for the
Lord must be exceeding magnifical.

YE . . . as lively stones, are built up a
spiritual house.—Know ye not that ye
are the temple of God, and that the Spirit
of God dwelleth in you? If any man
defile the temple of God, him shall God
destroy; for the temple of God is holy,
which temple ye are —Your body is the
temple of the Holy Ghost which is in you,
which ye have of God, and ye are not
your own. For ye are bought with a
price: therefore glorify God in your body,
and in your spirit, which are God's.—
What agreement hath the temple of God
with idols? for ye are the temple of the
living God; as God hath said, I will
dwell in them, and walk in them, and I
will be their God, and they shall be my
people.

Ye . . . are built upon the foundation
of the apostles and prophets, Jesus Christ
himself being the chief corner stone; in
whom all the building fitly framed together
groweth unto a holy temple in the Lord:
in whom ye also are builded together for
a habitation of God through the Spirit.

1 CHR 22, 5. 1 Pet. 2 5.—1 Cor 3. 16, 17 —
1 Cor 6 19, 20.—2 Cor 6. 16. Eph. 2. 10-22

M

8 *

AUGUST 17.

Pray one for another, that ye may be healed

ABRAHAM answered and said, Behold now, I have taken upon me to speak unto the Lord, which am but dust and ashes : peradventure there shall lack five of the fifty righteous : wilt thou destroy all the city for lack of five? And he said, If I find there forty and five, I will not destroy it.

Father, forgive them ; for they know not what they do.—Pray for them which despitefully use you, and persecute you

I pray for them · I pray not for the world, but for them which thou hast given me ; for they are thine. Neither pray I for these alone, but for them also which shall believe on me through their word. —Bear ye one another's burdens, and so fulfil the law of Christ.

The effectual fervent prayer of a right-eous man availeth much Elias was a man subject to like passions as we are, and he prayed earnestly that it might not rain : and it rained not on the earth by the space of three years and six months

Jᴀ 5. 16 Gen 18 27, 28 Luke 23 34 —Mat. 5 44. John 17. 9, 20.—Gal. 6. 2. Ja. 5 16, 17.
M

AUGUST 18.

What God is there in heaven or in earth,
that can do according to thy works, and
according to thy might?

WHO in the heaven can be compared
unto the LORD? who among the
sons of the mighty can be likened unto
the LORD? O LORD God of hosts, who
is a strong LORD like unto thee? or to thy
faithfulness round about thee?—Among
the gods there is none like unto thee, O
Lord ; neither are there any works like
unto thy works—For thy word's sake,
and according to thine own heart, hast
thou done all these great things, to make
thy servant know them. Wherefore thou
art great, O LORD God : for there is none
like thee, neither is there any God beside
thee, according to all that we have heard
with our ears

Eye hath not seen, nor ear heard, neither
have entered into the heart of man, the
things which God hath prepared for them
that love him. But God hath revealed
them unto us by his Spirit.—The secret
things belong unto the LORD our God :
but those things which are revealed belong
unto us and to our children.

DEUT. 3 24   Ps. 89 6, 8 —Ps 86 8 —
2 Sam. 7 21, 22   1 Cor 2. 9, 10.—Deut. 29 29
M

AUGUST 19.

As he which hath called you is holy, so be
ye holy in all manner of conversation

YE know how we exhorted . . . and
charged every one of you, . . . that
ye would walk worthy of God, who hath
called you unto his kingdom and glory.—
Ye should shew forth the praises of him
who hath called you out of darkness into
his marvellous light.

Ye were sometime darkness, but now
are ye light in the Lord : walk as children
of light : (for the fruit of the Spirit is in all
goodness and righteousness and truth ;)
proving what is acceptable unto the Lord
And have no fellowship with the unfruitful works of darkness, but rather reprove
them. — Being filled with the fruits of
righteousness, which are by Jesus Christ,
unto the glory and praise of God.

Let your light so shine before men, that
they may see your good works, and glorify
your Father which is in heaven.—Whether
therefore ye eat, or drink, or whatsoever
ye do, do all to the glory of God.

1 PET. 1. 15.   1 Thes. 2. 11, 12.—1 Pet. 2. 9.
Eph. 5 8-11 —Phil 1. 11 Mat. 5. 16.—
1 Cor. 10 31.

M

AUGUST 20.

God is not a man, that he should lie; neither the son of man, that he should repent.

THE Father of lights, with whom is no variableness, neither shadow of turning.—Jesus Christ, the same yesterday, and to day, and for ever.

His truth shall be thy shield and buckler.

God, willing more abundantly to shew unto the heirs of promise the immutability of his counsel, confirmed it by an oath; that by two immutable things, in which it was impossible for God to lie, we might have a strong consolation, who have fled for refuge to lay hold upon the hope set before us.

The faithful God, which keepeth covenant and mercy with them that love him and keep his commandments to a thousand generations.—All the paths of the LORD are mercy and truth unto such as keep his covenant and his testimonies.—Happy is he that hath the God of Jacob for his help, whose hope is in the LORD his God . . . which keepeth truth for ever.

NUM. 23. 19. Ja. 1. 17.—Heb. 13. 8   Ps. 91. 4. Heb. 6. 17, 18.   Deut. 7. 9.—Ps. 25. 10.—Ps. 146. 5, 6.

M

AUGUST 21.

Thou art my portion, O Lord.

ALL things are your's , . . . and ye are Christ's ; and Christ is God's.—Our Saviour Jesus Christ . . . gave himself for us.—God gave him to be the head over all things to the church.—Christ loved the church, and gave himself for it ; that he might present it to himself a glorious church, not having spot, or wrinkle, or any such thing ; but that it should be holy and without blemish.

My soul shall make her boast in the LORD.—I will greatly rejoice in the LORD, my soul shall be joyful in my God ; for he hath clothed me with the garments of salvation, he hath covered me with the robe of righteousness.

Whom have I in heaven but thee? and there is none upon earth that I desire beside thee. My flesh and my heart faileth : but God is the strength of my heart, and my portion for ever.—O my soul, thou hast said unto the LORD, Thou art my Lord. The LORD is the portion of mine inheritance and of my cup : thou maintainest my lot. The lines are fallen unto me in pleasant places ; yea, I have a goodly heritage.

Ps. 119 57   1 Cor. 3 21, 23 —Tit. 2 13, 14 —
Eph. 1 22 —Eph. 5 25, 27   Ps 34. 2 — Is 61
    10.   Ps 73 25, 26 —Ps 16 2, 5, 6.

M

AUGUST 22.

None of us liveth to himself, and no man dieth to himself.

WHETHER we live, we live unto the Lord ; and whether we die, we die unto the Lord : whether we live therefore, or die, we are the Lord's.—Let no man seek his own : but every man another's wealth,—Ye are bought with a price : therefore glorify God in your body, and in your spirit, which are God's.

Christ shall be magnified in my body, whether it be by life, or by death. For to me to live is Christ, and to die is gain. But if I live in the flesh, this is the fruit of my labour : yet what I shall choose I wot not. For I am in a strait betwixt two, having a desire to depart, and to be with Christ ; which is far better.

I through the law am dead to the law, that I might live unto God. I am crucified with Christ : nevertheless I live ; yet not I, but Christ liveth in me · and the life which I now live in the flesh I live by the faith of the Son of God, who loved me, and gave himself for me.

Rom. 14 7 Rom. 14. 8.—1 Cor. 10. 24.—1 Cor. 6. 20. Phil. 1. 20-23. Gal. 2. 19, 20.

AUGUST 23.

I have loved thee with an everlasting love: therefore with lovingkindness have I drawn thee

WE are bound to give thanks alway to God for you, brethren beloved of the Lord, because God hath from the beginning chosen you to salvation through sanctification of the Spirit and belief of the truth : whereunto he called you by our gospel, to the obtaining of the glory of our Lord Jesus Christ.—God . . . hath saved us, and called us with a holy calling, not according to our works, but according to his own purpose and grace, which was given us in Christ Jesus before the world began.—Thine eyes did see my substance, yet being unperfect ; and in thy book all my members were written, which in continuance were fashioned, when as yet there was none of them

God so loved the world, that he gave his only begotten Son, that whosoever believeth in him should not perish, but have everlasting life.

Herein is love, not that we loved God, but that he loved us, and sent his Son to be the propitiation for our sins.

JER. 31. 3   2 Thes. 2. 13, 14 —2 Tim. 1. 9 —Ps. 139. 16.   John 3. 16,   1 John 4. 10.

M

AUGUST 24

I know their sorrows.

A MAN of sorrows, and acquainted with grief.—Touched with the feeling of our infirmities.

Himself took our infirmities, and bare our sicknesses —Jesus . . . being wearied with his journey, sat thus on the well

When Jesus . . . saw her weeping, and the Jews also weeping which came with her, he groaned in the spirit, and was troubled.—Jesus wept—For in that he himself hath suffered being tempted, he is able to succour them that are tempted.

He hath looked down from the height of his sanctuary; from heaven did the LORD behold the earth; to hear the groaning of the prisoner; to loose those that are appointed to death.—He knoweth the way that I take : when he hath tried me, I shall come forth as gold — When my spirit was overwhelmed within me, then thou knewest my path.

He that toucheth you toucheth the apple of his eye —In all their affliction he was afflicted; and the angel of his presence saved them.

Ex 3. 7. Is. 53 3—Heb 4. 15 Mat 8 17—
John 4 6 John 11. 33 35.—Heb. 2 18. Ps.
102. 19 20.—Job 23 10.—Ps 142 3, Zec. 2. 8.
—Is 63 9

M

Look unto the rock whence ye are hewn, and to the hole of the pit whence ye are digged

BEHOLD, I was shapen in iniquity.—None eye pitied thee, . . . but thou wast cast out in the open field, to the loathing of thy person, in the day that thou wast born And when I passed by thee, and saw thee polluted in thine own blood, I said unto thee, . . . Live

He brought me up . . . out of a horrible pit, out of the miry clay, and set my feet upon a rock, and established my goings. And he hath put a new song in my mouth, even praise unto our God

When we were yet without strength, in due time Christ died for the ungodly. For scarcely for a righteous man will one die : yet peradventure for a good man some would even dare to die. But God commendeth his love toward us, in that, while we were yet sinners, Christ died for us.—God, who is rich in mercy, for his great love wherewith he loved us, even when we were dead in sins, hath quickened us together with Christ.

Is 51 1 Ps 51 5 —Ezek 16. 5, 6 Ps 40 2,
3 Rom. 5 6-8.—Eph 2 4, 5.
M

AUGUST 26.

Thou shalt make a plate of pure gold, and grave upon it, like the engravings of a signet,
HOLINESS TO THE LORD.

HOLINESS, without which no man shall see the Lord.—God is a Spirit and they that worship him must worship him in spirit and in truth.—I will be sanctified in them that come nigh me, and before all the people I will be glorified.—But we are all as an unclean thing, and all our righteousnesses are as filthy rags

This is the law of the house · Upon the top of the mountain the whole limit thereof round about shall be most holy. —Holiness becometh thine house, O LORD, for ever

For their sakes I sanctify myself, that they also might be sanctified through the truth.—Seeing . . . that we have a great high priest, that is passed into the heavens, Jesus the Son of God, let us . . . come boldly unto the throne of grace, that we may obtain mercy, and find grace to help in time of need.

Ex. 28 36. Heb 12 14 —John 4 24 —Lev 10. 3.—Is 64. 6 Ezek 43 12 —Ps 93 5. John 17 19 —Heb 4 14. 16

M

AUGUST 27.

Thy word is a lamp unto my feet, and a light unto my path.

BY the word of thy lips I have kept me from the paths of the destroyer. Hold up my goings in thy paths, that my footsteps slip not.

When thou goest, it shall lead thee; when thou sleepest, it shall keep thee; and when thou awakest, it shall talk with thee. For the commandment is a lamp; and the law is light —Thine ears shall hear a word behind thee, saying, This is the way, walk ye in it, when ye turn to the right hand, and when ye turn to the left.

I am the light of the world : he that followeth me shall not walk in darkness, but shall have the light of life.—We have also a . . . sure word of prophecy; whereunto ye do well that ye take heed, as unto a light that shineth in a dark place —Now we see through a glass, darkly; but then face to face: now I know in part; but then shall I know even as also I am known.—They need no candle, neither light of the sun; for the Lord God giveth them light : and they shall reign for ever and ever.

Ps 119 105. Ps 17 4, 5. Pro 6. 22, 23.—Is. 30. 21 John 8 12 —2 Pet 1 19.—1 Cor 13 12. —Rev. 22 5

M

AUGUST 28.

The accuser of our brethren is cast down, which accused them before our God day and night.

THEY overcame him by the blood of the Lamb, and by the word of their testimony.

Who shall lay any thing to the charge of God's elect? It is God that justifieth. Who is he that condemneth? It is Christ that died, yea, rather, that is risen again, who is even at the right hand of God, who also maketh intercession for us.

Having spoiled principalities and powers, he made a shew of them openly. —That through death he might destroy him that had the power of death, that is the devil; and deliver them who through fear of death were all their lifetime subject to bondage.—In all these things we are more than conquerors, through him that loved us.—Put on the whole armour of God, that ye may be able to stand against the wiles of the devil. And take the sword of the Spirit, which is the word of God —Thanks be to God, which giveth us the victory through our Lord Jesus Christ

REV. 12. 10. Rev. 12 11 Rom. 8 33, 34.
Col. 2 15.—Heb. 2 14, 15 —Rom. 8 37.—
Eph. 6. 11, 17 —1 Cor. 15. 57.

M

AUGUST 29.

Whoso trusteth in the Lord, happy is he

[ABRAHAM] staggered not at the promise of God through unbelief; but was strong in faith, giving glory to God; and being fully persuaded that, what he had promised, he was able also to perform —The children of Judah prevailed, because they relied upon the LORD God of their fathers

God is our refuge and strength, a very present help in trouble. Therefore will not we fear, though the earth be removed, and though the mountains be carried into the midst of the sea. —It is better to trust in the LORD than to put confidence in man It is better to trust in the LORD than to put confidence in princes. —The steps of a good man are ordered by the LORD. and he delighteth in his way. Though he fall, he shall not be utterly cast down. for the LORD upholdeth him with his hand.

O taste and see that the LORD is good: blessed is the man that trusteth in him. O fear the LORD, ye his saints: for there is no want to them that fear him.

PRO 16 20. Rom 4 20, 21 —2 Chr 13. 18.
Ps. 46 1, 2 —Ps 113. 8, 9 —Ps. 37 23, 24
Ps 34 8, 9.

M

The king held out the golden sceptre
So Esther drew near, and touched the top
of the sceptre.

IT shall come to pass, when he crieth
unto me, that I will hear; for I am
gracious.

We have known and believed the love
that God hath to us. God is love; and
he that dwelleth in love dwelleth in God,
and God in him. Herein is our love
made perfect, that we may have boldness
in the day of judgment · because as he is,
so are we in this world. There is no
fear in love; but perfect love casteth out
fear · because fear hath torment. He
that feareth is not made perfect in love.
We love him, because he first loved us.

Let us draw near with a true heart, in
full assurance of faith, having our hearts
sprinkled from an evil conscience, and
our bodies washed with pure water.

Through him we . . have access by
one Spirit unto the Father.—We have
boldness and access with confidence by
the faith of him.—Let us therefore come
boldly unto the throne of grace, that we
may obtain mercy, and find grace to help
in time of need.

EST 5. 2 Ex. 22 27 1 John 4 16-19 Heb.
10. 22. Eph. 2. 13.—Eph 3 12.—Heb 4 16.
M

AUGUST 31.

The free gift is of many offences unto
justification

THOUGH your sins be as scarlet, they shall be as white as snow; though they be red like crimson, they shall be as wool.

I, even I, am he that blotteth out thy transgressions for mine own sake, and will not remember thy sins Put me in remembrance : let us plead together : declare thou, that thou mayest be justified. —I have blotted out, as a thick cloud, thy transgressions, and, as a cloud, thy sins : return unto me ; for I have redeemed thee.

God so loved the world, that he gave his only begotten Son, that whosoever believeth in him should not perish, but have everlasting life. —Not as the offence, so also is the free gift. For if through the offence of one many be dead, much more the grace of God, and the gift by grace, which is by one man, Jesus Christ, hath abounded unto many. —And such were some of you : but ye are washed, but ye are sanctified, but ye are justified in the name of the Lord Jesus, and by the Spirit of our God.

Rom 5 16 Is 1 18 Is 43. 25, 26 —Is. 44 22. John 3 16. —Rom 5 15 —1 Cor. 6. 11.
M

SEPTEMBER 1.

The fruit of the Spirit is meekness

THE meek . . . . shall increase their joy in the LORD, and the poor among men shall rejoice in the Holy One of Israel.

Except ye be converted, and become as little children, ye shall not enter into the kingdom of heaven. Whosoever therefore shall humble himself as this little child, the same is greatest in the kingdom of heaven.—The ornament of a meek and quiet spirit, . . . is in the sight of God of great price.—Charity vaunteth not itself, is not puffed up.

Follow after meekness.—Take my yoke upon you and learn of me, for I am meek and lowly in heart.—He was oppressed, and he was afflicted, yet he opened not his mouth: he is brought as a lamb to the slaughter, and as a sheep before her shearers is dumb, so he openeth not his mouth.—Christ also suffered for us, leaving us an example, that ye should follow his steps: who did no sin, neither was guile found in his mouth: who, when he was re·viled, reviled not again, . . . but committed himself to him that judgeth righteously.

GAL. 5 22   Is. 29. 19.   Mat. 18. 3, 4.—1 Pet. 3 4—1 Cor 13, 4. 1 Tim. 6 11.—Mat. 11· 29. —Is. 53 7 —1 Pet 2 21-23.

M

SEPTEMBER 2.

Wait on the Lord be of good courage,
and he shall strengthen thine heart.

HAST thou not known? hast thou not heard, that the everlasting God, the LORD, the Creator of the ends of the earth, fainteth not, neither is weary? . . . He giveth power to the faint; and to them that have no might he increaseth strength.—Fear thou not, for I am with thee: be not dismayed; for I am thy God · I will strengthen thee; yea, I will help thee; yea, I will uphold thee with the right hand of my righteousness.—Thou hast been a strength to the poor, a strength to the needy in his distress, a refuge from the storm, a shadow from the heat, when the blast of the terrible ones is as a storm against the wall.

The trying of your faith worketh patience But let patience have her perfect work, that ye may be perfect and entire, wanting nothing.—Cast not away therefore your confidence, which hath great recompence of reward. For ye have need of patience, that, after ye have done the will of God, ye might receive the promise

Ps. 27. 14 Is 40 28, 29 —Is. 41 10 —Is. 25. 4
Ja. 1 3, 4 —Heb 10 35, 36.
M

SEPTEMBER 3.

Neither shall there be leaven seen with
thee in all thy quarters.

THE fear of the LORD is to hate evil.—
Abhor that which is evil.—Abstain
from all appearance of evil.—Looking
diligently lest any man fail of the grace
of God; lest any root of bitterness
springing up trouble you, and thereby
many be defiled.

If I regard iniquity in my heart, the
Lord will not hear me.

Know ye not that a little leaven lea·
veneth the whole lump? Purge out there·
fore the old leaven, that ye may be a new
lump, as ye are unleavened. For even
Christ our passover is sacrificed for us:
therefore let us keep the feast, not with
old leaven, neither with the leaven of
malice and wickedness; but with the un·
leavened bread of sincerity and truth.—
Let a man examine himself, and so let him
eat of that bread, and drink of that cup.

Let every one that nameth the name
of Christ depart from iniquity.—Such
an high priest became us, who is holy,
harmless, undefiled, separate from sin·
ners.—In him is no sin.

Ex 13 7   Pro 8 13.—Rom 12 9 —1 Thes. 5.
22 —Heb. 12 15. Ps 66. 18   1 Cor 5 6-8.
—1 Cor. 11 28. 2 Tim. 2. 19.—Heb 7. 26.
—1 John 3 5.

M

SEPTEMBER 4.

Sit still, my daughter.

TAKE heed, and be quiet; fear not, neither be fainthearted.—Be still, and know that I am God.—Said I not unto thee, that, if thou wouldest believe, thou shouldest see the glory of God?—The loftiness of man shall be bowed down, and the haughtiness of men shall be made low: and the LORD alone shall be exalted in that day.

Mary . . . sat at Jesus' feet, and heard his word. Mary hath chosen that good part, which shall not be taken away from her.—In returning and rest shall ye be saved; in quietness and in confidence shall be your strength.—Commune with your own heart upon your bed, and be still.

Rest in the LORD, and wait patiently for him: fret not thyself because of him who prospereth in his way, because of the man who bringeth wicked devices to pass.

He shall not be afraid of evil tidings: his heart is fixed, trusting in the LORD His heart is established.

He that believeth shall not make haste.

RUTH 3. 18. Is. 7 4.—Ps. 46. 10.—John 11. 40. —Is. 2 17. Luke 10 39, 42.—Is. 30 15.—Ps. 4 4 Ps. 37. 7. Ps. 112. 7, 8. Is 28 16.

M

SEPTEMBER 5.

As the body is one, and hath many
members so also is Christ

H E is the head of the body, the church.
—The head over all things to the
church, which is his body, the fulness of
him that filleth all in all.

We are members of his body, of his
flesh, and of his bones

A body hast thou prepared me.—Thine
eyes did see my substance, yet being unperfect ; and in thy book all my members
were written, which in continuance were
fashioned, when as yet there was none of
them.

Thine they were, and thou gavest them
me.—He hath chosen us in him before
the foundation of the world.—Whom he
did foreknow, he also did predestinate to
be conformed to the image of his Son.

Grow up into him in all things, which
is the head, even Christ · from whom
the whole body fitly joined together, and
compacted by that which every joint sup-
lieth, . . . maketh increase of the body
unto the edifying of itself in love.

1 Cor 12. 12   Col, 1 18.—Eph. 1. 22, 23
Eph. 5 30. Heb. 10. 5.—Ps. 139 16. John 17. 6.
—Eph. 1. 4.—Rom. 8 29. Eph. 4. 15, 16.

SEPTEMBER 6.

Let us lift up our heart with our hands unto God in the heavens

WHO is like unto the LORD our God, who dwelleth on high, who hum bleth himself to behold the things that are in heaven, and in the earth !—Unto thee, O LORD, do I lift up my soul.—I stretch forth my hands unto thee · my soul thirsteth after thee, as a thirsty land Hide not thy face from me, lest I be like unto them that go down into the pit. Cause me to hear thy lovingkindness in the morning; for in thee do I trust: cause me to know the way wherein I should walk ; for I lift up my soul unto thee.

Because thy lovingkindness is better than life, my lips shall praise thee. Thus will I bless thee while I live : I will lift up my hands in thy name.—Rejoice the soul of thy servant for unto thee, O Lord, do I lift up my soul. For thou, Lord, art good, and ready to forgive ; and plenteous in mercy unto all them that call upon thee

Whatsoever ye shall ask in my name, that will I do.

LAM 3 41 Ps 113 5, 6—Ps. 25. 1 —Ps 143 6-8. Ps 63 3, 4 —Ps. 86. 4, 5. John 14 13
M

Rejoicing in hope

THE hope which is laid up for you in heaven.—If in this life only we have hope in Christ, we are of all men most miserable.—We must through much tribulation enter into the kingdom of God. —Whosoever doth not bear his cross, and come after me, cannot be my disciple — No man should be moved by these afflictions : for yourselves know that we are appointed thereunto.

Rejoice in the Lord alway and again I say, Rejoice. —The God of hope fill you with all joy and peace in believing, that ye may abound in hope through the power of the Holy Ghost.—Blessed be the God and Father of our Lord Jesus Christ, which according to his abundant mercy hath begotten us again unto a lively hope by the resurrection of Jesus Christ from the dead —Whom having not seen, ye love ; in whom, though now ye see him not, yet believing, ye rejoice with joy unspeakable and full of glory —By whom also we have access by faith into this grace wherein we stand, and rejoice in hope of the glory of God.

Rom 12. 12. Col. 1 5 —1 Cor 15 19.— Acts 14 22 —Luke 14. 27.—1 Thes. 3 3. Philip 4 4 —Rom 15 13.—1 Pet. 1. 3.— 1 Pet 1. 8.—Rom. 5. 2.

M

SEPTEMBER 8.

*Thou art weighed in the balances,
and art found wanting*

THE LORD is a God of knowledge, and by him actions are weighed.

That which is highly esteemed among men is abomination in the sight of God —The LORD seeth not as man seeth; for man looketh on the outward appearance, but the LORD looketh on the heart. —Be not deceived; God is not mocked: for whatsoever a man soweth, that shall he also reap. For he that soweth to his flesh shall of the flesh reap corruption; but he that soweth to the Spirit shall of the Spirit reap life everlasting.

What is a man profited, if he shall gain the whole world, and lose his own soul? or what shall a man give in exchange for his soul?—What things were gain to me, those I counted loss for Christ.

Behold, thou desirest truth in the inward parts. — Thou hast proved mine heart; thou hast visited me in the night; thou hast tried me, and shalt find nothing.

DAN 5. 27. 1 Sam 2 3. Luke 16 15.—
1 Sam 16 7.—Gal 6 7, 8. Mat 16 26 —
Phil 3 7. Ps. 51 6.—Ps. 17. 3.

SEPTEMBER 9.

He hath filled the hungry with good things, and the rich he hath sent empty away

THOU sayest, I am rich, and increased with goods, and have need of nothing; and knowest not that thou art wretched, and miserable, and poor, and blind, and naked : I counsel thee to buy of me gold tried in the fire, that thou mayest be rich. . As many as I love, I rebuke and chasten : be zealous therefore and repent.

Blessed are they which do hunger and thirst after righteousness : for they shall be filled. — When the poor and needy seek water, and there is none, and their tongue faileth for thirst, I the LORD will hear them, I the God of Israel will not forsake them.—I am the LORD thy God, . . . open thy mouth wide, and I will fill it.

Wherefore do ye spend money for that which is not bread ? and your labour for that which satisfieth not ? hearken diligently unto me, and eat ye that which is good, and let your soul delight itself in fatness.—I am the bread of life.

LUKE 1 53 Rev 3 17-19 Mat 5 6.—
Is 41 17 —Ps 81 10. Is. 55 2.—John 6. 35
M

9

I will give them one heart, and one way,
that they may fear me for ever, for the
good of them, and of their children after
them.

A NEW heart . . . will I give you,
and a new spirit will I put within
you.—Good and upright is the LORD.
therefore will he teach sinners in the way,
The meek will he guide in judgment;
and the meek will he teach his way. All
the paths of the LORD are mercy and
truth unto such as keep his covenant and
his testimonies.

That they all may be one; as thou,
Father, art in me, and I in thee, that
they also may be one in us: that the
world may believe that thou hast sent me.

I . . . beseech you that ye walk worthy
of the vocation wherewith ye are called,
with all lowliness and meekness, . . .
endeavouring to keep the unity of the
Spirit in the bond of peace. There is
one body, and one Spirit, even as ye are
called in one hope of your calling; one
Lord, one faith, one baptism, one God
and Father of all, who is above all, and
through all, and in you all.

JER. 32. 39   Ezek. 36. 26 —Ps. 25. 8. 10
John 17. 21.   Eph. 4. 1-6

M

SEPTEMBER 11.

Be not conformed to this world; but be ye transformed by the renewing of your mind.

KNOW ye not that the friendship of the world is enmity with God? whosoever therefore will be a friend of the world is the enemy of God.

What fellowship hath righteousness with unrighteousness? and what communion hath light with darkness? And what concord hath Christ with Belial? or what part hath he that believeth with an infidel? And what agreement hath the temple of God with idols?—Love not the world, neither the things that are in the world. If any man love the world, the love of the Father is not in him. The world passeth away, and the lust thereof: but he that doeth the will of God abideth for ever.

In time past ye walked according to the course of this world, according to the prince of the power of the air, the spirit that now worketh in the children of disobedience.—Ye have not so learned Christ; if so be that ye have heard him, . . . as the truth is in Jesus.

Rom. 12. 2. Ja. 4. 4. 2 Cor. 6. 14-16.—
1 John 2. 15, 17. Eph. 2. 2.—Eph 4 20, 21
L

SEPTEMBER 12.

I have seen his ways, and will heal him.

I AM the LORD that healeth thee.

O LORD, thou hast searched me, and known me Thou knowest my down-sitting, and mine uprising, thou under-standest my thought afar off Thou com-passest my path and my lying down, and art acquainted with all my ways —Thou hast set our iniquities before thee, our secret sins in the light of thy countenance. —All things are naked and opened unto the eyes of him with whom we have to do.

Come now, and let us reason together, saith the LORD : Though your sins be as scarlet, they shall be as white as snow ; though they be red like crimson, they shall be as wool —He is gracious unto him, and saith, Deliver him from going down to the pit : I have found a ransom —He was wounded for our transgres-sions, he was bruised for our iniquities : the chastisement of our peace was upon him ; and with his stripes we are healed. —Thy faith hath made thee whole.

Is. 57. 18   Ex 15 26   Ps. 139. 1-3 —Ps 90. 8
—Heb 4. 13. Is 1 18 —Job 33 24 —
Is 53 5 —Mark 5. 34

M

SEPTEMBER 13.

If any man thirst, let him come unto me,
and drink.

MY soul longeth, yea, even fainteth for
the courts of the LORD : my heart
and my flesh crieth out for the living God.
—O God, thou art my God ; early will I
seek thee : my soul thirsteth for thee, my
flesh longeth for thee in a dry and thirsty
land where no water is , to see thy power
and thy glory, so as I have seen thee in
the sanctuary.

Ho, every one that thirsteth, come ye
to the waters, and he that hath no money;
come ye buy, and eat; yea, come, buy
wine and milk without money and without price.—The Spirit and the bride say,
Come. And let him that heareth say,
Come. And let him that is athirst come
And whosoever will, let him take the
water of life freely.—Whosoever drinketh
of the water that I shall give him shall
never thirst; but the water that I shall
give him shall be in him a well of water
springing up into everlasting life.—My
blood is drink indeed.

Eat, O friends; drink, yea, drink
abundantly, O beloved.

JOHN 7 37 Ps. 84 2 —Ps. 63. 1; 2. Is 55 1.
—Rev 22 17 —John 4 14 —John 6 55.
Cant 5. 1

M

SEPTEMBER 14.

I, even I, am he that comforteth you.

BLESSED be God, even the Father of our Lord Jesus Christ, the Father of mercies, and the God of all comfort ; who comforteth us in all our tribulation, that we may be able to comfort them which are in any trouble, by the comfort wherewith we ourselves are comforted of God. —Like as a father pitieth his children, so the LORD pitieth them that fear him For he knoweth our frame ; he remembereth that we are dust.—As one whom his mother comforteth, so will I comfort you.—Casting all your care upon him, for he careth for you

Thou, O Lord, art a God full of compassion, and gracious, longsuffering, and plenteous in mercy and truth

Another Comforter . . . even the Spirit of truth.—The Spirit . . . helpeth our infirmities.

God shall wipe away all tears from their eyes ; and there shall be no more death, neither sorrow, nor crying, neither shall there be any more pain : for the former things are passed away

Is. 51 12. 2 Cor. 1. 3, 4.—Ps. 103 13, 14 —
Is 66 13 —1 Pet 5 7 Ps 86 15 John 14.
16, 17 —Rom 8 26 Rev 21. 4

M

SEPTEMBER 15.

Sin shall not have dominion over you· for ye are not under the law, but under grace.

WHAT then? shall we sin, because we are not under the law, but under grace? God forbid —My brethren, ye . . . are become dead to the law by the body of Christ ; that ye should be married to another, even to him who is raised from the dead, that we should bring forth fruit unto God.—Being not without law to God, but under the law to Christ

The sting of death is sin : and the strength of sin is the law But thanks be to God, which giveth us the victory through our Lord Jesus Christ.

The law of the Spirit of life in Christ Jesus hath made me free from the law of sin and death.—Whosoever committeth sin is the servant of sin If the Son . . shall make you free, ye shall be free indeed.

Stand fast therefore in the liberty wherewith Christ hath made us free, and be not entangled again with the yoke of bondage.

Rom 6 14. Rom 6 15—Rom. 7 4.—
Cor 9 21 1 Cor. 15 56, 57 Rom. 8. 2 —
John 8 34. 36. Gal 5. 1.

M

SEPTEMBER 16.

The Lord pondereth the hearts.

THE LORD knoweth the way of the righteous : but the way of the ungodly shall perish.—The LORD will shew who are his, and who is holy.—Thy Father which seeth in secret himself shall reward thee openly.

Search me, O God, and know my heart: try me, and know my thoughts · and see if there be any wicked way in me, and lead me in the way everlasting.—There is no fear in love ; but perfect love casteth out fear

Lord, all my desire is before thee ; and my groaning is not hid from thee.—When my spirit was overwhelmed within me, then thou knewest my path.—He that searcheth the hearts knoweth what is the mind of the Spirit, because he maketh intercession for the saints according to the will of God

The foundation of God standeth sure, having this seal, The Lord knoweth them that are his. And, Let every one that nameth the name of Christ depart from iniquity.

PRO 21 2. Ps 1. 6.—Num 16 5.—Mat 6 6.
Ps 139. 23, 24.—1 John 4 18 Ps 38. 9.—
Ps 142. 3.—Rom 8 27 2 Tim 2 19.
M

A bruised reed shall he not break.

THE sacrifices of God are a broken spirit : a broken and a contrite heart, O God, thou wilt not despise.—He healeth the broken in heart, and bindeth up their wounds.—Thus saith the high and lofty One that inhabiteth eternity, whose name is Holy; I dwell in the high and holy place, with him also that is of a contrite and humble spirit, to revive the spirit of the humble, and to revive the heart of the contrite ones. For I will not contend for ever, neither will I be always wroth : for the spirit should fail before me, and the souls which I have made.

I will seek that which was lost, and bring again that which was driven away, and will bind up that which was broken, and will strengthen that which was sick. —Wherefore lift up the hands which hang down, and the feeble knees ; and make straight paths for your feet, lest that which is lame be turned out of the way ; but let it rather be healed.

Behold, your God . . . will come and save you.

MAT. 12. 20. Ps. 51. 17.—Ps 147. 3.—Is 57. 15, 16. Ezek. 34. 16.—Heb. 12 12, 13 Is 35. 4.

M

9 *

SEPTEMBER 18.

Open thou mine eyes, that I may behold
wondrous things out of thy law.

THEN opened he their understanding,
that they might understand the scriptures—It is given unto you to know the
mysteries of the kingdom of heaven, but
to them it is not given. —I thank thee, O
Father, Lord of heaven and earth, because
thou hast hid these things from the wise
and prudent, and hast revealed them unto
babes. Even so, Father: for so it seemed
good in thy sight —We have received,
not the spirit of the world, but the spirit
which is of God, that we might know the
things that are freely given to us of God.
—How precious also are thy thoughts
unto me, O God! how great is the sum of
them! If I should count them, they are
more in number than the sand —O the
depth of the riches both of the wisdom
and knowledge of God! how unsearchable
are his judgments, and his ways past finding out! For who hath known the mind
of the Lord? or who hath been his counsellor? For of him, and through him,
and to him are all things : to whom be
glory for ever. Amen.

Ps. 119 18. Luke 24 45—Mat 13 11 —
Mat. 11 25, 26.—1 Cor. 2. 12 —Ps 139 17, 18
—Rom. 11. 33 34, 36.

M

The God of all grace

I WILL proclaim the name of the LORD before thee, and will be gracious to whom I will be gracious —He is gracious unto him, and saith, Deliver him from going down to the pit · I have found a ransom. — Being justified freely by his grace, thr ugh the redemption that is in Christ Jesus. whom God hath set forth to be a propitiation through faith in his blood, to declare his righteousness for the remission of sins that are past, through the forbearance of God.—Grace and truth came by Jesus Christ.

By grace are ye saved through faith; and that not of yourselves; it is the gift of God —Grace, mercy, and peace, from God our Father and Jesus Christ our Lord.—Unto every one of us is given grace according to the measure of the gift of Christ.—As every man hath received the gift, even so minister the same one to another, as good stewards of the manifold grace of God.—He giveth more grace.

Grow in grace, and in the knowledge of our Lord and Saviour Jesus Christ. To him be glory both now and for ever.

1 PET 5 10   Ex. 33 19.—Job 33 24 —
Rom 3 24, 25 —John 1 17.   Eph. 2 8 —
1 Tim 1. 2 —Eph. 4 7.—1 Pet. 4. 10.—
Ja. 4 6. 2 Pet. 3 18.

M

SEPTEMBER 20.

Happy is the man that findeth wisdom, and the man that getteth understanding.

WHOSO findeth me findeth life, and shall obtain favour of the LORD

Thus saith the LORD, Let not the wise man glory in his wisdom, neither let the mighty man glory in his might : . . . but let him that glorieth glory in this, that he understandeth and knoweth me, that I am the LORD.—The fear of the LORD is the beginning of wisdom.

What things were gain to me, those I counted loss for Christ. Yea doubtless, and I count all things but loss for the excellency of the knowledge of Christ Jesus my Lord : for whom I have suffered the loss of all things, and do count them but dung, that I may win Christ.—In whom are hid all the treasures of wisdom and knowledge.—Counsel is mine, and sound wisdom : I am understanding ; I have strength.

Christ Jesus, . . . is made unto us wisdom, and righteousness, and sanctification, and redemption.

He that winneth souls is wise.

Pro. 3. 13   Pro. 8. 35   Jer 9. 23, 24.—
Pro. 9. 10.   Phil 3. 7, 8.—Col. 2 3 —
Pro. 8. 14   1 Cor. 1. 20.   Pro. 11. 10
M

SEPTEMBER 21.

We know that all things work together
for good to them that love God.

SURELY the wrath of man shall praise
thee; the remainder of wrath shalt
thou restrain.—Ye thought evil against
me : but God meant it unto good.

All things are your's, whether . . .
the world, or life, or death, or things
present, or things to come ; all are your's ;
and ye are Christ's ; and Christ is God's.

All things are for your sakes, that
the abundant grace might through the
thanksgiving of many redound to the
glory of God. For which cause we faint
not ; but though our outward man perish,
yet the inward man is renewed day by
day. For our light affliction, which is
but for a moment, worketh for us a far
more exceeding and eternal weight of
glory.

My brethren, count it all joy when ye
fall into divers temptations ; knowing
this, that the trying of your faith worketh
patience. But let patience have her perfect work, that ye may be perfect and
entire, wanting nothing.

Rom. 8 28. Ps. 76. 10.—Gen. 50 20
1 Cor 3 21-23 2 Cor. 4 15-17 Ja 1. 2-4.
M

SEPTEMBER 22.

My meditation of him shall be sweet;
I will be glad in the Lord.

AS the apple tree among the trees of
the wood, so is my beloved among
the sons   I sat down under his shadow
with great delight, and his fruit was
sweet to my taste —For who in the
heaven can be compared unto the LORD?
who among the sons of the mighty can
be likened unto the LORD?

My beloved is white and ruddy, the
chiefest among ten thousand.—One pearl
of great price.—The prince of the kings
of the earth

His head is as the most fine gold, his
locks are bushy, and black as a raven.
—The head over all things.—He is the
head of the body, the church

His cheeks are as a bed of spices, as
sweet flowers.—He could not be hid.

His lips like lilies, dropping sweet
smelling myrrh.—Never man spake like
this man.

His countenance is as Lebanon, excellent as the cedars.—Make thy face to
shine upon thy servant —LORD, lift thou
up the light of thy countenance upon us.

Ps 104 34   Cant. 2. 3 —Ps 89 6   Cant. 5. 10.
—Mat. 13 46.—Rev. 1. 5   Cant 5 11.—
Eph 1 22 —Col 1. 18 Cant 5 13 —Mark 7 24
Cant 5 13 —John 7 46   Cant 5 15 —
Ps 31 16 —Ps 4 6

M

Our God hath not forsaken us

BELOVED, think it not strange concerning the fiery trial which is to try
you, as though some strange thing happened unto you.—If ye endure chastening,
God dealeth with you as with sons ; for
what son is he whom the father chasteneth
not? But if ye be without chastisement,
whereof all are partakers, then are ye
bastards, and not sons

The LORD your God proveth you, to
know whether ye love the LORD your
God with all your heart and with all your
soul

The LORD will not forsake his people
for his great name's sake : because it
hath pleased the LORD to make you his
people.—Can a woman forget her sucking child, that she should not have compassion on the son of her womb? yea,
they may forget, yet will I not forget
thee.—Happy is he that hath the God
of Jacob for his help, whose hope is in
the LORD his God

Shall not God avenge his own elect,
which cry day and night unto him,
though he bear long with them? I tell
you that he will avenge them speedily.

EZR. 9. 9. 1 Pet. 4. 12 —Heb. 12 7, 8
Deut. 13 3. 1 Sam 12 22 —Is 49 15 —
Ps 145. 5 Luke 13. 7, 8

M

SEPTEMBER 24.

It is good for me to draw near to God.

LORD, I have loved the habitation of thy house, and the place where thine honour dwelleth.—A day in thy courts is better than a thousand   I had rather be a doorkeeper in the house of my God, than to dwell in the tents of wickedness. —Blessed is the man whom thou choosest, and causest to approach unto thee, that he may dwell in thy courts   we shall be satisfied with the goodness of thy house, even of thy holy temple.

The LORD is good unto them that wait for him, to the soul that seeketh him.— Therefore will the LORD wait that he may be gracious unto you, and therefore will he be exalted, that he may have mercy upon you : for the LORD is a God of judgment   blessed are all they that wait for him.

Having therefore, brethren, boldness to enter into the holiest by the blood of Jesus, by a new and living way, which he hath consecrated for us , . . . let us draw near with a true heart in full assurance of faith, having our hearts sprinkled from an evil conscience.

Ps. 73 28. Ps. 26 8.—Ps. 84 10.—Ps. 65. 4.
Lam 3. 25 —Is 30. 18   Heb. 10 19, 20, 22.
M

SEPTEMBER 25.

Let patience have her perfect work,
that ye may be perfect and entire,
wanting nothing.

NOW for a season, if need be, ye are in heaviness through manifold temptations : that the trial of your faith, being much more precious than of gold that perisheth, though it be tried with fire, might be found unto praise and honour and glory at the appearing of Jesus Christ.—We glory in tribulations   . knowing that tribulation worketh patience ; and patience, experience ; and experience, hope.

It is good that a man should both hope and quietly wait for the salvation of the LORD —Ye have in heaven a better and an enduring substance. Cast not away therefore your confidence, which hath great recompence of reward For ye have need of patience, that, after ye have done the will of God, ye might receive the promise.—Our Lord Jesus Christ himself, and God, even our Father, which hath loved us, and hath given us everlasting consolation and good hope through grace, comfort your hearts

JA. 1 4 1 Pet. 1 6, 7 —Rom 5. 3, 4
Lam. 3 26 —Heb 10. 34 36.—2 Thes. 2 16, 17.
M

A God of truth and without iniquity, just and right is he

HIM that judgeth righteously —We must all appear before the judgment seat of Christ; that every one may receive the things done in his body, according to that he hath done, whether it be good or bad —Every one of us shall give account of himself to God.—The soul that sinneth it shall die

Awake, O sword, against my shepherd, and against the man that is my fellow, saith the LORD of hosts: smite the shepherd.—The LORD hath laid on him the iniquity of us all —Mercy and truth are met together: righteousness and peace have kissed each other.—Mercy rejoiceth against judgment

The wages of sin is death: but the gift of God is eternal life through Jesus Christ our Lord.

A just God and a Saviour; there is none beside me —Just, and the justifier of him which believeth in Jesus.—Justified freely by his grace through the redemption that is in Christ Jesus

DEUT. 32. 4   1 Pet. 2 23 —2 Cor. 5. 10 — Rom. 14 12 —Ezek 18 4 Zec 13. 7 —Is. 53 6. —Ps 85 10.—Ja. 2 13   Rom. 6. 23   Is 45 21 —Rom 3. 26.—Rom 3. 24

M

SEPTEMBER 27.

Humble yourselves under the mighty
hand of God, that he may exalt
you in due time.

EVERY one that is proud in heart is
an abomination to the LORD: though
hand join in hand, he shall not be un-
punished.

O LORD, thou art our father; we are
the clay, and thou our potter; and we
all are the work of thy hand Be not
wroth very sore, O LORD, neither remember iniquity for ever: behold, see,
we beseech thee, we are all thy people.
—Thou hast chastised me, and I was
chastised, as a bullock unaccustomed to
the yoke: turn thou me, and I shall be
turned; for thou art the LORD my God.
Surely after that I was turned, I re-
pented; and after that I was instructed,
I smote upon my thigh: I was ashamed,
yea, even confounded, because I did bear
the reproach of my youth.—It is good
for a man that he bear the yoke in his
youth.

Affliction cometh not forth of the dust,
neither doth trouble spring out of the
ground; yet man is born unto trouble, as
the sparks fly upward.

1 Pet. 5. 6. Pro. 16. 5. Is. 64 8, 9.—
Jer. 31. 18 19.—Lam. 3. 27. Job 5 6, 7.
M

They shall put my name upon the
children of Israel; and I will
bless them.

O LORD our God, other lords beside
thee have had dominion over us ; but
by thee only will we make mention of
thy name.—We are thine : thou never
barest rule over them ; they were not
called by thy name.

All people of the earth shall see that
thou art called by the name of the LORD ;
and they shall be afraid of thee.—The
LORD will not forsake his people for his
great name's sake : because it hath pleased
the LORD to make you his people.

O Lord, hear ; O Lord, forgive ; O
Lord, hearken and do ; defer not, for
thine own sake, O my God : for thy city
and thy people are called by thy name.
—Help us, O God of our salvation, for
the glory of thy name : and deliver us,
and purge away our sins, for thy name's
sake. Wherefore should the heathen say,
Where is their God?—The name of the
LORD is a strong tower : the righteous
runneth into it, and is safe.

NUM. 6 27. Is. 26. 13.—Is 63 19. Deut. 28. 32.
—1 Sam. 12. 22. Dan. 9. 19.—Ps. 79. 9, 10.
—Pro 18. 10.

M

SEPTEMBER 29.

Hereby perceive we the love of God, because he laid down his life for us

THE love of Christ, which passeth knowledge.—Greater love hath no man than this, that a man lay down his life for his friends.—Ye know the grace of our Lord Jesus Christ, that, though he was rich, yet for your sakes he became poor, that ye through his poverty might be rich.—Beloved, if God so loved us, we ought also to love one another.—Be ye kind one to another, tenderhearted, forgiving one another, even as God for Christ's sake hath forgiven you.—Forbearing one another, and forgiving one another, if any man have a quarrel against any : even as Christ forgave you, so also do ye.—For even the Son of man came not to be ministered unto, but to minister, and to give his life a ransom for many.—Christ . . suffered for us, leaving us an example, that ye should follow his steps.

Ye also ought to wash one another's feet. For I have given you an example, that ye should do as I have done to you.—We ought to lay down our lives for the brethren.

1 JOHN 3 16   Eph 3 19.—John 15 13 —2 Cor 8 9.—1 John 4 11.—Eph 4 32.—Col. 3 13.—Mark 10 45 —1 Pet. 2 21. John 13 15.—
1 John 3 16

M

He knoweth the way that I take : when he hath tried me, I shall come forth as gold.

HE knoweth our frame.—He doth not afflict willingly nor grieve the children of men.

The foundation of God standeth sure, having this seal, The Lord knoweth them that are his. And, Let every one that nameth the name of Christ depart from iniquity. But in a great house there are not only vessels of gold and of silver, but also of wood and of earth ; and some to honour, and some to dishonour. If a man therefore purge himself from these, he shall be a vessel unto honour, sanctified, and meet for the master's use, and prepared unto every good work.

He shall sit as a refiner and purifier of silver ; and he shall purify the sons of Levi, and purge them as gold and silver, that they may offer unto the LORD an offering in righteousness.—I . . . will re fine them as silver is refined, . . . they shall call on my name, and I will hear them : I will say, It is my people : and they shall say, The LORD is my God.

Job 23 10 Ps. 103. 14 —Lam. 3. 33. 2 Tim. 2. 19-21. Mal. 3. 3.—Zec. 13 9.

M

OCTOBER 1.

The fruit of the Spirit is temperance.

EVERY man that striveth for the
mastery is temperate in all things.
Now they do it to obtain a corruptible
crown; but we an incorruptible. I
therefore so run, not as uncertainly; so
fight I, not as one that beateth the air :
but I keep under my body, and bring it
into subjection : lest that by any means,
when I have preached to others, I myself
should be a castaway

Be not drunk with wine, wherein is
excess; but be filled with the Spirit.

If any man will come after me, let him
deny himself, and take up his cross, and
follow me.

Let us not sleep, as do others ; but let
us watch and be sober. For they that
sleep sleep in the night : and they that be
drunken are drunken in the night. But
let us, who are of the day, be sober.—
Denying ungodliness and worldly lusts,
we should live soberly, righteously, and
godly, in this present world ; looking for
that blessed hope, and the glorious
appearing of the great God and our
Saviour Jesus Christ.

GAL. 5. 22. 1 Cor 9. 25-27. Eph. 5 18. Mat.
16. 24. 1 Thes. 5. 6-8.—Tit. 2. 12, 13.

M

OCTOBER 2.

The goat shall bear upon him all their in-
iquities unto a land not inhabited; and he
shall let go the goat in the wilderness.

AS far as the east is from the west, so
far hath he removed our transgressions from us —In those days, and in that
time, saith the LORD, the iniquity of
Israel shall be sought for, and there shall
be none ; and the sins of Judah, and they
shall not be found : for I will pardon
,them whom I reserve —Thou wilt cast
' all their sins into the depths of the sea.
Who is a God like unto thee, that pardon
eth iniquity ?

All we like sheep have gone astray :
we have turned every one to his own way ;
and the LORD hath laid on him the iniquity of us all.—He shall bear their
iniquities. Therefore will I divide him a
portion with the great, and he shall divide
the spoil with the strong, because he hath
poured out his soul unto death ; and he
was numbered with the transgressors ;
and he bare the sin of many, and made
intercession for the transgressors —The
Lamb of God, which taketh away the
sin of the world.

LEV 16 22   Ps 103 12—J^r. 50 20 —Mic·
7· 19, 18   Is 53 6 —Is 53· 11, 12 —John 1 29
M

Unto him that loved us, and washed us from our sins in his own blood.

MANY waters cannot quench love, neither can the floods drown it. Love is strong as death —Greater love hath no man than this, that a man lay down his life for his friends.

Who his own self bare our sins in his own body on the tree, that we, being dead to sins, should live unto righteous-ness : by whose stripes ye were healed.
—In whom we have redemption through his blood, the forgiveness of sins, according to the riches of his grace

Ye are washed, . . . ye are sanctified, . . ye are justified in the name of the Lord Jesus, and by the Spirit of our God.
—Ye are a chosen generation, a royal priesthood, a holy nation, a peculiar people; that ye should shew forth the praises of him who hath called you out of darkness into his marvellous light

I beseech you . . . brethren, by the mercies of God, that ye present your bodies a living sacrifice, holy, acceptable unto God, which is your reasonable service.

REV 1 5   Cant. 8 7 6.—John 15 13   1 Pet. 2 24.—Eph. 1 7   1 Cor 6 11.—1 Pet. 2 9   Rom 12 1.

M

OCTOBER 4.

Moses wist not that the skin of his face shone while he talked with him.

NOT unto us, O LORD, not unto us, but unto thy name give glory.—Lord, when saw we thee an hungered, and fed thee ? or thirsty, and gave thee drink ?—In lowliness of mind, let each esteem other better than themselves.—Be clothed with humility.

[Jesus] was transfigured before them : and his face did shine as the sun, and his raiment was white as the light.—All that sat in the council, looking stedfastly on [Stephen], saw his face as it had been the face of an angel.—The glory which thou gavest me, I have given them.—We all, with open face beholding as in a glass the glory of the Lord, are changed into the same image from glory to glory, even as by the Spirit of the Lord.

Ye are the light of the world. A city that is set on a hill cannot be hid. Neither do men light a candle, and put it under a bushel, but on a candlestick ; and it giveth light unto all that are in the house.

Ex. 34 29. Ps. 115 1.—Mat 25 37 —Phil. 2 3. —1 Pet. 5 5 Mat 17. 2.—Acts 6 15 —John 17 22.—2 Cor 3 18 Mat. 5. 14, 15.
M

OCTOBER 5.

Call upon me in the day of trouble. I will deliver thee, and thou shalt glorify me.

WHY art thou cast down, O my soul? and why art thou disquieted within me? hope thou in God. for I shall yet praise him, who is the health of my countenance, and my God —LORD, thou hast heard the desire of the humble. thou wilt prepare their heart, thou wilt cause thine ear to hear —For thou, Lord, art good, and ready to forgive ; and plenteous in mercy unto all them that call upon thee

Jacob said unto his household, . . . Let us arise, and go up to Beth-el ; and I will make there an altar unto God, who answered me in the day of my distress, and was with me in the way which I went.

I love the LORD, because he hath heard my voice and my supplications. Because he hath inclined his ear unto me, therefore will I call upon him as long as I live. The sorrows of death compassed me, and the pains of hell gat hold upon me. . . . Then called I upon the name of the LORD.

Ps. 50. 15   Ps 42. 11.—Ps. 10 17 —Ps. 86. 5.
Gen 35 2, 3.   Ps. 116. 1-4.
M

OCTOBER 6

The Lord God omnipotent reigneth.

I KNOW that thou canst do every thing.
—The things which are impossible
with men are possible with God.—He
doeth according to his will in the army of
heaven, and among the inhabitants of the
earth and none can stay his hand, or
say unto him, What doest thou?—There
is none that can deliver out of my hand:
I will work, and who shall let it?

Abba, Father, all things are possible
unto thee

Believe ye that I am able to do this?
They said unto him, Yea, Lord Then
touched he their eyes, saying, According
to your faith be it unto you.—Lord, if
thou wilt, thou canst make me clean.
And Jesus put forth his hand, and touched
him, saying, I will, be thou clean—The
mighty God.—All power is given unto
me in heaven and in earth.

Some trust in chariots, and some in
horses but we will remember the name
of the LORD our God—Be strong and
courageous, be not afraid nor dismayed,
. . . there be more with us than with
him.

REV 19 6 Job 42. 2—Luke 18 27—Dan.
4. 35—Is. 43 13 Mark 14 36. Mat 9 28, 29
—Mat 8. 2, 3—Is 9 6—Mat 28 18. Ps.
20 7—2 Chr 32 7.

M

OCTOBER 7.

The meek will he teach his way.

BLESSED are the meek.

I returned, and saw under the sun, that the race is not to the swift, nor the battle to the strong, neither yet bread to the wise, nor yet riches to men of understanding, nor yet favour to men of skill —A man's heart deviseth his way : but the LORD directeth his steps

Unto thee lift I up mine eyes, O thou that dwellest in the heavens. Behold, as the eyes of servants look unto the hand of their masters, and as the eyes of a maiden unto the hand of her mistress ; so our eyes wait upon the LORD our God.—Cause me to know the way wherein I should walk ; for I lift up my soul unto thee.

O our God, wilt thou not judge them ? for we have no might against this great company that cometh against us ; neither know we what to do : but our eyes are upon thee.

If any of you lack wisdom, let him ask of God, that giveth to all men liberally, and upbraideth not ; and it shall be given him.

Ps. 25. 9   Mat. 5 5.   Ecc 9 11.—Pro 16 9.
Ps 123 1, 2 —Ps 142. 8   2 Chr. 20. 12   Ja. 1 5.
M

OCTOBER 8.

I will not fear what man shall do unto me.

WHO shall separate us from the love of Christ? shall tribulation, or distress, or persecution, or famine, or nakedness, or peril, or sword? Nay, in all these things we are more than conquerors through him that loved us.

Be not afraid of them that kill the body, and after that have no more that they can do. But I will forewarn you whom ye shall fear: Fear him, which after he hath killed hath power to cast into hell; yea, I say unto you, Fear him.

Blessed are they which are persecuted for righteousness' sake: for their's is the kingdom of heaven. Blessed are ye, when men shall revile you, and persecute you, and shall say all manner of evil against you falsely, for my sake. Rejoice, and be exceeding glad: for great is your reward in heaven —None of these things move me, neither count I my life dear unto myself, so that I might finish my course with joy.—I will speak of thy testimonies . . . before kings, and will not be ashamed.

HEB. 13. 6. Rom 8 35, 37. Luke 12 4, 5. Mat. 5 10-12.—Acts 20. 24 —Ps 119. 46.
M

OCTOBER 9.

Thou art a God ready to pardon, gracious
and merciful.

THE Lord is not slack concerning his
promise, as some men count slackness ; but is longsuffering to us-ward, not
willing that any should perish, but that
all should come to repentance.—The
longsuffering of our Lord is salvation.

For this cause I obtained mercy, that
in me first Jesus Christ might shew forth
all longsuffering, for a pattern to them
which should hereafter believe on him to
life everlasting.—Whatsoever things were
written aforetime were written for our
learning, that we through patience and
comfort of the scriptures might have hope.

Despisest thou the riches of his goodness and forbearance and longsuffering ;
not knowing that the goodness of God
leadeth thee to repentance ?

Rend your heart, and not your garments, and turn unto the LORD your
God . for he is gracious and merciful,
slow to anger, and of great kindness, and
repenteth him of the evil

NEH. 9 17. 2 Pet. 3 9.—2 Pet. 3 15. 1 Tim.
1 16.—Rom. 15 4. Rom. 2. 4 Joel 2. 13.
M

OCTOBER 10.

The whole family in heaven and earth.

ONE God and Father of all, who is above all, and through all, and in you all.—Ye are all the children of God by faith in Christ Jesus —That in the dispensation of the fulness of times, he might gather together in one all things in Christ, both which are in heaven, and which are on earth ; even in him

He is not ashamed to call them brethren —Behold my mother and my brethren! Whosoever shall do the will of my Father which is in heaven, the same is my brother, and sister, and mother.—Go to my brethren, and say unto them, I ascend unto my Father, and your Father.

I saw under the altar the souls of them that were slain for the word of God, and for the testimony which they held : . . and white robes were given unto every one of them , and it was said unto them, that they should rest for a little season, until their fellowservants also and their brethren, that should be killed as they were, should be fulfilled.—That they without us should not be made perfect.

EPH. 3 15 Eph. 4 6 —Gal 3 26.—Eph. 1 10.
Heb. 2. 11.—Mat 12 49, 50 —John 20 17.
Rev 6 9-11.—Heb. 11. 40

M

Be not far from me, for trouble is near.

HOW long wilt thou forget me, O
LORD? for ever? how long wilt thou
hide thy face from me? How long shall
I take counsel in my soul, having sorrow
in my heart daily?—Hide not thy face
far from me; put not thy servant away
in anger: thou hast been my help; leave
me not, neither forsake me, O God of
my salvation

He shall call upon me, and I will answer him I will be with him in trouble;
I will deliver him, and honour him.—
The LORD is nigh unto all them that call
upon him, to all that call upon him in
truth He will fulfil the desire of them
that fear him : he also will hear their cry,
and will save them.

I will not leave you comfortless · I
will come to you —Lo, I am with you
alway, even unto the end of the world.

God is our refuge and strength, a very
present help in trouble —Truly my soul
waiteth upon God : from him cometh my
salvation. My soul, wait thou only upon
God ; for my expectation is from him.

Ps. 22 11   Ps. 13 1, 2 —Ps 27. 9   Ps 91 15.
—Ps 145 18, 19 John 14 18.—Mat 28. 20.
Ps 46 1 —Ps 62 1, 5
M   10

OCTOBER 12.

God was in Christ, reconciling the world unto himself, not imputing their trespasses unto them.

IT pleased the Father, that in him should all fulness dwell ; and, having made peace through the blood of his cross, by him to reconcile all things unto himself. —Mercy and truth are met together ; righteousness and peace have kissed each other.

I know the thoughts that I think toward you, saith the LORD, thoughts of peace, and not of evil.—Come now, and let us reason together, saith the LORD ; Though your sins be as scarlet, they shall be as white as snow ; though they be red like crimson, they shall be as wool.

Who is a God like unto thee, that pardoneth iniquity ?

Acquaint now thyself with him, and be at peace —Work out your own salvation with fear and trembling For it is God which worketh in you both to will and to do of his good pleasure —LORD, thou wilt ordain peace for us : for thou also hast wrought all our works in us

2 COR 5. 19.   Col. 1. 19, 20.—Ps 85 10   Jer. 29 11.—Is. 1 18.   Mic 7 18   Job 22 21 —
Phil 2. 12, 13.—Is 26, 12

M

OCTOBER 13.

From the first day that thou didst set
thine heart to chasten thyself before thy
God, thy words were heard.

THUS saith the high and lofty One
that inhabiteth eternity, whose name
is Holy; I dwell in the high and holy
place, with him also that is of a contrite
and humble spirit, to revive the spirit of
the humble, and to revive the heart of the
contrite ones —The sacrifices of God are
a broken spirit : a broken and a contrite
heart, O God, thou wilt not despise.—
Though the LORD be high, yet hath he
respect unto the lowly : but the proud he
knoweth afar off.—Humble yourselves
therefore under the mighty hand of God,
that he may exalt you in due time.—God
resisteth the proud, but giveth grace unto
the humble. Submit yourselves therefore
to God.

Thou, Lord, art good, and ready to
forgive ; and plenteous in mercy unto all
them that call upon thee. Give ear, O
LORD, unto my prayer; and attend to
the voice of my supplications. In the
day of my trouble I will call upon thee :
for thou wilt answer me.

DAN. 10. 12. Is. 57 15 —Ps. 51. 17 —Ps. 138.
6 —1 Pet. 5. 6.—Ja. 4 6, 7. Ps 86. 5-7
M

OCTOBER 14.

Christ both died, and rose, and revived,
that he might be Lord both of the dead
and living

IT pleased the LORD to bruise him ; he
hath put him to grief : when thou
shalt make his soul an offering for sin, he
shall see his seed, he shall prolong his
days, and the pleasure of the LORD shall
prosper in his hand. He shall see of the
travail of his soul, and shall be satisfied:
by his knowledge shall my righteous servant justify many ; for he shall bear their
iniquities.—Ought not Christ to have
suffered these things, and to enter into
his glory?—We thus judge, that if one
died for all, then were all dead : and that
he died for all, that they which live should
not henceforth live unto themselves, but
unto him which died for them, and rose
again

Let all the house of Israel know assur
edly, that God hath made that same
Jesus, whom ye have crucified, both
Lord and Christ.—Who verily was foreordained before the foundation of the
world, but was manifest in these last
times for you, who by him do believe in
God.

ROM. 14. 9. Is. 53. 10, 11.—Luke 24 26.—
2 Cor 5 14, 15. Acts 2 36—1 Pet. 1 20, 21.
M

OCTOBER 15.

God is my defence.

THE LORD is my rock, and my fortress, and my deliverer ; the God of my rock ; in him will I trust he is my shield, and the horn of my salvation, my high tower, and my refuge, my saviour. —The LORD is my strength and my shield ; my heart trusted in him, and I am helped therefore my heart greatly rejoiceth ; and with my song will I praise him

When the enemy shall come in like a flood, the Spirit of the LORD shall lift up a standard against him —We may boldly say, The LORD is my helper, and I will not fear what man shall do unto me —The LORD is my light and my salvation ; whom shall I fear? the LORD is the strength of my life ; of whom shall I be afraid?

As the mountains are round about Jerusalem, so the LORD is round about his people from henceforth even for ever. —Because thou hast been my help, therefore in the shadow of thy wings will I rejoice.

For thy name's sake lead me, and guide me.

Ps 59 9. 2 Sam 22 2, 3.—Ps. 28 7 Is 59. 19.—Heb 13 6 —Ps 27 1 Ps 125 2.—
Ps. 63 7 Ps. 31 3

M

OCTOBER 16.

Not slothful in business; fervent in
spirit; serving the Lord

WHATSOEVER thy hand findeth to
do, do it with thy might; for there is
no work, nor device, nor knowledge, nor
wisdom, in the grave, whither thou goest.
—Whatsoever ye do, do it heartily, as to
the Lord, and not unto men; knowing
that of the Lord ye shall receive the
reward of the inheritance. for ye serve
the Lord Christ.—Whatsoever good thing
any man doeth, the same shall he receive
of the Lord.

I must work the works of him that sent
me, while it is day. the night cometh,
when no man can work.—Wist ye not that
I must be about my Father's business?—
The zeal of thine house hath eaten me up.

Brethren, give diligence to make your
calling and election sure; for if ye do
these things, ye shall never fall.—We
desire that every one of you do shew the
same diligence to the full assurance of
hope unto the end that ye be not slothful, but followers of them who through
faith and patience inherit the promises.
—So run, that ye may obtain

ROM 12 11. Ecc. 9 10.—Col. 3 23, 24 —
Eph 6 8 John 9 4—Luke 2 49.—John 2. 17.
2 Pet 1 10.—Heb. 6. 11, 12 —1 Cor 9 24

M

OCTOBER 17.

In thy name shall they rejoice all the
day; and in thy righteousness shall
they be exalted.

I N the LORD have I righteousness and
strength : even to him shall men
come ; and all that are incensed against
him shall be ashamed. In the LORD
shall all the seed of Israel be justified,
and shall glory.—Be glad in the LORD,
and rejoice, ye righteous · and shout for
joy, all ye that are upright in heart.

The righteousness of God without the
law is manifested, being witnessed by
the law and the prophets ; even the
righteousness of God which is by faith
of Jesus Christ unto all and upon all
them that believe. To declare . . . at
this time his righteousness : that he might
be just, and the justifier of him which
believeth in Jesus.

Whom having not seen, ye love; in
whom, though now ye see him not, yet
believing, ye rejoice with joy unspeakable and full of glory

Rejoice in the Lord alway : and again
I say, Rejoice

Ps 89 16. Is. 45. 24, 25 —Ps. 32 11 Rom. 3.
21, 22, 26. 1 Pet. 1 8. Phil. 4 4

OCTOBER 18.

One of the soldiers with a spear pierced
his side, and forthwith came there
out blood and water

BEHOLD the blood of the covenant,
which the LORD hath made with you.
—The life of the flesh is in the blood :
and I have given it to you upon the altar
to make an atonement for your souls —It
is not possible that the blood of bulls and
of goats should take away sins.

Jesus said unto them, This is my blood
of the new testament, which is shed for
many —By his own blood he entered in
once into the holy place, having obtained
eternal redemption for us.—Peace through
the blood of his cross

Ye know that ye were not redeemed
with corruptible things, as silver and
gold, . . . but with the precious blood
of Christ, as of a lamb without blemish
and without spot.

Then will I sprinkle clean water upon
you, and ye shall be clean : . . . from all
your idols, will I cleanse you —Let us
draw near with a true heart in full assurance of faith, having our hearts
sprinkled from an evil conscience.

JOHN 19 34   Ex 24 8 —Lev 17 11 —Heb.
10 4   Mark 14 24 —Heb 9 12 —Col 1 20.
1 Pet 1 18, 19   Ezek 36 25 —Heb 10 22
M

OCTOBER 19.

The Lord shall be thy confidence, and shall keep thy foot from being taken

SURELY the wrath of man shall praise thee : the remainder of wrath shalt thou restrain.—The king's heart is in the hand of the LORD, as the rivers of water : he turneth it whithersoever he will.—When a man's ways please the LORD, he maketh even his enemies to be at peace with him

I wait for the LORD, my soul doth wait, and in his word do I hope. My soul waiteth for the Lord more than they that watch for the morning : I say, more than they that watch for the morning.— I sought the LORD, and he heard me, and delivered me from all my fears

The eternal God is thy refuge, and underneath are the everlasting arms : and he shall thrust out the enemy from before thee; and shall say, Destroy them. —Blessed is the man that trusteth in the LORD, and whose hope the LORD is.

What shall we then say to these things? If God be for us, who can be against us?

Pro 3 26. Ps 76 10 —Pro 21. 1.—Pro. 16 7 Ps 130. 5, 6.—Ps 34. 4. Deut. 33. 27.— Jer. 17 7 Rom. 8 31   10 *

M

I delight in the law of God after the
inward man

O HOW love I thy law ! it is my meditation all the day.—Thy words were
found, and I did eat them ; and thy word
was unto me the joy and rejoicing of mine
heart.—I sat down under his shadow with
great delight, and his fruit was sweet to
my taste.—I have esteemed the words of
his mouth more than my necessary food.

I delight to do thy will, O my God:
yea, thy law is within my heart.—My
meat is to do the will of him that sent
me, and to finish his work.

The statutes of the LORD are right,
rejoicing the heart : the commandment
of the LORD is pure, enlightening the
eyes More to be desired are they than
gold, yea, than much fine gold sweeter
also than honey and the honeycomb.

Be ye doers of the word, and not
hearers only, deceiving your own selves.
For if any be a hearer of the word, and
not a doer, he is like unto a man beholding his natural face in a glass.

ROM 7 22. Ps 119 97 —Jer 15 16 —Cant.
2 3 —Job 23 12 Ps 40 8 —John 4 34 Ps
19 8, 10. Ja. 1 22, 23.

M

OCTOBER 21.

Of his fulness have all we received,
and grace for grace.

THIS is my beloved Son, in whom I am well pleased — Behold, what manner of love the Father hath bestowed upon us, that we should be called the sons of God.

His Son, whom he hath appointed heir of all things — If children, then heirs; heirs of God, and joint heirs with Christ, if so be that we suffer with him, that we may be also glorified to gether

I and my Father are one. The Father is in me, and I in him.—My Father, and your Father; and . . my God, and your God — I in them, and thou in me, that they may be made perfect in one.

The Church, which is his body, the fulness of him that filleth all in all

Having therefore these promises, dearly beloved, let us cleanse ourselves from all filthiness of the flesh and spirit, perfecting holiness in the fear of God

JOHN 1 16. Mat. 17 5 — 1 John 3 1 Heb. 1 2 —Rom 8 17 John 10. 30, 38.—John 20 17 —John 17. 23 Eph 1 22, 23 2 Cor 7 1.
M

OCTOBER 22.

O God, my heart is fixed

THE LORD is my light and my salvation; whom shall I fear? the LORD is the strength of my life; of whom shall I be afraid?

Thou wilt keep him in perfect peace, whose mind is stayed on thee: because he trusteth in thee —He shall not be afraid of evil tidings: his heart is fixed, trusting in the LORD. His heart is established, he shall not be afraid, until he see his desire upon his enemies.

What time I am afraid, I will trust in thee.—In the time of trouble he shall hide me in his pavilion in the secret of his tabernacle shall he hide me; he shall set me up upon a rock. And now shall mine head be lifted up above mine enemies round about me. therefore will I offer in his tabernacle sacrifices of joy: I will sing, yea, I will sing praises unto the LORD

The God of all grace, who hath called us unto his eternal glory by Christ Jesus, after that ye have suffered awhile, make you perfect, stablish, strengthen, settle you. To him be glory and dominion for ever and ever

Ps. 108 1   Ps. 27. 1.   Is. 26. 3 —Ps. 112. 7, 8.
Ps 56 3 – Ps 27. 5, 6.   1 Pet. 5 10, 11
M

OCTOBER 23.

A man's life consisteth not in the abundance of the things which he possesseth

A LITTLE that a righteous man hath is better than the riches of many wicked —Better is little with the fear of the LORD than great treasure and trouble therewith —Godliness with contentment is great gain Having food and raiment let us be therewith content

Give me neither poverty nor riches; feed me with food convenient for me lest I be full, and deny thee, and say, Who is the LORD? or lest I be poor, and steal, and take the name of my God in vain — Give us this day our daily bread

Take no thought for your life, what ye shall eat, or what ye shall drink ; nor yet for your body, what ye shall put on. Is not the life more than meat, and the body than raiment ?—When I sent you without purse, and scrip, and shoes, lacked ye anything? And they said, Nothing.— Let your conversation be without covet‧ousness: and be content with such things as ye have : for he hath said, I will never leave thee, nor forsake thee

LUKE 12. 15 Ps 37. 16 —Pro. 15 16.— 1 Tim. 6 6, 8. Pro 30 8, 9 —Mat 6. 11. Mat 6. 25.—Luke 22 35 —Heb 13 5.
M

OCTOBER 24.

*I am cast out of thy sight; yet I will look
again toward thy holy temple*

ZION said, The LORD hath forsaken
me, and my Lord hath forgotten me.
Can a woman forget her sucking child,
that she should not have compassion on
the son of her womb? yea, they may forget, yet will I not forget thee.

I forgat prosperity. And I said, My
strength and my hope is perished from
the LORD.—Awake, why sleepest thou,
O LORD? arise, cast us not off for ever.
—Why sayest thou, O Jacob, and speak-
est, O Israel, My way is hid from the
LORD, and my judgment is passed over
from my God?—In a little wrath I hid
my face from thee for a moment; but with
everlasting kindness will I have mercy on
thee, saith the LORD thy Redeemer.

Why art thou cast down, O my soul?
and why art thou disquieted within me?
hope in God : for I shall yet praise him,
who is the health of my countenance.—
We are troubled on every side, yet not
distressed ; we are perplexed, but not in
despair ; persecuted, but not forsaken ;
cast down, but not destroyed.

JON 2 4 Is. 49. 14, 15 Lam. 3. 17, 18 —
Ps 44. 23.—Is 40. 27.—Is. 54. 8
Ps 43. 5.—2 Cor. 4 8, 9.

OCTOBER 25.

Lo, I am with you alway, even unto the
end of the world.

IF two of you shall agree on earth as
touching any thing that they shall ask,
it shall be done for them of my Father
which is in heaven. For where two or
three are gathered together in my name,
there am I in the midst of them.

He that hath my commandments, and
keepeth them, he it is that loveth me:
and he that loveth me shall be loved of
my Father, and I will love him, and will
manifest myself to him.

Lord, how is it that thou wilt manifest
thyself unto us, and not unto the world?
. . . If a man love me, he will keep my
words: and my Father will love him, and
we will come unto him, and make our
abode with him

Unto him that is able to keep you from
falling, and to present you faultless before
the presence of his glory with exceeding
joy, to the only wise God our Saviour, be
glory and majesty, dominion and power,
both now and ever. Amen.

MAT. 28. 20. Mat. 18. 19, 20. John 14. 21.
John 14. 22, 23. Jude 24, 25.

M

OCTOBER 26.

The Lord reigneth.

FEAR ye not me? saith the LORD: will ye not tremble at my presence, which have placed the sand for the bound of the sea by a perpetual decree, that it cannot pass it: and though the waves thereof toss themselves, yet can they not prevail; though they roar, yet can they not pass over it?—Promotion cometh neither from the east, nor from the west, nor from the south. But God is the judge: he putteth down one, and setteth up another.

He changeth the times and the seasons: he removeth kings, and setteth up kings. he giveth wisdom unto the wise, and knowledge to them that know understanding.—Ye shall hear of wars and rumours of wars: see that ye be not troubled.

If God be for us, who can be against us?—Are not two sparrows sold for a farthing? and one of them shall not fall on the ground without your Father. The very hairs of your head are all numbered. Fear ye not therefore, ye are of more value than many sparrows.

Ps. 99 1 Jer. 5 22 —Ps 75 6, 7 Dan. 2. 21 —Mat 24 6 Rom 8 31.—Mat 10 29-31.
M

OCTOBER 27.

Himself took our infirmities, and bare
our sicknesses.

THEN shall the priest command to take
for him that is to be cleansed two
birds alive and clean, and cedar wood,
and scarlet, and hyssop : and the priest
shall command that one of the birds be
killed in an earthen vessel over running
water . as for the living bird, he shall
take it, and the cedar wood, and the
scarlet, and the hyssop, and shall dip
them and the living bird in the blood of
the bird that was killed over the running
water . and he shall sprinkle upon him
that is to be cleansed from the leprosy
seven times, and shall pronounce him
clean, and shall let the living bird loose
into the open field.

Behold a man full of leprosy · who
seeing Jesus fell on his face, and besought
him, saying, Lord, if thou wilt, thou canst
make me clean —And Jesus, moved with
compassion, put forth his hand, and touched
him, and saith unto him, I will ; be thou
clean   And as soon as he had spoken,
immediately the leprosy departed from
him, and he was cleansed.

MAT 8 17. Lev. 14 4-7 Luke ٤ 12.—
Mark 1 41, 42

M

OCTOBER 28.

He saw that there was no man, and wondered that there was no intercessor : therefore his arm brought salvation unto him.

SACRIFICE and offering thou didst not desire : mine ears hast thou opened : burnt offering and sin offering hast thou not required. Then said I, Lo, I come : in the volume of the book it is written of me, I delight to do thy will, O my God : yea, thy law is within my heart —I lay down my life, that I might take it again No man taketh it from me, but I lay it down of myself. I have power to lay it down, and I have power to take it again.

There is no God else beside me : a just God and a Saviour ; there is none beside me. Look unto me, and be ye saved, all the ends of the earth : for I am God, and there is none else.—There is none other name under heaven given among men, whereby we must be saved

Ye know the grace of our Lord Jesus Christ, that, though he was rich, yet for your sakes he became poor, that ye through his poverty might be rich

Is 59 16   Ps. 40 6-8.—John 10. 17, 18.
Is. 45 21, 22 —Acts 4 12   2 Cor 8. 9

He is altogether lovely.

MY meditation of him shall be sweet.
—My beloved is . . . the chiefest
among ten thousand — A chief corner
stone, elect, precious: and he that believeth on him shall not be confounded.

Thou art fairer than the children of
men : grace is poured into thy lips —God
. . . hath highly exalted him, and given
him a name which is above every name.—
It pleased the Father that in him should
all fulness dwell.

Whom having not seen, ye love; in
whom, though now ye see him not, yet
believing, ye rejoice with joy unspeakable
and full of glory.

I count all things but loss, for the excellency of the knowledge of Christ Jesus
my Lord : for whom I have suffered the
loss of all things, and do count them but
dung, that I may win Christ, and be
found in him, not having mine own righteousness which is of the law, but that which
is through the faith of Christ, the righteousness which is of God by faith.

CANT. 5 16. Ps. 104 34.—Cant 5 10.—
1 Pet. 2 6 Ps 45 2 —Phil 2 9.—Col 1 19.
1 Pet 1 8. Phil 3 8, 9.
M

It is good that a man should both hope and quietly wait for the salvation of the Lord.

HATH God forgotten to be gracious? hath he in anger shut up his tender mercies?—I said in my haste, I am cut off from before thine eyes nevertheless thou heardest the voice of my supplications when I cried unto thee.

Shall not God avenge his own elect, which cry day and night unto him, though he bear long with them? I tell you that he will avenge them speedily.—Wait on the LORD, and he shall save thee —Rest in the LORD, and wait patiently for him : fret not thyself because of him who prospereth in his way, because of the man who bringeth wicked devices to pass.

Ye shall not need to fight in this battle: set yourselves, stand ye still, and see the salvation of the LORD

Let us not be weary in well doing . . . in due season we shall reap, if we faint not.—Behold, the husbandman waiteth for the precious fruit of the earth, and hath long patience for it, until he receive the early and latter rain

LAM. 3 26   Ps 77 9 —Ps. 31. 22.   Luke 18 7, 8.—Pro 20. 22 —Ps 37 7.   2 Chr. 20. 17 Gal 6 9 —Ja. 5. 7.

M

OCTOBER 31.

Not by might, nor by power, but by my
Spirit, saith the Lord of hosts

WHO hath directed the Spirit of the
LORD, or being his counsellor hath
taught him?
God hath chosen the foolish things of
the world to confound the wise ; and God
hath chosen the weak things of the world
to confound the things which are mighty ;
and base things of the world, and things
which are despised, hath God chosen,
yea, and things which are not, to bring
to nought things that are : that no flesh
should glory in his presence.

The wind bloweth where it listeth,
and thou hearest the sound thereof, but
canst not tell whence it cometh, and
whither it goeth : so is every one that is
born of the Spirit —Born not of blood,
nor of the will of the flesh, nor of the
will of man, but of God.

My Spirit remaineth among you : fear
ye not. —The battle is not your's, but
God's.

The LORD saveth not with sword and
spear : for the battle is the LORD's.

Zec. 4 6. Is. 40. 13 1 Cor 1 27 29 John 3 3.
—John 1 13. Hag 2 5 —2 Chr 20 15.
1 Sam 17 47

M

NOVEMBER 1.

Blessed is the man that heareth me,
watching daily at my gates, waiting at
the posts of my doors

BEHOLD, as the eyes of servants look
unto the hand of their masters, and
as the eyes of a maiden unto the hand of
her mistress · so our eyes wait upon the
LORD our God, until that he have mercy
upon us

A continual burnt offering throughout
your generations at the door of the tabernacle of the congregation before the
LORD where I will meet you, to speak
there unto thee —In all places where I
record my name I will come unto thee,
and I will bless thee

Where two or three are gathered together in my name, there am I in the
midst of them

The hour cometh, and now is, when
the true worshippers shall worship the
Father in spirit and in truth : for the
Father seeketh such to worship him.
God is a Spirit : and they that worship
him must worship him in spirit and in
truth.

Praying always with all prayer and
supplication in the Spirit

Pro 3 34   Ps. 123. 2.   Ex 29 42 —Ex 20. 24
   Mat 18 20.   John 4 22. 24   Eph 6 18.
M

NOVEMBER 2.

Ever follow that which is good

FOR even hereunto were ye called : because Christ also suffered for us, leaving us an example, that ye should follow his steps : who did no sin, neither was guile found in his mouth : who, when he was reviled, reviled not again ; . . but committed himself to him that judgeth righteously.—Consider him that endured such contradiction of sinners against himself, lest ye be wearied and faint in your minds

Let us lay aside every weight, and the sin which doth so easily beset us, and let us run with patience the race that is set before us, looking unto Jesus the author and finisher of our faith ; who for the joy that was set before him endured the cross, . . . and is set down at the right hand of the throne of God.

Finally, brethren, whatsoever things are true, whatsoever things are honest, whatsoever things are just, whatsoever things are pure, whatsoever things are lovely, whatsoever things are of good report ; if there be any virtue, and if there be any praise, think on these things

1 THES 5 15   1 Pet. 2 21-23 —Heb 12 3
Heb 12 1, 1 Phil 4 8.

M

NOVEMBER 3.

The ways of the Lord are right, and the just shall walk in them but the transgressors shall fall therein.

UNTO you . . . which believe he is precious : but unto them which be disobedient, . . . a stone of stumbling, and a rock of offence —The way of the LORD is strength to the upright : but destruc tion shall be to the workers of iniquity.

He that hath ears to hear, let him hear.—Whoso is wise, and will observe these things, even they shall understand the lovingkindness of the LORD —The light of the body is the eye : if therefore thine eye be single, thy whole body shall be full of light. But if thine eye be evil, thy whole body shall be full of darkness —If any man will do his will, he shall know of the doctrine, whether it be of God —Whosoever hath, to him shall be given, and he shall have more abundance.

He that is of God heareth God's words · ye therefore hear them not, because ye are not of God —Ye will not come unto me, that ye might have life —My sheep hear my voice, and I know them, and they follow me.

Hos 14 9   1 Pet 2. 7, 8 —Pro. 10 29
Mat 11. 15 —Ps 107 43 —Mat 6 22 —
John 7. 17 —Mat 13 12 John 8 47 —
John 5 40 —John 10 27

M

NOVEMBER 4.

Now for a season, if need be, ye are in heaviness through manifold temptations.

BELOVED, think it not strange concerning the fiery trial which is to try you, as though some strange thing happened unto you ; but rejoice, inasmuch as ye are partakers of Christ's sufferings ; that, when his glory shall be revealed, ye may be glad also with exceeding joy. — The exhortation . . . speaketh unto you as unto children, My son, despise not thou the chastening of the Lord, nor faint when thou art rebuked of him. — Now no chastening for the present seemeth to be joyous, but grievous : nevertheless afterward it yieldeth the peaceable fruit of righteousness unto them which are exercised thereby.

We have not a high priest which cannot be touched with the feeling of our infirmities ; but was in all points tempted like as we are, yet without sin — For in that he himself hath suffered being tempted, he is able to succour them that are tempted. — God is faithful, who will not suffer you to be tempted above that ye are able.

1 Pet 1 6. 1 Pet 4 12, 13 — Heb 12 5 —
Heb 12. 11. Heb 4 15 — Heb 2 18 —
1 Cor. 10 13

M

NOVEMBER 5.

Take thou also unto thee principal spices,
and thou shalt make it an oil of
holy ointment

UPON man's flesh shall it not be poured, neither shall ye make any other like it, after the composition of it : it is holy, and it shall be holy unto you. —One Spirit. —Diversities of gifts, but the same Spirit

Thy God hath anointed thee with the oil of gladness above thy fellows —God anointed Jesus of Nazareth with the Holy Ghost and with power —God giveth not the Spirit by measure unto him

Of his fulness have all we received — As the same anointing teacheth you of all things, and is truth, and is no lie, and even as it hath taught you, ye shall abide in him — He which . . hath anointed us, is God , who hath also sealed us, and given the earnest of the Spirit in our hearts

The fruit of the Spirit is love, joy, peace, longsuffering, gentleness, good· ness, faith, meekness, temperance : against such there is no law

Ex 30. 23, 25   Ex 30 32 —Eph 4 4 —
1 Cor 12 4   Ps 45 7 —Acts 10 38 —John 3 34.
John 1 16 —1 John 2 27 —2 Cor 1 21, 22.—
Gal 5 22, 23
M

When Christ, who is our life, shall appear,
then shall ye also appear with him
in glory.

I AM the resurrection, and the life : he
that believeth in me, though he were
dead, yet shall he live —God hath given
to us eternal life, and this life is in his
Son. He that hath the Son hath life ;
and he that hath not the Son of God
hath not life.

The Lord himself shall descend from
heaven with a shout, with the voice of
the archangel, and with the trump of
God : and the dead in Christ shall rise
first : then we which are alive and re
main shall be caught up together with
them in the clouds, to meet the Lord in
the air : and so shall we ever be with the
Lord. Wherefore comfort one another
with these words.—When he shall appear,
we shall be like him ; for we shall see
him as he is.—It is sown in dishonour ;
it is raised in glory : it is sown in weak·
ness ; it is raised in power.

If I go and prepare a place for you, I
will come again, and receive you unto
myself ; that where I am, there ye may
be also.

Col. 3. 4   John 11. 25.—1 John 5 11, 12.
1 Thes. 4 16 18.—1 John 3. 2.   1 Cor. 15. 43.
John 14. 3

M

NOVEMBER 7.

Oh that men would praise the Lord for
his goodness, and for his wonderful
works to the children of men

O TASTE and see that the LORD is
good : blessed is the man that
trusteth in him.—How great is thy goodness, which thou hast laid up for them
that fear thee !

This people have I formed for myself ;
they shall shew forth my praise —Having predestinated us unto the adoption of
children by Jesus Christ to himself, according to the good pleasure of his will,
to the praise of the glory of his grace,
wherein he hath made us accepted in the
beloved   That we should be to the
praise of his glory, who first trusted in
Christ.

How great is his goodness, and how
great is his beauty !—The LORD is good
to all : and his tender mercies are over
all his works.   All thy works shall praise
thee, O LORD ; and thy saints shall bless
thee   They shall speak of the glory of
thy kingdom, and talk of thy power ; to
make known to the sons of men his
mighty acts, and the glorious majesty of
his kingdom

Ps 107. 8.   Ps 34 8 —Ps 31 19.   Is 43 21 —
Eph 1. 5, 6, 12.   Zec 9 17 —Ps 145 9 12
M

NOVEMBER 8.

Let us, who are of the day, be sober, putting on the breastplate of faith and love; and for an helmet, the hope of salvation.

GIRD up the loins of your mind, be sober, and hope to the end for the grace that is to be brought unto you at the revelation of Jesus Christ —Stand therefore, having your loins girt about with truth, and having on the breastplate of righteousness; above all, taking the shield of faith, wherewith ye shall be able to quench all the fiery darts of the wicked And take the helmet of salvation, and the sword of the Spirit, which is the word of God.

He will swallow up death in victory; and the Lord GOD will wipe away tears from off all faces; and the rebuke of his people shall he take away from off all the earth : for the LORD hath spoken it. And it shall be said in that day, Lo, this is our God; we have waited for him, and he will save us : this is the LORD; we have waited for him,' we will be glad and rejoice in his salvation.

Faith is the substance of things hoped for, the evidence of things not seen.

1 THES 5. 8   1 Pet 1 13 —Eph 6 14, 16, 17.
    Is 25 8, 9   Heb 11 1.

M

I have laid help upon one that is
mighty; I have exalted one chosen
out of the people

I, EVEN I, am the LORD; and beside
me there is no saviour.—There is one
God, and one mediator between God
and men, the man Christ Jesus.—There
is none other name under heaven given
among men, whereby we must be saved.

The mighty God.—Who made himself
of no reputation, and took upon him the
form of a servant, and was made in the
likeness of men: and being found in
fashion as a man, he humbled himself,
and became obedient unto death, even
the death of the cross. Wherefore God
also hath highly exalted him, and given
him a name which is above every name
—We see Jesus, who was made a little
lower than the angels for the suffering of
death, crowned with glory and honour;
that he by the grace of God should taste
death for every man.—Forasmuch . . .
as the children are partakers of flesh and
blood, he also himself likewise took part
of the same.

Ps 89 19 Is 43 11.—1 Tim 2 5.—Acts 4 12
Is 9 6.—Phil 2 7-9.—Heb 2 9.—Heb. 2 14.
M

Fruitful in every good work, and
increasing in the knowledge of God

I BESEECH you, . . . brethren, by
the mercies of God, that ye present
your bodies a living sacrifice, holy, acceptable unto God, which is your reasonable service. And be not conformed to
this world : but be ye transformed by
the renewing of your mind, that ye may
prove what is that good, and acceptable,
and perfect, will of God —As ye have
yielded your members servants to uncleanness and to iniquity unto iniquity ;
even so now yield your members servants
to righteousness unto holiness —In Christ
Jesus neither circumcision availeth any
thing, nor uncircumcision, but a new
creature. And as many as walk according to this rule, peace be on them, and
mercy.

Herein is my Father glorified, that
ye bear much fruit ; so shall ye be my
disciples —Ye have not chosen me, but
I have chosen you, and ordained you,
that ye should go and bring forth fruit,
and that your fruit should remain

Col. 1. 10. Rom. 12. 1, 2.—Rom. 6. 19.—
Gal. 6. 15, 16. John 15. 8.—John 15. 16
M

He led them on safely

I LEAD in the way of righteousness, in the midst of the paths of judgment.

Behold, I send an Angel before thee, to keep thee in the way, and to bring thee into the place which I have prepared — In all their affliction he was afflicted, and the angel of his presence saved them : in his love and in his pity he redeemed them ; and he bare them, and carried them all the days of old.

They got not the land in possession by their own sword, neither did their own arm save them : but thy right hand, and thine arm, and the light of thy countenance, because thou hadst a favour unto them. —So didst thou lead thy people, to make thyself a glorious name

Lead me, O LORD, in thy righteousness because of mine enemies ; make thy way straight before my face —O send out thy light and thy truth : let them lead me ; let them bring me unto thy holy hill, and to thy tabernacles Then will I go unto the altar of God, unto God my exceeding joy : yea, upon the harp will I praise thee, O God.

Ps 78 53   Pro 8 20.   Ex. 23 20 —Is 63 9
Ps 44 3 —Is 63 14   Ps 5 8 —Ps 43 3 4
M

NOVEMBER 12.

Godly sorrow worketh repentance not to be repented of

PETER remembered the word of Jesus, which said unto him, Before the cock crow, thou shalt deny me thrice. And he went out, and wept bitterly —If we confess our sins, he is faithful and just to forgive us our sins, and to cleanse us from all unrighteousness.—The blood of Jesus Christ his Son cleanseth us from all sin

Mine iniquities have taken hold upon me, so that I am not able to look up; they are more than the hairs of my head : therefore my heart faileth me Be pleased, O LORD, to deliver me : O LORD, make haste to help me.

Turn thou to thy God : keep mercy and judgment, and wait on thy God continually

The sacrifices of God are a broken spirit : a broken and a contrite heart, O God, thou wilt not despise.—He healeth the broken in heart —He hath shewed thee, O man, what is good : and what doth the LORD require of thee, but to do justly, and to love mercy, and to walk humbly with thy God ?

2 COR. 7. 10 Mat. 26 75 —1 John 1 9 —
1 John 1 7 Ps 40. 12, 13 Hos 12 6
 Ps 51 17 —Ps. 147 3 —Mic 6 8.

M   I T

Christ loved the church, and gave himself for it; that he might sanctify and cleanse it with the washing of water by the word.

WALK in love, as Christ also hath loved us, and hath given himself for us an offering and a sacrifice to God for a sweetsmelling savour.

Being born again, not of corruptible seed, but of incorruptible, by the word of God, which liveth and abideth for ever.—Sanctify them through thy truth: thy word is truth.—Except a man be born of water and of the Spirit, he cannot enter into the kingdom of God.

Not by works of righteousness which we have done, but according to his mercy he saved us, by the washing of regeneration, and renewing of the Holy Ghost.—Thy word hath quickened me.

The law of the LORD is perfect, converting the soul: the testimony of the LORD is sure, making wise the simple. The statutes of the LORD are right, rejoicing the heart: the commandment of the LORD is pure, enlightening the eyes

EPH 5. 25, 26. Eph. 5 2. 1 Pet 1 23.—John 17. 17.—John 3 5. Tit 3 5.—Ps 119. 50. Ps 19. 7, 8

M

Thou art my help and my deliverer;
make no tarrying, O my God.

THE steps of a good man are ordered
by the LORD : and he delighteth in
his way.   Though he fall, he shall not be
utterly cast down   for the LORD upholdeth him with his hand —In the fear of
the LORD is strong confidence   and his
children shall have a place of refuge.

Who art thou, that thou shouldest be
afraid of a man that shall die, and of the
son of man which shall be made as grass;
and forgettest the LORD thy maker?

I am with thee to delivei thee —Be
strong and of a good courage, fear not,
nor be afraid of them : for the LORD thy
God, he it is that doth go with thee ; he
will not fail thee, nor forsake thee.

I will sing of thy power , yea, I will
sing aloud of thy mercy in the morning :
for thou hast been my defence and refuge
in the day of my trouble.—Thou art my
hiding place ; thou shalt preserve me
from trouble; thou shalt compass me
about with songs of deliverance.

Ps 40. 17   Ps 37 23, 24 —Pro 14 26.
Is 51 12, 13   Jer. 1 8 —Deut. 31. 6.
Ps 59. 16.—Ps. 32. 7

M

NOVEMBER 15.

God is faithful, by whom ye were
called unto the fellowship of his Son
Jesus Christ our Lord

LET us hold fast the profession of our
faith without wavering; for he is
faithful that promised —God hath said,
I will dwell in them, and walk in them;
and I will be their God, and they shall
be my people.—Truly our fellowship is
with the Father, and with his Son Jesus
Christ —Rejoice, inasmuch as ye are
partakers of Christ's sufferings; that,
when his glory shall be revealed, ye may
be glad also with exceeding joy.

That Christ may dwell in your hearts
by faith; that ye, being rooted and
grounded in love, may be able to comprehend with all saints what is the
breadth, and length, and depth, and
height; and to know the love of Christ,
which passeth knowledge, that ye might
be filled with all the fulness of God.

Whosoever shall confess that Jesus is
the Son of God, God dwelleth in him,
and he in God.—And he that keepeth
his commandments dwelleth in him, and
he in him.

1 COR. 1 9   Heb 10 23 —2 Cor 6 16.—
1 John 1 3 —1 Pet 4 13   Eph 3 17-19
1 John 4 15 —1 Johr 3 24.

M

NOVEMBER 16.

Sanctify them through thy truth: thy
word is truth.

NOW ye are clean through the word
which I have spoken unto you.—
Let the word of Christ dwell in you
richly in all wisdom.

Wherewithal shall a young man cleanse
his way? by taking heed thereto according to thy word. With my whole heart
have I sought thee : O let me not wander
from thy commandments.

When wisdom entereth into thine heart,
and knowledge is pleasant unto thy soul :
discretion shall preserve thee, understanding shall keep thee.

My foot hath held his steps, his way
have I kept, and not declined Neither
have I gone back from the commandment
of his lips; I have esteemed the words of
his mouth more than my necessary food.
—I have more understanding than all my
teachers: for thy testimonies are my
meditation.—If ye continue in my word,
then are ye my disciples indeed; and ye
shall know the truth, and the truth shall
make you free.

JOHN 17. 17. John 15. 3 —Col. 3 16. Ps. 119.
9, 10. Pro. 2. 10, 11. Job 23 12.—Ps. 119. 99.
—John 8. 31 32.

M

Thy thoughts are very deep

WE . . . do not cease to pray for you, and to desire that ye might be filled with the knowledge of his will in all wisdom and spiritual understanding.— That ye, being rooted and grounded in love, may be able to comprehend with all saints what is the breadth, and length, and depth, and height ; and to know the love of Christ, which passeth knowledge, that ye might be filled with all the fulness of God.

O the depth of the riches both of the wisdom and knowledge of God ! how unsearchable are his judgments, and his ways past finding out !—My thoughts are not your thoughts, neither are your ways my ways, saith the LORD. For as the heavens are higher than the earth, so are my ways higher than your ways, and my thoughts than your thoughts.—Many, O LORD my God, are thy wonderful works which thou hast done, and thy thoughts which are to us-ward . they cannot be reckoned up in order unto thee : if I would declare and speak of them, they are more than can be numbered.

Ps. 92. 5. Col. 1. 9.—Eph. 3. 17-19. Rom. 11. 33—Is. 55. 8, 9.—Ps. 40. 5

NOVEMBER 18.

He stayeth his rough wind in the day of the east wind

LET us fall now into the hand of the LORD; for his mercies are great.—I am with thee, saith the LORD, to save thee : .. I will correct thee in measure, and will not leave thee altogether un·punished.—He will not always chide : neither will he keep his anger for ever. He hath not dealt with us after our sins ; nor rewarded us according to our iniquities. For he knoweth our frame; he remembereth that we are dust.—I will spare them, as a man spareth his own son that serveth him.

God is faithful, who will not suffer you to be tempted above that ye are able ; but will with the temptation also make a way to escape, that ye may be able to bear it.—Satan hath desired to have you, that he may sift you as wheat : but I have prayed for thee, that thy faith fail not

Thou hast been a strength to the poor, a strength to the needy in his distress, a refuge from the storm, a shadow from the heat, when the blast of the terrible ones is as a storm against the wall

Is 27. 8. 2 Sam. 24 14.—Jer. 30. 11.— Ps. 103 9, 10, 14.—Mal. 3 17. 1 Cor. 10. 13.—Luke 22 31, 32. Is. 25. 4

M

By their fruits ye shall know them.

LITTLE children, let no man deceive you : he that doeth righteousness is righteous, even as he is righteous.— Doth a fountain send forth at the same place sweet water and bitter? Can the fig tree, my brethren, bear olive berries? either a vine, figs? so can no fountain both yield salt water and fresh. Who is a wise man and endued with knowledge among you? let him shew out of a good conversation his works with meekness of wisdom.—Having your conversation honest among the Gentiles : that, whereas they speak against you as evildoers, they may by your good works, which they shall behold, glorify God in the day of visitation.

Either make the tree good, and his fruit good ; or else make the tree corrupt, and his fruit corrupt : for the tree is known by his fruit.—A good man out of the good treasure of the heart bringeth forth good things : and an evil man out of the evil treasure bringeth forth evil things.

What could have been done more to my vineyard, that I have not done in it?

MAT. 7. 20. 1 John 3. 7.—Ja. 3. 11-13.—1 Pet. 2. 12. Mat. 12. 33.—Mat. 12. 35. Is. 5. 4.
M

NOVEMBER 20.

When I sit in darkness, the Lord shall
be a light unto me.

WHEN thou passest through the waters,
I will be with thee ; and through
the rivers, they shall not overflow thee :
when thou walkest through the fire,
thou shalt not be burned ; neither shall
the flame kindle upon thee. For I am
the LORD thy God, the Holy One of
Israel, thy Saviour —I will bring the
blind by a way that they knew not ; I
will lead them in paths that they have
not known : I will make darkness light
before them, and crooked things straight.
These things will I do unto them, and
not forsake them.

Yea, though I walk through the valley
of the shadow of death, I will fear no
evil : for thou art with me ; thy rod and
thy staff they comfort me.—What time
I am afraid, I will trust in thee. In God
I will praise his word, in God I have
put my trust ; I will not fear what flesh
can do unto me.—The LORD is my light
and my salvation ; whom shall I fear ?
the LORD is the strength of my life ; of
whom shall I be afraid ?

Mic 7 8. Is 43 2, 3 —Is. 42 16. Ps 23 4
—Ps 56 3, 4 —Ps. 27. 1

M   II *

NOVEMBER 21.

Him that cometh to me I will in no wise cast out.

IT shall come to pass, when he crieth unto me, that I will hear; for I am gracious.—I will not cast them away, neither will I abhor them, to destroy them utterly, and to break my covenant with them : for I am the LORD their God.—I will remember my covenant with thee in the days of thy youth, and I will establish unto thee an everlasting covenant.

Come now, and let us reason together, saith the LORD. Though your sins be as scarlet, they shall be as white as snow; though they be red like crimson, they shall be as wool —Let the wicked forsake his way, and the unrighteous man his thoughts : and let him return unto the LORD, and he will have mercy upon him; and to our God, for he will abundantly pardon.—Lord, remember me when thou comest into thy kingdom. And Jesus said unto him, Verily I say unto thee, To day shalt thou be with me in paradise.

A bruised reed shall he not break, and the smoking flax shall he not quench.

JOHN 6. 37 Ex. 22. 27.—Lev 26 44.—
Ezek. 16. 60. Is 1. 18 —Is. 55. 7.—
Luke 23. 42, 43 Is 42. 3.

M

NOVEMBER 22.

Praying in the Holy Ghost.

GOD is a Spirit · and they that worship him must worship him in spirit and in truth.—We . . have access by one Spirit unto the Father.

O my Father, if it be possible, let this cup pass from me : nevertheless not as I will, but as thou wilt.

The Spirit - - - helpeth our infirmities : for we know not what we should pray for as we ought . but the Spirit itself maketh intercession for us with groanings which cannot be uttered. And he that searcheth the hearts knoweth what is the mind of the Spirit, because he maketh intercession for the saints according to the will of God.—This is the confidence that we have in him, that, if we ask any thing according to his will, he heareth us.—When he, the Spirit of truth, is come, he will guide you into all truth.

Praying always with all prayer and supplication in the Spirit, and watching thereunto with all perseverance and supplication for all saints.

JUDE 20. John 4. 24.—Eph. 2. 18. Mat. 26. 39. Rom. 8. 26, 27.—1 John 5. 14.—John 16. 13.
Eph. 6. 18.

M

NOVEMBER 23.

*Whoso hearkeneth unto me shall dwell
safely, and shall be quiet from
fear of evil.*

LORD, thou hast been our dwelling
place in all generations.—He that
dwelleth in the secret place of the most
High shall abide under the shadow of
the Almighty.—His truth shall be thy
shield and buckler.

Your life is hid with Christ in God.—
He that toucheth you toucheth the apple
of his eye.—Fear ye not, stand still, and
see the salvation of the LORD. The
LORD shall fight for you, and ye shall
hold your peace.—God is our refuge and
strength, a very present help in trouble.

Jesus spake unto them, saying, Be of
good cheer; it is I; be not afraid.—
Why are ye troubled? and why do
thoughts arise in your hearts? Behold
my hands and my feet, that it is I myself: handle me, and see; for a spirit
hath not flesh and bones, as ye see me
have.—I know whom I have believed,
and am persuaded that he is able to
keep that which I have committed unto
him against that day.

PRO 1 33   Ps. 90. 1.—Ps 91 1.—Ps 91. 4.
Col 3 3.—Zec. 2. 8.—Ex 14 13, 14.—Ps 46 1
Mat 14. 27.—Luke 24 38, 39.—2 Tim 1 12
M

My mother and my brethren are these
which hear the word of God, and do it.

BOTH he that sanctifieth and they who
are sanctified are all of one : for
which cause he is not ashamed to call
them brethren : saying, I will declare thy
name unto my brethren , in the midst of
the church will I sing praise unto thee.—
In Jesus Christ neither circumcision availeth any thing, nor uncircumcision ; but
faith which worketh by love.—Ye are my
friends, if ye do whatsoever I command
you.—Blessed are they that hear the word
of God, and keep it.

Not every one that saith unto me, Lord,
Lord, shall enter into the kingdom of
heaven ; but he that doeth the will of my
Father which is in heaven —My meat is
to do the will of him that sent me.

If we say that we have fellowship with
him, and walk in darkness, we lie, and
do not the truth —Whoso keepeth his
word, in him verily is the love of God
perfected . hereby know we that we are
in him.

LUKE 8 21. Heb 2. 11, 12 —Gal. 5 6 —John
15 14 —Luke 11. 28. Mat 7 21 —John 4 34.
1 John 1. 6 —1 John 2. 5.

M

NOVEMBER 25.

Being made free from sin, ye became the
servants of righteousness

YE cannot serve God and Mammon.
—When ye were the servants of sin,
ye were free from righteousness. What
fruit had ye then in those things whereof
ye are now ashamed? for the end of those
things is death But now being made
free from sin, and become servants to
God, ye have your fruit unto holiness, and
the end everlasting life.

Christ is the end of the law for right.
eousness to every one that believeth.

If any man serve me, let him follow
me ; and where I am, there shall also my
servant be : if any man serve me, him
will my Father honour.—Take my yoke
upon you, and learn of me : for I am
meek and lowly in heart : and ye shall
find rest unto your souls For my yoke
is easy, and my burden is light.

O LORD our God, other lords beside
thee have had dominion over us ; but by
thee only will we make mention of thy
name.—I will run the way of thy commandments, when thou shalt enlarge my
heart.

ROM. 6. 18. Mat 6 24 —Rom. 6. 19-22
Rom 10. 4 John 12. 26.—Mat. 11 29, 30.
Is. 26 13 —Ps 119. 32.

M

NOVEMBER 26.

The Lord delighteth in thee

THUS saith the LORD that created thee, . . . Fear not : for I have redeemed thee. I have called thee by thy name ; thou art mine—Can a woman forget her sucking child, that she should not have compassion on the son of her womb ? yea, they may forget, yet will I not forget thee Behold, I have graven thee upon the palms of mine hands : thy walls are continually before me.

The steps of a good man are ordered by the LORD : and he delighteth in his way.—My delights were with the sons of men.—The LORD taketh pleasure in them that fear him, in those that hope in his mercy.—They shall be mine, saith the LORD of hosts, in that day when I make up my jewels and I will spare them, as a man spareth his own son that serveth him.

You, that were sometime alienated and enemies in your mind by wicked works, yet now hath he reconciled in the body of his flesh through death, to present you holy and unblameable and unreproveable in his sight.

Is. 62. 4. Is. 43 1.—Is. 49. 15, 16. Ps 37. 23.
—Pro. 8. 31 —Ps. 147 11.—Mal. 3 17.
Col 1. 21, 22

M

NOVEMBER 27.

I SAW . . . the Lord sitting upon a
throne, high and lifted up, and his
train filled the temple. Above it stood
the seraphims And one cried unto
another, and said, Holy, holy, holy, is
the LORD of hosts; the whole earth is
full of his glory.—These things said Esaias,
when he saw his glory, and spake of him.
—Upon the likeness of the throne was
the likeness . . . of a man above upon it.
As the appearance of the bow that is in
the cloud in the day of rain, so was the
appearance of the brightness round about.
This was the appearance of the likeness
of the glory of the LORD.

I beseech thee, shew me thy glory.
And he said, Thou canst not see my face :
for there shall no man see me, and live.—
No man hath seen God at any time ; the
only begotten Son, which is in the bosom
of the Father, he hath declared him.—
God, who commanded the light to shine
out of darkness, hath shined in our hearts,
to give the light of the knowledge of the
glory of God in the face of Jesus Christ.

JOHN 17 22. Is. 6 1-3.—John 12 41.—Ezek. 1.
26, 28 Ex 33 18, 20.—John 1. 18 —2 Cor. 4. 6.
M

NOVEMBER 28.

As the body without the spirit is dead, so faith without works is dead also.

NOT every one that saith, . . . Lord, Lord, shall enter into the kingdom of heaven; but he that doeth the will of my Father which is in heaven —Holiness, without which no man shall see the Lord. —Add to your faith virtue; and to virtue knowledge; and to knowledge temperance; and to temperance patience; and to patience godliness; and to godliness brotherly kindness; and to brotherly kindness charity. For if these things be in you, and abound, they make you that ye shall neither be barren nor unfruitful in the knowledge of our Lord Jesus Christ. But he that lacketh these things is blind, and cannot see afar off, and hath forgotten that he was purged from his old sins. Wherefore the rather, brethren, give diligence to make your calling and election sure: for if ye do these things, ye shall never fall.

By grace are ye saved through faith; and that not of yourselves; it is the gift of God.

JA 2 26. Mat. 7. 21.—Heb. 12. 14 —2 Pet. 1. 5-9. Eph. 2. 8.

M

We shall be satisfied with the goodness of thy house

ONE thing have I desired of the LORD, that will I seek after ; that I may dwell in the house of the LORD all the days of my life, to behold the beauty of the LORD, and to enquire in his temple.

Blessed are they which do hunger and thirst after righteousness · for they shall be filled.—He hath filled the hungry with good things ; and the rich he hath sent empty away

He satisfieth the longing soul, and filleth the hungry soul with goodness.—I am the bread of life : he that cometh to me shall never hunger ; and he that believeth on me shall never thirst

How excellent is thy lovingkindness, O God ! therefore the children of men put their trust under the shadow of thy wings.   They shall be abundantly satisfied with the fatness of thy house ; and thou shalt make them drink of the river of thy pleasures.   For with thee is the fountain of life : in thy light shall we see light.

Ps. 65 4   Ps 27 4.   Mat. 5. 6.—Luke 1. 53
Ps. 107. 0.—John 6. 35.   Ps. 36. 7-9
M

NOVEMBER 30.

The Lord of peace himself give you peace
always by all means   The Lord be with
you all

PEACE, from him which is, and which
was, and which is to come.—The
peace of God, which passeth all understanding, shall keep your hearts and minds
through Christ Jesus.

Jesus himself stood in the midst of them,
and saith unto them, Peace be unto you.
—Peace I leave with you, my peace I
give unto you : not as the world giveth,
give I unto you   Let not your heart be
troubled, neither let it be afraid.

The Comforter . . even the Spirit of
truth.—The fruit of the Spirit is love, joy,
peace —The Spirit itself beareth witness
with our spirit, that we are the children
of God

My presence shall go with thee, and I
will give thee rest.   And he said unto
him, If thy presence go not with me,
carry us not up hence.   For wherein shall
it be known here that I and thy people
have found grace in thy sight ? is it not
in that thou goest with us ?

2 THES. 3. 16.   Rev. 1. 4.—Phil. 4. 7.   Luke
24. 36.—John 14. 27   John 15. 26.—Gal 5. 22.—
Rom. 8. 16   Ex. 33. 14-16.

M

DECEMBER 1.

A man shall be as a hiding place from the wind, and a covert from the tempest

FORASMUCH .. as the children are partakers of flesh and blood, he also himself likewise took part of the same.—The man that is my fellow, saith the LORD of hosts.—I and my Father are one.

He that dwelleth in the secret place of the most High shall abide under the shadow of the Almighty.—There shall be a tabernacle for a shadow in the daytime from the heat, and for a place of refuge, and for a covert from storm and from rain.—The LORD is thy shade upon thy right hand. The sun shall not smite thee by day, nor the moon by night.

When my heart is overwhelmed : lead me to the rock that is higher than I — Thou art my hiding place; thou shalt preserve me from trouble.—Thou hast been a strength to the poor, a strength to the needy in his distress, a refuge from the storm, a shadow from the heat, when the blast of the terrible ones is as a storm against the wall.

Is 32. 2.   Heb 2. 17.—Zec. 13. 7.—John 10 30.
Ps. 91. 1.—Is 4 6—Ps 121 5, 6. Ps 61. 2.—
Ps 32. 7.—Is 25 4
M

DECEMBER 2.

Ye have an unction from the Holy One, and ye know all things

GOD anointed Jesus of Nazareth with the Holy Ghost and with power.—It pleased the Father that in him should all fulness dwell.—Of his fulness have all we received, and grace for grace.

Thou anointest my head with oil.—The anointing which ye have received of him abideth in you, and ye need not that any man teach you : but as the same anointing teacheth you of all things, and is truth, and is no lie, and even as it hath taught you, ye shall abide in him.

The Comforter, which is the Holy Ghost, whom the Father will send in my name, he shall teach you all things, and bring all things to your remembrance, whatsoever I have said unto you

The Spirit also helpeth our infirmities : for we know not what we should pray for as we ought . but the Spirit itself maketh intercession for us with groanings which cannot be uttered.

1 JOHN 2. 20. Acts 10. 38.—Col. 1. 19.—John 1 16. Ps. 23. 5.—1 John 2. 27 John 14 26. Rom 8 26

M

DECEMBER 3.

I would seek unto God, and unto God would I commit my cause.

IS any thing too hard for the LORD?—Commit thy way unto the LORD; trust also in him ; and he shall bring it to pass.—Be careful for nothing ; but in every thing by prayer and supplication, with thanksgiving, let your requests be made known unto God.—Casting all your care upon him, for he careth for you.

Hezekiah received the letter from the hand of the messengers, and read it : and Hezekiah went up unto the house of the LORD, and spread it before the LORD. And Hezekiah prayed unto the LORD.

It shall come to pass, that before they call, I will answer ; and while they are yet speaking, I will hear.—The effectual fervent prayer of a righteous man availeth much.

I love the LORD, because he hath heard my voice and my supplications. Because he hath inclined his ear unto me, therefore will I call upon him as long as I live.

JOB 5. 8. Gen. 18. 14.—Ps. 37. 5.—Phil. 4. 6.—1 Pet. 5. 7. Is. 37. 14, 15 Is. 65. 24.—Ja. 5. 16. Ps. 116. 1, 2.

M

DECEMBER 4.

Where shall wisdom be found?

IF any of you lack wisdom, let him ask of God, that giveth to all men liberally, and upbraideth not ; and it shall be given him. But let him ask in faith, nothing wavering —Trust in the LORD with all thine heart ; and lean not unto thine own understanding. In all thy ways acknowledge him, and he shall direct thy paths —The only wise God.— Be not wise in thine own eyes ; fear the Lord, and depart from evil.

Ah, Lord GOD ! behold, I cannot speak : for I am a child But the LORD said unto me, Say not, I am a child · for thou shalt go to all that I shall send thee, and whatsoever I command thee thou shalt speak Be not afraid of their faces : for I am with thee to deliver thee, saith the LORD.

Whatsoever ye shall ask the Father in my name, he will give it you. Hitherto nave ye asked nothing in my name : ask, and ye shall receive, that your joy may be full.—All things whatsoever ye shall ask in prayer, believing, ye shall receive.

JOB 28. 12. Ja. 1 5, 6 —Pro. 3 5, 6.—1 Tim. 1. 17 —Pro. 3. 7. Jer. 1. 6-8 John 16. 23, 24. —Mat. 21 22.

M

DECEMBER 5.

It is good for me that I have been afflicted; that I might learn thy statutes

THOUGH he were a Son, yet learned he obedience by the things which he suffered.—We suffer with him, that we may be also glorified together For I reckon that the sufferings of this present time are not worthy to be compared with the glory which shall be revealed in us.

He knoweth the way that I take · when he hath tried me, I shall come forth as gold. My foot hath held his steps, his way have I kept, and not declined.

Thou shalt remember all the way which the LORD thy God led thee these forty years in the wilderness, to humble thee, and to prove thee, to know what was in thine heart, whether thou wouldest keep his commandments, or no Thou shalt also consider in thine heart, that, as a man chasteneth his son, so the LORD thy God chasteneth thee. Therefore thou shalt keep the commandments of the LORD thy God, to walk in his ways, and to fear him.

Ps 119. 71 Heb 5. 8 —Rom 8 17, 18
Job 23 10, 11 Deut 8 2, 5. 6.
M

It is God which worketh in you.

NOT that we are sufficient of ourselves to think any thing as of ourselves; but our sufficiency is of God.—A man can receive nothing, except it be given him from heaven —No man can come to me, except the Father which hath sent me draw him . and I will raise him up at the last day —And I will give them one heart, and one way, that they may fear me for ever.

Do not err, my beloved brethren. Every good gift and every perfect gift is from above, and cometh down from the Father of lights, with whom is no variableness, neither shadow of turning Of his own will begat he us with the word of truth, that we should be a kind of first-fruits of his creatures.

For we are his workmanship, created in Christ Jesus unto good works, which God hath before ordained that we should walk in them.

LORD, thou wilt ordain peace for us: for thou also hast wrought all our works in us.

PHIL 2 13 2 Cor 3. 5.—John 3. 27 —John 6. 44 —Jer. 32. 39 Ja. 1. 16-18. Eph 2 10. Is. 26. 12

M

DECEMBER 7.

He hath made him to be sin for us, who knew no sin; that we might be made the righteousness of God in him.

THE LORD hath laid on him the iniquity of us all —Who his own self bare our sins in his own body on the tree, that we, being dead to sins, should live unto righteousness : by whose stripes ye were healed.—As by one man's disobedience many were made sinners, so by the obedience of one shall many be made righteous.

After that the kindness and love of God our Saviour toward man appeared, not by works of righteousness which we have done, but according to his mercy he saved us, by the washing of regeneration, and renewing of the Holy Ghost ; which he shed on us abundantly through Jesus Christ our Saviour ; that being justified by his grace, we should be made heirs according to the hope of eternal life.— There is therefore now no condemnation to them which are in Christ Jesus, who walk not after the flesh, but after the Spirit

The LORD our Righteousness

2 COR. 5. 21   Is. 53. 6 —1 Pet. 2 24 —Rom. 5. 19.   Tit. 3. 4-7.—Rom 8 1   Jer 23 6.
M

DECEMBER 8.

By love serve one another.

BRETHREN, if a man be overtaken in a fault, ye which are spiritual, restore such an one in the spirit of meekness; considering thyself, lest thou also be tempted. Bear ye one another's burdens, and so fulfil the law of Christ.

Brethren, if any of you do err from the truth, and one convert him; let him know, that he which converteth the sinner from the error of his way shall save a soul from death, and shall hide a multitude of sins. —Seeing ye have purified your souls in obeying the truth through the Spirit unto unfeigned love of the brethren, see that ye love one another with a pure heart fervently.—Owe no man any thing, but to love one another: for he that loveth another hath fulfilled the law.—Be kindly affectioned one to another in brotherly love; in honour preferring one another.— Yea, all of you be subject one to another, and be clothed with humility: for God resisteth the proud, and giveth grace to the humble.

We . . . that are strong ought to bear the infirmities of the weak, and not to please ourselves.

GAL. 5. 13   Gal. 6 1, 2.   Ja. 5. 19, 20.—1 Pet.
1. 22.—Rom. 13. 8.—Rom. 12 10.—1 Pet. 5. 5.
Rom. 15. 1.

M

DECEMBER 9.

To do justice and judgment is more acceptable to the Lord than sacrifice.

HE hath shewed thee, O man, what is good; and what doth the LORD require of thee, but to do justly, and to love mercy, and to walk humbly with thy God?—Hath the LORD as great delight in burnt offerings and sacrifices, as in obeying the voice of the LORD? Behold, to obey is better than sacrifice, and to hearken than the fat of rams.—To love him with all the heart, and with all the understanding, and with all the soul, and with all the strength, and to love his neighbour as himself, is more than all whole burnt offerings and sacrifices.

Therefore turn thou to thy God: keep mercy and judgment, and wait on thy God continually.—Mary . . . sat at Jesus' feet, and heard his word. One thing is needful: and Mary hath chosen that good part, which shall not be taken away from her.

It is God which worketh in you both to will and to do of his good pleasure.

PRO. 21. 3 Mic. 6. 8.—1 Sam. 15. 22.—Mark 12. 33 Hos 12. 6.—Luke 10. 39, 42 Phil. 2 13.

M

DECEMBER 10.

No man is able to pluck them out of my
Father's hand.

I KNOW whom I have believed, and
am persuaded that he is able to keep
that which I have committed unto him
against that day.—The Lord shall deliver
me from every evil work, and will preserve
me unto his heavenly kingdom —We are
more than conquerors through him that
loved us. For I am persuaded, that
neither death, nor life, nor angels, nor
principalities, nor powers, nor things present, nor things to come, nor height, nor
depth, nor any other creature, shall be
able to separate us from the love of God,
which is in Christ Jesus our Lord.—Your
life is hid with Christ in God.

Hath not God chosen the poor of this
world rich in faith, and heirs of the kingdom which he hath promised to them that
love him?

Our Lord Jesus Christ himself, and
God, even our Father, which hath loved
us, and hath given us everlasting consolation and good hope through grace, comfort
your hearts, and stablish you in every
good word and work.

JOHN 10. 29.   2 Tim. 1. 12.—2 Tim. 4. 18.—
Rom. 8 38, 39.—Col. 3. 3   Ja. 2. 5.
2 Thes 2 16, 17.

M

DECEMBER 11.

Let not your good be evil spoken of.

ABSTAIN from all appearance of evil. —Providing for honest things, not only in the sight of the Lord, but also in the sight of men —For so is the will of God, that with well doing ye may put to silence the ignorance of foolish men.

But let none of you suffer as a murderer, or as a thief, or as an evildoer, or as a busybody in other men's matters. Yet if any man suffer as a Christian, let him not be ashamed ; but let him glorify God on this behalf.

Brethren, ye have been called unto liberty ; only use not liberty for an occasion to the flesh, but by love serve one another. —Take heed lest by any means this liberty of your's become a stumbling-block to them that are weak —Whoso shall offend one of these little ones which believe in me, it were better for him that a millstone were hanged about his neck, and that he were drowned in the depth of the sea —Inasmuch as ye have done it unto one of the least of these my brethren, ye have done it unto me.

ROM. 14 16. 1 Thes 5. 22 —2 Cor 8. 21.—
1 Pet. 2. 15 1 Pet 4 15, 16 Gal 5. 13 —
1 Cor. 8. 9.—Mat. 18 6.—Mat. 25 40

M

DECEMBER 12.

The Lord is in the midst of thee.

FEAR thou not; for I am with thee: be not dismayed , for I am thy God: I will strengthen thee; yea, I will help thee; yea, I will uphold thee with the right hand of my righteousness.—Strengthen ye the weak hands, and confirm the feeble knees. Say to them that are of a fearful heart, Be strong, fear not: behold, your God will come with vengeance, even God with a recompence ; he will come and save you. —The LORD thy God in the midst of thee is mighty ; he will save, he will rejoice over thee with joy ; he will rest in his love, he will joy over thee with singing. —Wait on the LORD: be of good courage, and he shall strengthen thine heart

I heard a great voice out of heaven, saying, Behold, the tabernacle of God is with men, and he will dwell with them, and they shall be his people, and God himself shall be with them, and be their God   And God shall wipe away all tears from their eyes ; and there shall be no more death. neither sorrow, nor crying, neither shall there be any more pain.

ZEP. 3. 15   Is. 41 10.—Is 35 3, 4.—Zep 3. 17. —Ps 27, 14   Rev 21 3, 4.

M

DECEMBER 13.

Be strong in the grace that is in
Christ Jesus

STRENGTHENED with all might,
according to his glorious power.—As
ye have therefore received Christ Jesus
the Lord, so walk ye in him : rooted and
built up in him, and stablished in the faith,
as ye have been taught, abounding therein
with thanksgiving.—Trees of righteousness, the planting of the LORD, that he
might be glorified.—Built upon the foundation of the apostles and prophets, Jesus
Christ himself being the chief corner stone;
in whom all the building fitly framed to·
gether groweth unto a holy temple in the
Lord : in whom ye also are builded together for a habitation of God through
the Spirit.

I commend you to God, and to the
word of his grace, which is able to build
you up, and to give you an inheritance
among all them which are sanctified.—
Being filled with the fruits of righteous
ness, which are by Jesus Christ, unto the
glory and praise of God

Fight the good fight of faith.—In no-·
thing terrified by your adversaries ⁄

2 TIM 2 1   Col 1 11.—Col 2. 6, 7.—Is 61. 3
—Eph 2. 20-22. Acts 20. 32—Phil. 1. 11
      1 Tim. 6 12 —Phil 1 28

M

Make his praise glorious.

THIS people have I formed for myself; they shall shew forth my praise.—I will cleanse them from all their iniquity, whereby they have sinned against me; and I will pardon all their iniquities, whereby they have sinned, and whereby they have transgressed against me. And it shall be to me a name of joy, a praise and an honour before all the nations of the earth.—By him therefore let us offer the sacrifice of praise to God continually, that is, the fruit of our lips giving thanks to his name.

I will praise thee, O Lord my God, with all my heart: and I will glorify thy name for evermore. For great is thy mercy toward me: and thou hast delivered my soul from the lowest hell.—Who is like unto thee, O LORD, . . . glorious in holiness, fearful in praises, doing wonders?—I will praise the name of God with a song, and will magnify him with thanksgiving.—They sing the song of Moses the servant of God, and the song of the Lamb, saying, Great and marvellous are thy works, Lord God Almighty.

Ps. 66. 2. Is. 43. 21.—Jer. 33. 8, 9.—Heb. 13. 15.
Ps. 86. 12, 13.—Ex. 15. 11.—Ps. 69. 30.—Rev. 15. 3.

M   12

DECEMBER 15.

Bear ye one another's burdens, and so
fulfil the law of Christ.

LOOK not every man on his own things,
but every man also on the things of
others.   Let this mind be in you, which
was also in Christ Jesus : who . . took
upon him the form of a servant.—Even
the Son of man came not to be ministered
unto, but to minister, and to give his life
a ransom for many.—He died for all, that
they which live should not henceforth live
unto themselves, but unto him which died
for them, and rose again.

When Jesus . .   saw her weeping, and
the Jews also weeping which came with
her, he groaned in the spirit, and was
troubled.   Jesus wept. — Rejoice with
them that do rejoice, and weep with them
that weep.

Be ye all of one mind, having compassion one of another, love as brethren, be
pitiful, be courteous : not rendering evil
for evil, or railing for railing : but con-
trariwise blessing ; knowing that ye are
thereunto called, that ye should inherit a
blessing.

GAL 6. 2.   Phil. 2 4, 5, 7 —Mark 10 45.—
2 Cor 5. 15.   John 11. 33, 35.—Rom. 12. 15.
1 Pet. 3. 8, 9.

M

Having loved his own which were in the world, he loved them unto the end.

I PRAY for them: I pray not for the world, but for them which thou hast given me; for they are thine. And all mine are thine, and thine are mine; and I am glorified in them. I pray not that thou shouldest take them out of the world, but that thou shouldest keep them from the evil They are not of the world, even as I am not of the world.

As the Father hath loved me, so have I loved you: continue ye in my love.— Greater love hath no man than this, that a man lay down his life for his friends. Ye are my friends, if ye do whatsoever I command you —A new commandment I give unto you, That ye love one another; as I have loved you, that ye also love one another

He which hath begun a good work in you will perform it until the day of Jesus Christ —Christ . . loved the church, and gave himself for it; that he might sanctify and cleanse it with the washing of water by the word.

JOHN 13. 1. John 17. 9, 10, 15, 16. John 15. 9 —John 15. 13, 14 —John 13 34. Phil 1. 6. —Eph. 5. 25, 26.

M

DECEMBER 17.

Quicken us, and we will call upon
thy name.

IT is the Spirit that quickeneth.—The
Spirit also helpeth our infirmities : for
we know not what we should pray for as
we ought : but the Spirit itself maketh
intercession for us with groanings which
cannot be uttered And he that searcheth
the hearts knoweth what is the mind of
the Spirit, because he maketh intercession
for the saints according to the will of
God.—Praying always with all prayer and
supplication in the Spirit, and watching
thereunto with all perseverance.

I will never forget thy precepts : for
with them thou hast quickened me.—
The words that I speak unto you, they
are spirit, and they are life.—The letter
killeth, but the spirit giveth life.—If ye
abide in me, and my words abide in you,
ye shall ask what ye will, and it shall be
done unto you.—This is the confidence
that we have in him, that, if we ask any
thing according to his will, he heareth us.

No man can say that Jesus is the Lord
but by the Holy Ghost.

Ps 80 18.   John 6 63.—Rom. 8. 26, 27.—
Eph. 6. 18   Ps. 119. 93 —John 6. 63 —2 Cor. 3.
6.—John 15. 7.—1 John 5. 14.   1 Cor. 12. 3.

DECEMBER 18.

Let us come boldly unto the throne of
grace, that we may obtain mercy, and
find grace to help in time of need.

BE careful for nothing ; but in every
thing by prayer and supplication with
thanksgiving let your requests be made
known unto God. And the peace of
God, which passeth all understanding,
shall keep your hearts and minds through
Christ Jesus.—Ye have not received the
spirit of bondage again to fear ; but ye
have received the Spirit of adoption,
whereby we cry, Abba, Father

I said not unto the seed of Jacob,
Seek ye me in vain —Having therefore,
. . boldness to enter into the holiest by
the blood of Jesus, by a new and living
way, which he hath consecrated for us
through the veil, that is to say, his flesh ;
and having an high priest over the house
of God ; let us draw near with a true
heart in full assurance of faith, having
our hearts sprinkled from an evil conscience, and our bodies washed with pure
water —We may boldly say, The Lord
is my helper, and I will not fear what
man shall do unto me

Heb. 4 16. Phil 4. 6, 7.—Rom 8 15. Is.
45. 19.—Heb 10. 19-22.—Heb. 13. 6.

DECEMBER 19.

Unto the upright there ariseth light
in the darkness.

WHO is among you that feareth the LORD, that obeyeth the voice of his servant, that walketh in darkness, and hath no light? let him trust in the name of the LORD, and stay upon his God.— Though he fall, he shall not be utterly cast down : for the LORD upholdeth him with his hand —The commandment is a lamp, and the law is light.

Rejoice not against me, O mine enemy : when I fall, I shall arise ; when I sit in darkness, the LORD shall be a light unto me. I will bear the indignation of the LORD, because I have sinned against him, until he plead my cause, and execute judgment for me . he will bring me forth to the light, and I shall behold his righteousness.

The light of the body is the eye : if therefore thine eye be single, thy whole body shall be full of light. But if thine eye be evil, thy whole body shall be full of darkness. If therefore the light that is in thee be darkness, how great is that darkness !

Ps. 112. 4. Is. 50. 10.—Ps. 37. 24.—Pro 6. 23
Mic 7. 8, 9. Mat 6. 22, 23.

M

He hath chosen us in Him before the foundation of the world.

THAT we should be holy and without blame before him in love

God hath from the beginning chosen you to salvation through sanctification of the Spirit and belief of the truth: whereunto he called you, . to the obtaining of the glory of our Lord Jesus Christ.—Whom he did foreknow, he also did predestinate to be conformed to the image of his Son, that he might be the firstborn among many brethren. Moreover whom he did predestinate, them he also called; and whom he called, them he also justified; and whom he justified, them he also glorified.—Elect according to the foreknowledge of God the Father, through sanctification of the Spirit, unto obedience and sprinkling of the blood of Jesus Christ.

A new heart also will I give you, and a new spirit will I put within you: and I will take away the stony heart out of your flesh, and I will give you a heart of flesh.—God hath not called us unto uncleanness, but unto holiness

EPH. 1. 4. Eph. 1. 4. 2 Thes 2. 13, 14.—Rom. 8 29, 30.—1 Pet 1. 2 Ezek 36. 26 — 1 Thes 4 7.

M

DECEMBER 21.

The days of thy mourning shall be ended.

THE whole creation groaneth and travaileth in pain together until now. And not only they, but ourselves also, which have the firstfruits of the Spirit, even we ourselves groan within ourselves, waiting for the adoption, to wit, the redemption of our body.—We that are in this tabernacle do groan, being burdened: not for that we would be unclothed, but clothed upon, that mortality might be swallowed up of life

These are they which came out of great tribulation, and have washed their robes, and made them white in the blood of the Lamb. Therefore are they before the throne of God, and serve him day and night in his temple. and he that sitteth on the throne shall dwell among them They shall hunger no more, neither thirst any more, neither shall the sun light on them, nor any heat For the Lamb which is in the midst of the throne shall feed them, and shall lead them unto living fountains of waters; and God shall wipe away all tears from their eyes

Is 60. 20. Rom 8 22, 23 —2 Cor. 5. 4
Rev. 7 14-17

M

DECEMBER 22.

Your work of faith.

THIS is the work of God, that ye believe on him whom he hath sent.

Faith, if it hath not works, is dead, being alone.—Faith worketh by love.—He that soweth to his flesh, shall of the flesh reap corruption; but he that soweth to the Spirit shall of the Spirit reap life everlasting.—We are his workmanship, created in Christ Jesus unto good works, which God hath before ordained that we should walk in them.—Who gave himself for us, that he might redeem us from all iniquity, and purify unto himself a peculiar people, zealous of good works.

We are bound to thank God always for you, brethren, as it is meet, because that your faith groweth exceedingly, and the charity of every one of you all toward each other aboundeth. Wherefore also we pray always for you, that our God would count you worthy of this calling, and fulfil all the good pleasure of his goodness, and the work of faith with power.—It is God which worketh in you both to will and to do of his good pleasure.

1 THES. 1. 3. John 6. 29. Ja. 2. 17.—Gal. 5. 6. —Gal. 6. 8.—Eph. 2. 10.—Tit. 2. 14. 2 Thes 1. 3, 11.—Phil. 2. 13.

M   12 *

DECEMBER 23.

Let him take hold of my strength, that he may make peace with me.

I KNOW the thoughts that I think toward you, saith the LORD, thoughts of peace, and not of evil —There is no peace, saith the LORD, unto the wicked.

In Christ Jesus ye who sometime were far off are made nigh by the blood of Christ. For he is our peace.

It pleased the Father that in him should all fulness dwell: and having made peace through the blood of his cross, by him to reconcile all things unto himself.—Christ Jesus: whom God hath set forth to be a propitiation through faith in his blood, to declare his righteousness for the remission of sins that are past : . . . that he might be just, and the justifier of him which believeth in Jesus.—If we confess our sins, he is faithful and just to forgive us our sins, and to cleanse us from all unrighteousness.

Trust ye in the LORD for ever, for in the LORD JEHOVAH is everlasting strength.

Is. 27 5 Jer. 29. 11 —Is. 48 22 Eph. 2. 13, 14 Col. 1 19, 20.—Rom. 3 24-26.—1 John 1 9. Is. 26 4.

M

DECEMBER 24.

If ye live after the flesh, ye shall die : but if ye through the Spirit do mortify the deeds of the body, ye shall live.

NOW the works of the flesh are manifest, which are these ; Adultery, fornication, . . . and such like : of the which I tell you before, as I have also told you in time past, that they which do such things shall not inherit the kingdom of God. But the fruit of the Spirit is love, joy, peace, longsuffering, gentleness, goodness, faith, meekness, temperance : against such there is no law. And they that are Christ's have crucified the flesh with the affections and lusts. If we live in the Spirit, let us also walk in the Spirit.

The grace of God that bringeth salvation hath appeared to all men, teaching us that, denying ungodliness and worldly lusts, we should live soberly, righteously, and godly, in this present world ; looking for that blessed hope, and the glorious appearing of the great God and our Saviour Jesus Christ ; who gave himself for us, that he might redeem us from all iniquity.

Rom. 8 13. Gal. 5. 19, 21, 25. Tit. 2. 11-14.
M

DECEMBER 25.

The kindness and love of God our
Saviour toward man appeared.

I HAVE loved thee with an everlasting love.

In this was manifested the love of God toward us, because that God sent his only begotten Son into the world, that we might live through him. Herein is love, not that we loved God, but that he loved us, and sent his Son to be the propitiation for our sins.

When the fulness of the time was come, God sent forth his Son, made of a woman, made under the law, to redeem them that were under the law, that we might receive the adoption of sons — The Word was made flesh, and dwelt among us, (and we beheld his glory, the glory as of the only begotten of the Father,) full of grace and truth —Great is the mystery of godliness . God was manifest in the flesh.

As the children are partakers of flesh and blood, he also himself likewise took part of the same ; that through death he might destroy him that had the power of death, that is, the devil.

Tit. 3. 4. Jer. 31. 3. 1 John 4 9, 10 Gal. 4 4. 5 —John 1 14.—1 Tim. 3. 16 Heb 2 14

M

DECEMBER 26.

Be ye stedfast, unmoveable, always
abounding in the work of the Lord.

YE know that your labour is not in vain
in the Lord.—As ye have . . . received Christ Jesus the Lord, so walk ye
in him : rooted and built up in him, and
stablished in the faith, as ye have been
taught, abounding therein with thanksgiving.—He that shall endure unto the
end, the same shall be saved.—That on
the good ground are they, which in an
honest and good heart, having heard the
word, keep it, and bring forth fruit with
patience.

By faith ye stand.

I must work the works of him that sent
me, while it is day: the night cometh,
when no man can work.

He that soweth to his flesh shall of the
flesh reap corruption ; but he that soweth
to the Spirit shall of the Spirit reap life
everlasting. And let us not be weary in
well doing : for in due season we shall
reap, if we faint not. As we have therefore opportunity, let us do good unto all
men, especially unto them who are of the
household of faith.

1 Cor 15. 58. 1 Cor 15. 58.—Col. 2 6, 7 —
Mat. 24 13.—Luke 8 15. 2 Cor. 1 24.
John 9. 4. Gal. 6. 8-10.

M

DECEMBER 27.

We look not at the things which are seen:
. . . for the things which are seen are
temporal; but the things which are not
seen are eternal.

H ERE have we no continuing city.—
Ye have in heaven a better and an
enduring substance.

Fear not, little flock; for it is your
Father's good pleasure to give you the
kingdom.

Now for a season, if need be, ye are in
heaviness through manifold temptations.
—There the wicked cease from troubling;
and there the weary be at rest.

We that are in this tabernacle do groan,
being burdened.—God shall wipe away all
tears from their eyes; and there shall be
no more death, neither sorrow, nor crying,
neither shall there be any more pain: for
the former things are passed away.

The sufferings of this present time are
not worthy to be compared with the
glory which shall be revealed in us.—
Our light affliction, . . . worketh for us
a far more exceeding and eternal weight
of glory.

2 COR. 4. 18.   Heb. 13 14.—Heb. 10. 34.   Luke
12. 32.   1 Pet. 1. 6.—Job 3. 17.   2 Cor. 5 4.—
    Rev 21. 4   Rom. 8. 18.—2 Cor 4 17.
M

DECEMBER 28.

Thy sins be forgiven thee.

I WILL forgive their iniquity, and I
will remember their sin no more.—
Who can forgive sins but God only?

I, even I, am he that blotteth out thy
transgressions for mine own sake, and
will not remember thy sins.—Blessed is
he whose transgression is forgiven, whose
sin is covered. Blessed is the man unto
whom the LORD imputeth not iniquity.
—Who is a God like unto thee, that
pardoneth iniquity?

God for Christ's sake hath forgiven
you.—The blood of Jesus Christ his Son
cleanseth us from all sin. If we say
that we have no sin, we deceive ourselves, and the truth is not in us. If
we confess our sins, he is faithful and
just to forgive us our sins, and to cleanse
us from all unrighteousness.

As far as the east is from the west, so far
hath he removed our transgressions from
us.—Sin shall not have dominion over you:
for ye are not under the law, but under
grace. Being then made free from sin,
ye became the servants of righteousness.

MARK 2. 5. Jer. 31. 34.—Mark 2. 7 Is. 43. 25.
—Ps. 32. 1, 2 —Mic. 7. 18 Eph. 4. 32.—1 John
1. 7-9 Ps. 103. 12.—Rom. 6. 14, 18.

M

DECEMBER 29.

Understanding what the will of the Lord is

THIS is the will of God, even your sanctification.—Acquaint now thyself with him, and be at peace: thereby good shall come unto thee.—This is life eternal, that they might know thee the only true God, and Jesus Christ, whom thou hast sent

We know that the Son of God is come, and hath given us an understanding, that we may know him that is true, and we are in him that is true, even in his Son Jesus Christ.

We . . . do not cease to pray for you, and to desire that ye might be filled with the knowledge of his will in all wisdom and spiritual understanding.—The God of our Lord Jesus Christ, the Father of glory, . . . give unto you the spirit of wisdom and revelation in the knowledge of him: the eyes of your understanding being enlightened; that ye may know what is the hope of his calling, and what the riches of the glory of his inheritance in the saints, and what is the exceeding greatness of his power to us-ward who believe.

EPH. 5. 17. 1 Thes 4 3.—Job 22 21.—John 17 3. 1 John 5 20. Col. 1. 9.—Eph 1 17-19.

DECEMBER 30.

Blameless in the day of our Lord Jesus Christ.

YOU, that were sometime alienated and enemies in your mind by wicked works, yet now hath he reconciled in the body of his flesh through death, to present you holy and unblameable and unreproveable in his sight : if ye continue in the faith grounded and settled, and be not moved away from the hope of the gospel —That ye may be blameless and harmless, the sons of God, without rebuke, in the midst of a crooked and perverse nation, among whom ye shine as lights in the world.

Wherefore, beloved, seeing that ye look for such things, be diligent that ye may be found of him in peace, without spot, and blameless —That ye may be sincere and without offence till the day of Christ.

Now unto him that is able to keep you from falling, and to present you faultless before the presence of his glory with exceeding joy, to the only wise God our Saviour, be glory and majesty, dominion and power, both now and ever.

1 Cor. 1. 8. Col. 1. 21-23.—Phil. 2. 15. 2 Pet. 3. 14 —Phil. 1 10. Jude 24, 25

M

DECEMBER 31.

The Lord thy God bare thee, as a man doth bear his son, in all the way that ye went, until ye came into this place.

I BARE you on eagles' wings, and brought you unto myself.—In his love and in his pity he redeemed them; and he bare them, and carried them all the days of old.—As an eagle stirreth up her nest, fluttereth over her young, spreadeth abroad her wings, taketh them, beareth them on her wings: so the LORD alone did lead him.

Even to your old age I am he; and even to hoar hairs will I carry you: I have made, and I will bear; even I will carry, and will deliver you.—This God is our God for ever and ever; he will be our guide even unto death.

Cast thy burden upon the LORD, and he shall sustain thee.—Take no thought for your life, what ye shall eat, or what ye shall drink; nor yet for your body, what ye shall put on. For your heavenly Father knoweth that ye have need of all these things.

Hitherto hath the LORD helped us.

DEUT. 1. 31. Ex. 19. 4.—Is. 63 9.—Deut. 32 11, 12. Is 46. 4 —Ps 48. 14. Ps. 55. 22.— Mat. 6. 25, 32. 1 Sam. 7 12.

M

FOR

SPECIAL OCCASIONS

EASTER.

Jesus said . . I am the resurrection and the life: he that believeth in me, though he were dead, yet shall he live: and whosoever liveth and believeth in me shall never die.

I KNOW that my Redeemer liveth . . . and though, after my skin, worms destroy this body, yet in my flesh shall I see God

The LORD is risen indeed.—Now is Christ risen from the dead, and become the first fruits of them that slept For since by man came death, by man came also the resurrection of the dead —O death, where is thy sting? O grave, where is thy victory?

If ye then be risen with Christ, seek those things which are above.—Lay not up for yourselves treasures upon earth . . . but lay up for yourselves treasures in heaven, where neither moth nor rust doth corrupt, and where thieves do not break through nor steal.

Christ . . in that he died, he died unto sin, once: but in that he liveth, he liveth unto God. Likewise reckon ye also yourselves to be dead indeed unto sin, but alive unto God through Jesus Christ our Lord.

JOHN 11 25-26.—Job 19. 25-26.—Luke 24 34 — 1 Cor. 15 20-21. 55 —Col. 3. 1 —Mat. 6. 19-20. —Rom. 6 9-11.

M

THANKSGIVING DAY.

Blessing, and glory, and wisdom, and thanksgiving, and honour, and power, and might,
be unto our God for ever and ever.

THIS is the day which the LORD has
made; we will rejoice and be glad
in it.

Thou visitest the earth, and waterest it;
thou greatly enrichest it with the river of
God, which is full of water: thou pre-
parest them corn, when thou hast so provided for it. Thou waterest the ridges
thereof abundantly; thou settlest the
furrows thereof; thou makest it soft with
showers; thou blessest the springing
thereof. Thou crownest the year with
thy goodness; and thy paths drop fatness.

They that plow iniquity and sow
wickedness, reap the same.—Whatsoever a man soweth, that shall he also
reap.—He which soweth sparingly shall
reap also sparingly; and he which soweth
bountifully shall reap also bountifully.

The children of Israel brought in
abundance the first fruits of corn, wine,
and oil, and honey, and of all the increase
of the field.—Freely ye have received,
freely give.—Give alms of such things as
ye have.

REV. 7. 12.—Ps. 118. 24.—Ps. 65. 9-11.—Job 4. 8.
—Gal. 6. 7.—2 Cor. 9. 6.—2 Chron. 31. 5.—
Mat. 10. 8.—Luke 11. 41.

M

FOR A BIRTHDAY.

The Lord bless thee, and keep thee.

THE LORD that made heaven and earth bless thee.—God, even our Father.--—The living God, who giveth us richly all things to enjoy.

Your heavenly Father knoweth that ye have need of all these things.—For the Father himself loveth you

No good thing will he withhold from them that walk uprightly.—He layeth up sound wisdom for the righteous. he is a buckler to them that walk uprightly —Blessed are they that keep his testimonies, and that seek him with the whole heart

He that keepeth thee will not slumber. Behold, he that keepeth Israel shall neither slumber nor sleep —The LORD shall be thy confidence, and shall keep thy foot from being taken.—Thou wilt keep him in perfect peace whose mind is stayed on thee, because he trusteth in thee.

The LORD of peace himself give you peace always by all means

NUM 6 24. Ps. 134 3 —2 Thes 2 16.—1 Tim. 6. 17. Mat. 6 32—John 16 27. Ps 84. 11 — Pro 2. 7 —Ps 119 2 —Ps 121 3, 4 —Pro. 3 26.—Is. 26. 3. 2 Thes. 3 16.

M

FOR A BIRTHDAY.

O send out thy light and thy truth: let
them lead me

WHERE is the way where light
dwelleth?—The LORD shall be
unto thee an everlasting light.—God is
light, and in him is no darkness at all.
If we walk in the light as he is in the
light, we have fellowship one with another,
and the blood of Jesus Christ his Son
cleanseth us from all sin

Shew me thy ways, O LORD;
Lead me in thy truth, and teach me: for
thou art the God of my salvation; on
thee do I wait all the day.—Thy word is
a lamp unto my feet, and a light unto my
path.—Thy word is truth.

The LORD is my light and my salvation;
whom shall I fear?—He leadeth me in
the paths of righteousness for his name's
sake Surely goodness and mercy shall
follow me all the days of my life: and I
will dwell in the house of the LORD for
ever

Ps 43 3   Job 38 19 —Is. 60 19 —1 John
1. 5, 7   Ps. 25 4, 5 —Ps 119 105 —John 17.
      17 Ps 27. 1 —Ps 23 3, 6

AFFLICTION.

Save me, O God; for the waters are come in unto my soul.

O MY Father, if it be possible, let this cup pass from me : nevertheless not as I will, but as thou wilt.—Being in an agony.—Jesus wept.

Surely he hath borne our griefs, and carried our sorrows.—We have not an high priest which cannot be touched with the feeling of our infirmities ; but was in all points tempted like as we are, yet without sin —Let us therefore come boldly unto the throne of grace, that we may find grace to help in time of need.

He careth for you.—I have called thee by thy name ; thou art mine.—When thou passest through the waters, I will be with thee ; and through the rivers, they shall not overflow thee —I will never leave thee, nor forsake thee.

Though he slay me, yet will I trust in him.—My flesh and my heart faileth : but God is the strength of my heart, and my portion for ever.

Ps. 69 1 Mat. 26. 39.—Luke 22. 44.—John 11. 35 Is. 53 4 —Heb. 4. 15, 16 1 Pet. 5. 7 —Is. 43. 1, 2.—Heb. 13. 5· Job 13. 15 —Ps. 73. 26.
M

FOR SICKNESS.

Lord, behold, he whom thou lovest is sick

SURELY he hath borne our griefs, and carried our sorrows.—Himself took our infirmities, and bare our sicknesses.—He, being full of compassion.—Like as a father pitieth his children, so the LORD pitieth them that fear him.—For he knoweth our frame

Who shall separate us from the love of Christ? shall tribulation, or distress.—Whom the LORD loveth he chasteneth.—Now no chastening for the present seemeth to be joyous, but grievous : nevertheless afterward it yieldeth the peaceable fruit of righteousness unto them which are exercised thereby.—We know that all things work together for good to them that love God

The LORD said unto me, My grace is sufficient for thee : for my strength is made perfect in weakness. Most gladly therefore will I rather glory in my infirmities, that the power of Christ may rest upon me.

JOHN 11 3. Is 53. 4.—Mat 8 17.—Ps 78. 38. —Ps 103. 13, 14 Rom. 8, 35.—Heb 12 6, 11 —Rom 8 28. 2 Cor. 12. 9.

M

BEREAVEMENT.

Father, I will that they also, whom thou hast given me, be with me where I am

HE shall return no more to his house, neither shall his place know him any more

Whilst we are at home in the body, we are absent from the LORD : we are willing rather to be absent from the body, and to be present with the LORD.—I am in a strait betwixt two, having a desire to depart, and to be with Christ; which is far better.—Whether we live or die, we are the LORD's.

Ye have in heaven a better and an enduring substance.—It doth not yet appear what we shall be : but we know that, when he shall appear, we shall be like him ; for we shall see him as he is.—Now we see through a glass, darkly ; but then face to face.—I will behold thy face in righteousness : I shall be satisfied, when I awake, with thy likeness.

So shall we ever be with the LORD. Wherefore comfort one another with these words.

JOHN 17 24 Job 7 10. 2 Cor 5. 6-8 —1 Cor, 1. 23 —Rom. 14 8 Heb 10 34 —1 John 3 2 —1 Cor. 13 12.—Ps. 17 15 1 Thes 4 17, 18

FOR TIMES OF ANXIETY.

*Neither know we what to do ‧ but our
eyes are upon thee*

O GOD, thou knowest my foolishness ;
and my sins are not hid from thee —
Teach me to do thy will ; for thou art my
God.—Lead me, O LORD, in thy righteousness, make thy way straight before
my face.—My times are in thy hand.

If any of you lack wisdom, let him ask
of God, that giveth to all men liberally,
and upbraideth not ; and it shall be given
him. But let him ask in faith, nothing
wavering.—Who is among you that feareth the LORD, that walketh in darkness,
and hath no light? let him trust in the
name of the LORD, and stay upon his
God.

In the multitude of my thoughts within
me, thy comforts delight my soul.—Why
art thou cast down, O my soul? and why
art thou disquieted in me? Hope thou
in God.

Jesus . . . said unto them, Why are ye
so fearful? how is it that ye have no
faith?—Now faith is the evidence of
things not seen.

2 CHR 20. 12. Ps. 69 5.—Ps. 143. 10.—Ps. 5.
8.—Ps 31 15. Ja 1 5, 6.—Is 50 10. Ps. 94.
   19.—Ps. 42 5. Mark 4 40.—Rev. 11. 1.
   M

DAILY LIGHT
ON THE DAILY PATH

The Morning Hour

LIST OF THE DAILY TEXTS

ARRANGED IN BIBLE ORDER

GENESIS

13. 10, 11.	Mar. 22.
15 6.	Mar. 24.
16. 13.	Jan. 29.
21. 1.	April 24.
22. 14.	Mar. 10.
24. 63.	Mar. 30
28. 16.	May 2.
32 20	April 5
32. 28.	May 31.
39 3.	June 8
41. 52.	Mar. 2.

EXODUS.

2. 9.	June 20.
3. 7	Aug. 24
12. 11	June 2
12 43.	July 2.
13. 7.	Sept. 3.

M

19. 6.	July 16.
25. 21, 22.	June 18.
28 12.	May 23.
28. 36.	Aug. 26.
30. 23, 25.	Nov. 5.
33 14	July 12.
34. 29.	Oct. 4.

LEVITICUS.

1. 3, 4.	April 22.
1 4	Mar 17.
4. 12.	Feb. 17.
16. 22.	Oct. 2.
17. 11.	May 29.
20. 8.	Feb. 21.

NUMBERS.

6. 24.	Mar. 11.
6 25, 26.	Mar. 12.
6. 27.	Sept. 28.

LIST OF THE DAILY TEXTS

10. 33.	June 24	
23 19.	Aug. 20	
31 23	June 12	
33 55.	Jan. 31.	

EZRA.

9. 9. — Sept. 23.

NEHEMIAH.

5. 19. — Jan 7.
8 10 — Aug. 14.
9 17. — Oct. 9.

DEUTERONOMY

1. 31. — Dec. 31.
3 24. — Aug 18.
8 10, 11. — Feb. 7
12 9 — Jan. 4
13. 17. — April 20
17. 16. — Feb. 4.
18 18. — April 18.
29. 29. — June 15.
32. 4 — Sept 26
33. 25. — Jan. 28.

ESTHER.

5 2. — Aug 30.

JOB.

5. 8. — Dec. 3.
19. 25. — June 28.
23. 10. — Sept. 30.
28 12. — Dec. 4.

JOSHUA.

1. 18. — Mar. 28.

RUTH.

3 18. — Sept. 4.

I SAMUEL.

7. 3. — April 2.
12. 24. — April 29.

I CHRONICLES.

4 10. — Feb 2
4. 10. — June 26.
22. 5. — Aug. 16

PSALMS.

9 10. — Jan. 8.
18. 18. — April 23.
22 11. — Oct. 11.
25 9. — Oct. 7.
25. 12. — Feb. 22.
27 14. — Sept. 2.
31 19. — May 25.
31 22. — April 16.
40 17. — Nov. 14.
48 14. — Jan. 22.
50 15. — Oct. 5.
50 23. — April 17.
51. 2. — May 19
59. 9. — Oct. 15.
60 4. — Jan. 9.

M

63 5, 6.	April 14.	
65. 1.	Jan 11	
65. 4.	Nov. 29.	
66 2	Dec. 14	
73. 28.	Sept 24.	
78 53.	Nov 11.	
80 18.	Dec. 17	
85 10.	May 6.	
89 16	Oct 17.	
89. 19.	Nov 9	
90 17.	Jan. 6.	
92 5.	Nov. 17.	
99 1	Oct. 26.	
104 34.	Sept. 22	
107 7.	Jan. 3.	
107 8.	Nov. 7	
108 1.	Oct. 22.	
112 4.	Dec. 19.	
119 18	Sept 18	
119 25.	Jan. 15.	
119 57.	Aug 21.	
119 71	Dec. 5	
119 105.	Aug 27.	
119 130	Mar. 20.	

PROVERBS.

1 33.	Nov 23.
2 6.	Feb 19.
2 8	Mar. 6.
3 5, 6.	Mar 3.
3 9.	April 13
3 12	Aug 6.
3 13	Sept 20
3 26.	Oct 19.

M

4 18	Aug. 8.
8 34	Nov. 1.
10 19.	April 11.
11 18	Mar 27
16. 20.	Aug 29.
20 9.	Feb. 15.
21 2.	Sept 16.
21 3.	Dec. 9.
27 1.	Feb 29.

CANTICLES.

1. 3	Feb. 16.
1 5	April 10.
2 6.	April 26.
4 7.	Aug. 9.
5 16.	Oct 29.
7. 10.	July 13.

ISAIAH.

9 6.	Jan. 20.
26 3	Jan. 13.
27. 5	Dec. 23.
27 8.	Nov 18.
32 2	Dec. 1
38. 14.	Mar. 5.
38. 14.	Mar. 18.
38. 17	Mar 8.
38. 17.	Jan. 17.
42. 10.	Jan. 2.
43. 1	April 9.
51 1	Aug 25.
51. 12.	Sept 14.
53 10.	May 8.
53. 11.	Feb. 20.

54. 5.	Mar. 7.	
57. 18.	Sept 12	
59. 1.	May 4.	
59. 16.	Oct 28	
60. 20.	Dec. 21.	
62. 4	Nov. 26.	
64. 1.	July 29.	

JEREMIAH.

15. 20.	July 11.
17. 17.	Feb. 18.
31. 3.	Aug 23.
32. 39.	Sept 10.
50. 34.	April 15.

LAMENTATIONS.

3. 26.	Oct. 30.
3. 31, 32.	Aug. 12.
3. 40.	Feb. 26
3. 41	Sept 6.

EZEKIEL.

1. 26.	Feb. 13.
20. 19	May 17
36. 37.	Feb 24

DANIEL.

5. 27.	Sept. 8.
10. 12.	Oct. 13.

HOSEA.

14. 9.	Nov. 3.

M

JONAH.

2. 4.	Oct. 24.
4. 2.	July 17.

MICAH.

7. 8.	Nov. 20.

NAHUM.

1. 7.	May 27.

ZEPHANIAH.

3. 15	Dec. 12.
3. 17	June 6.

HAGGAI.

2. 4.	Feb. 3.
2. 9.	June 4.

ZECHARIAH.

3. 4.	July 9.
4. 6.	Oct. 31.

MALACHI.

3. 16.	Feb. 11.
3. 17.	Feb. 12.

MATTHEW.

1. 21.	April 25.
3. 15	Feb. 14.
4. 1.	July 7.

5 48.	May	3
6 10	July	15
6 31, 32.	May	5
7 20.	Nov	19
8 17.	Oct	27
10 24	July	10
12 20.	Sept	17.
12 34.	July	14
24 6.	May	7
25 13	June	3
25 14, 15	Mar	26
25 34.	Mar	29
28 20	Oct	25

MARK

2 5	Dec	28

LUKE

1 49.	July	19
1 50	Aug	3
1 53	Sept	9
8 21	Nov	24
11 34.	Feb	10
12 15	Oct.	23
15 13	June	10.
15 20	June	11.
16 25	Feb	9
17 10	June	5
18 1	June	7.

JOHN

1 16	Oct	21
1 29.	April	28
3 16.	Feb.	28

M

5 26.	May	18.
6 37	Nov	21
7 37.	Sept.	13.
7 46	June	9
10 3	July	18.
10 7.	April	19
10 10.	Feb.	5
10 29	Dec	10.
13 1.	Dec.	16.
13 23	July	4.
14 16, 17	June	23
14 26	Aug.	7
14 27	May	22
14 28	Jan	14
15 2.	Jan	21
15 4	June	13
15 15	Feb	8
17 15.	Aug	10.
17 16	July	20.
17 17	Nov	16
17 22	Nov.	27.
19 30	Aug.	4
19 34	Oct.	18.

ACTS

3 26	Mar.	19.
20 19.	Jan	19.

ROMANS

1 1.	May	16
3 1	July	21.
3 22	Jan.	25
5 5.	Jan.	23

5. 14.	Jan 18	4 18	Dec. 27.
5. 16.	Aug 31	5 19	Oct. 12.
6 4	Aug 5	5 21	Dec 7.
6. 10	July 22	6 10	April 7.
6 11	Feb 27.	7 10.	Nov 12.
6. 14.	Sept 15		
6 18	Nov 25	GALATIANS	
7 22	Oct 20	5 13	Dec 8
8 3.	April 12.	5 22.	Mar 1
8 13.	Dec. 24.	5 22	April 1
8. 17	July 3	5 22	May 1
8. 28	Sept 21.	5 22	June 1.
12 2	Sept. 11	5 22	July 1
12 11.	Oct 16.	5 22	Aug. 1.
12 12.	July 24	5 22	Sept 1
12 12	Sept 7	5 22	Oct 1
14 7	Aug 22.	6 2	Dec 15.
14 9	Oct 14		
14 16	Dec 11	EPHESIANS	

1 CORINTHIANS

		EPHESIANS	
		1 4	Dec 20.
		3 15.	Oct. 10
1 5.	April 8	4 30	May 24.
1 8	Dec 30	5 2	July 28
1 9.	Nov 15	5 15, 16.	June 16.
7. 29	April 27	5 17	Dec 29.
12 12.	Sept 5	5 25, 26	Nov 13
15 24	July 23	6 10	May 21
15 34	May 11		
15 58.	Dec. 26.	PHILIPPIANS	

2 CORINTHIANS.

		PHILIPPIANS	
		2 13.	Dec. 6
		3 10	May 14
1. 5	June 14	3 13, 14.	Jan. 1.
4. 4	July 27.	3 20.	May 28.

M

4. 1.   April 21
4 5   Jan. 24.
4. 6.   June 17.
4. 19   Mar. 31.

COLOSSIANS.

1. 10.   Nov. 10.
1 19.   Jan. 16.
3 1   July 30
3. 2   Mar. 4
3 3   June 22.
3. 4.   Nov. 6.
4. 6.   July 6

1 THESSALONIANS.

1. 3   Dec. 22
5 8   Nov. 8.
5. 15   Nov. 2
5 23   Jan. 10.

2 THESSALONIANS.

3 16   Nov. 30.

1 TIMOTHY.

1. 14   Feb. 6.
2 5   Mar. 13.
2 8   May 13
4. 16   May 20.
6. 17   Mar. 9

2 TIMOTHY.

2 1   Dec. 13.
2 3   July 31.

TITUS.

2 10.   Mar 14.
3 4   Dec 25

HEBREWS.

2. 10   Mar 15.
2 14   Aug. 11
4. 3   Jan. 5.
4 11.   May 30.
4. 16   Dec 18.
7 25   April 6.
11 1   May 9.
11 8   July 26
11 16   Aug. 13
12. 1. 2   Jan. 30.
12 14   June 19
12 24.   Feb 23
13 5   Mar 25.
13 6   Oct 8
13 13, 14   Jan. 26.
13 20   May 26.
13 21.   Aug 15

JAMES.

1. 4   Sept 25.
2. 26   Nov. 28.
4 7   Feb 25.
4 14   Mar. 16.
5 16.   Aug. 17.

1 PETER.

1 6   Nov 4.
1 8   Feb. 1.

M

1	15	Aug 19	4	16	July 5.
2	21	June 21	5	3	June 29.
5	6.	Sept 27			
5	10	Sept 19			

JUDE

20	Nov 22.
25	Jan 12

2 PETER.

3	8, 9	April 3

1 JOHN.

REVELATION

			1	5	Oct 3.
1	9	July 8	1	17	April 4
2	5	April 30	3	2	Mar. 21.
2	20	Dec 2	3	19	June 30.
3	2	June 25	4	8	Mar 23.
3	5	Jan 27	6	17	June 27
3	8	May 10	12	10	Aug 28.
3	14	July 25	13	8	Aug. 2.
3	16	Sept. 29	19.	6	Oct 6.
4	7	May 12.	21	4.	May 15.

M

Lightning Source UK Ltd.
Milton Keynes UK
UKHW021901220421
382471UK00003B/126